Cognitive Behavioural Therapy

FOR

DUMMIES®

Cognitive Behavioural Therapy FOR DUMMIES®

by Rob Willson and Rhena Branch

JOHN WILEY & SONS, LTD

Cognitive Behavioural Therapy For Dummies®

Published by
John Wiley & Sons, Ltd
The Atrium
Southern Gate
Chichester
West Sussex
PO19 8SQ
England

E-mail (for orders and customer service enquires): cs-books@wiley.co.uk

Visit our Home Page on www.wiley.com

Wiley also publishes its books in a variety of electronic formats. Some content that appears in print may not be available in electronic books.

British Library Cataloguing in Publication Data: A catalogue record for this book is available from the British Library.

ISBN-13: 978-0-470-01838-5 (PB)

ISBN-10: 0-470-01838-0 (PB)

Printed and bound in Great Britain by Bell and Bain Ltd, Glasgow

10 9 8 7 6 5 4 3 2 1

WILEY

About the Authors

Rob Willson, BSc, MSc, Dip SBHS, has worked for the Priory Hospital North London for a number of years as a CBT therapist. Rob also teaches and supervises trainee therapists at Goldsmith's College, University of London, and has his own practice in North London. His first book was *Overcoming Obsessive Compulsive Disorder* (Constable & Robinson, 2005), co-written with Dr David Veale.

Rob has done numerous newspaper and radio interviews about CBT. More rarely he's appeared on television discussing understanding and treating body image problems. His particular interests include the research and treatment of obsessional problems, and applying CBT in group and self-help formats.

Rhena Branch, MSc, Dip CBT, is an accredited CBT therapist and works with the Priory Hospital North London as a CBT therapist. She also has her own practice in North London and supervises on the Masters' course at Goldsmith College, University of London.

Dedication

To our children, Felix, Atticus, Emma, and Lucy.

Authors' Acknowledgements

From Rob: I'm hugely grateful to Rhena for agreeing to write this book with me, and thereby making the process substantially more entertaining. Thank you Rhena for your intelligent and hard working attitude, sharp wit, and consistently good company. A great deal of gratitude is due to my family and friends who have been more than patient with my absences whilst writing this book.

From Rhena: First and foremost I'd like to thank Rob for inviting me to co-author the book. Also, thank you Rob for your support with my clinical work and for good solid supervision in the not so distant past (and mostly I appreciate your unerring sense of humour and your friendship!). Hal, for looking after the boys. And, last but never least, thanks to my tabby cat Jack (who harbours grandiose ideas of being an ocelot), for providing Rob and myself with hours of entertainment at his expense.

From both of us: So many researchers, therapists, and authors deserve acknowledgement for influencing our understanding and practice of CBT, and therefore the content of this book. Founding fathers Albert Ellis and Aaron T. Beck deserve special mention of course, but there are many, many others, such as (in no particular order): Ray DiGuiseppe, Mary-Anne Layden, Jaqueline Persons, David A Clarke, Adrian Wells, Paul Salkovskis, Christine Padesky, David Burns, Kevin Gournay, Stanley Rachman, David Veale, and David M. Clarke. Special acknowledgment is due to Windy Dryden for teaching us so much and teaching us well.

Finally thanks to all our patients (clients!), past and present, for letting us get to know you and learn from you.

Publisher's Acknowledgements

We're proud of this book; please send us your comments through our Dummies online registration form located at www.dummies.com/register/.

Some of the people who helped bring this book to market include the following:

Acquisitions, Editorial, and Media Development

Project Editor: Rachael Chilvers

Development Editor: Brian Kramer

Content Editor: Simon Bell

Copy Editor: Colette Holden

Proofreader: Juliet Booker

Technical Editor: David Kingdon, Professor of Mental Health Care Delivery, University of Southampton

Executive Editor: Jason Dunne

Executive Project Editor: Amie Jackowski Tibble

Cover Photo: © Ray Massey/Image Bank/Getty Images

Cartoons: Rich Tennant, www.the5thwave.com

Special Help: Zoë Wykes

Composition Services

Project Coordinator: Maridee Ennis

Layout and Graphics: Carl Byers, Andrea Dahl, Denny Hager, Joyce Haughey, Heather Ryan

Proofreader: Susan Moritz

Indexer: TECHBOOKS Production Services

Publishing and Editorial for Consumer Dummies

    Diane Graves Steele, Vice President and Publisher, Consumer Dummies

    Joyce Pepple, Acquisitions Director, Consumer Dummies

    Kristin A. Cocks, Product Development Director, Consumer Dummies

    Michael Spring, Vice President and Publisher, Travel

    Kelly Regan, Editorial Director, Travel

Publishing for Technology Dummies

    Andy Cummings, Vice President and Publisher, Dummies Technology/General User

Composition Services

    Gerry Fahey, Vice President of Production Services

    Debbie Stailey, Director of Composition Services

Contents at a Glance

Introduction 1

Part I: Introducing CBT Basics 7

Chapter 1: You Feel the Way You Think....................................9
Chapter 2: Spotting Errors in Your Thinking 19
Chapter 3: Tackling Toxic Thoughts 39
Chapter 4: Behaving like a Scientist: Designing and
Conducting Behavioural Experiments 49
Chapter 5: Pay Attention! Refocusing and Retraining Your Awareness....................61

Part II: Charting the Course: Defining Problems and Setting Goals 71

Chapter 6: Exploring Emotions...73
Chapter 7: Identifying Solutions That Cause You Problems 95
Chapter 8: Setting Your Sights on Goals 107

Part III: Putting CBT into Action 117

Chapter 9: Standing Up to Anxiety and Facing Fear...............119
Chapter 10: Deconstructing and Demolishing Depression 129
Chapter 11: Overcoming Obsessions.....................................143
Chapter 12: Overcoming Low Self-esteem by Accepting Yourself 159
Chapter 13: Cooling Down Your Anger 175

Part IV: Looking Backwards and Moving Forwards 189

Chapter 14: Taking a Fresh Look at Your Past 191
Chapter 15: Moving New Beliefs from Your Head to Your Heart....................209
Chapter 16: Heading for a Healthier and Happier Life.............223
Chapter 17: Overcoming Obstacles to Progress.....................233
Chapter 18: Psychological Gardening: Maintaining Your CBT Gains....................243
Chapter 19: Working with the Professionals 253

Part V: The Part of Tens 265

Chapter 20: Ten Healthy Attitudes for Living 267
Chapter 21: Ten Self-Esteem Boosters That Don't Work 275
Chapter 22: Ten Ways to Lighten Up......................................281
Chapter 23: Ten Books to Add to Your Library 289

Appendix A: Resources 293

Appendix B: Forms...297

Index 309

Table of Contents

Introduction 1

About This Book...1
Conventions Used in This Book 2
What You're Not to Read 2
Foolish Assumptions 3
How This Book Is Organised..3
    Part I: Introducing CBT Basics...................................3
    Part II: Charting the Course: Defining Problems
       and Setting Goals 3
    Part III: Putting CBT into Action 4
    Part IV: Looking Backwards and Moving Forwards 4
    Part V: The Part of Tens..5
    Appendixes...5
Icons Used in This Book..5
Where to Go from Here..6

Part 1: Introducing CBT Basics 7

Chapter 1: You Feel the Way You Think 9

Using Scientifically Tested Methods.................................9
Understanding CBT..11
    Combining science, philosophy, and behaviour 11
    Progressing from problems to goals............................12
Making the Thought–Feeling Link....................................12
    Emphasising the meanings you attach to events.........13
    Acting out 13
Learning Your ABCs 14
Characterising CBT 16

Chapter 2: Spotting Errors in Your Thinking 19

Catastrophising: Turning Mountains Back Into Molehills........20
All-or-Nothing Thinking: Finding Somewhere in Between 21
Fortune-telling: Stepping Away from the Crystal Ball.............23
Mind-Reading: Taking Your Guesses with a Pinch of Salt 24
Emotional Reasoning: Reminding Yourself That Feelings
    Aren't Facts 26
Overgeneralising: Avoiding the Part/Whole Error 27
Labelling: Giving Up the Rating Game 28
Making Demands: Thinking Flexibly 30
Mental Filtering: Keeping an Open Mind...........................31

Disqualifying the Positive: Keeping the Baby When Throwing Out
the Bathwater 33
Low Frustration Tolerance: Realising You Can Bear the 'Unbearable'....34
Personalising: Removing Yourself from the Centre of the Universe........35

Chapter 3: Tackling Toxic Thoughts **39**
Catching NATs..39
Making the thought–feeling link 40
Becoming more objective about your thoughts.............................40
Stepping Through the ABC Form I 40
Creating Constructive Alternatives: Completing the ABC Form II..........44

**Chapter 4: Behaving like a Scientist: Designing and Conducting
Behavioural Experiments** **49**
Seeing for Yourself: Reasons for Doing Behavioural Experiments 50
Testing Out Predictions...50
Seeking Evidence to See Which Theory Best Fits the Facts 53
Conducting Surveys..55
Making Observations...57
Ensuring Successful Behavioural Experiments 57
Keeping Records of Your Experiments...58

**Chapter 5: Pay Attention! Refocusing and Retraining
Your Awareness** **61**
Training in Task Concentration...62
Choosing to concentrate 62
Tuning in to tasks and the world around you..............................65
Tackling the task concentration record sheet 66
Becoming More Mindful 68
Being present in the moment...68
Letting your thoughts pass by...68
Discerning when not to listen to yourself 69
Incorporating mindful daily tasks 70

*Part II: Charting the Course: Defining Problems
and Setting Goals* **71**

Chapter 6: Exploring Emotions **73**
Naming Your Feelings 74
Thinking What to Feel..75
Understanding the Anatomy of Emotions...76
Comparing Healthy and Unhealthy Emotions 77
Spot the difference in thinking 86
Spot the difference in behaving, and ways you want to behave....88
Spot the difference in what you focus on....................................89
Spotting Similarities in Your Physical Sensations................................90

Identifying Feelings about Feelings..91
Defining Your Emotional Problems 92
    Making a statement 92
    Rating your emotional problem..93

Chapter 7: Identifying Solutions That Cause You Problems 95

When Feeling Better Can Make Your Problems Worse..............................95
Getting Over Depression Without Getting Yourself Down 97
Loosening Your Grip on Control 97
Feeling Secure in an Uncertain World...98
Surmounting the Side Effects of Excessive Safety-Seeking 100
Wending Your Way Out of Worry..102
Preventing the Perpetuation of Your Problems 103
Helping Yourself: Putting the Petals on Your Vicious Flower.................104

Chapter 8: Setting Your Sights on Goals 107

Putting SPORT Into Your Goals 107
Homing In on How You Want to Be Different 108
    Setting goals in relation to your current problems.......................109
    Making a statement 110
Maximising Your Motivation...110
    Identifying inspiration for change 110
    Focusing on the benefits of change 111
    Completing a cost–benefit analysis 111
    Recording your progress...113

Part III: Putting CBT into Action 117

Chapter 9: Standing Up to Anxiety and Facing Fear 119

Acquiring Anti-Anxiety Attitudes 119
    Thinking realistically about the probability of bad events...........119
    Avoiding extreme thinking 120
    Taking the fear out of fear 120
Attacking Anxiety..122
    Winning by not fighting 122
    Defeating fear with FEAR 122
    Repeatedly confronting your fears 123
    Keeping your exposure challenging but not overwhelming.........123
    Shedding safety behaviours...125
    Recording your fear-fighting 125
Overriding Common Anxieties 125
    Socking it to social anxiety..126
    Waging war on worry..126
    Pounding on panic 126
    Assaulting agoraphobia...127
    Dealing with post-traumatic stress disorder 127
    Hitting back at fear of heights..127

Chapter 10: Deconstructing and Demolishing Depression **129**

Understanding the Nature of Depression 130
Looking at What Fuels Depression..131
Going Round and Round in Your Head: Ruminative Thinking..............132
Catching yourself in the act 133
Arresting ruminations before they arrest you...........................134
Activating Yourself as an Antidepressant 135
Tackling inactivity 135
Dealing with the here and now: Solving problems.....................136
Taking care of yourself and your environment..........................138
Getting a Good Night's Sleep 138
Setting realistic sleep expectations 139
Making your bedroom oh so cosy..140
Managing Suicidal Thoughts..141

Chapter 11: Overcoming Obsessions **143**

Identifying and Understanding Obsessional Problems 144
Understanding obsessive-compulsive disorder (OCD) 145
Recognising health anxiety 146
Understanding body dysmorphic disorder (BDD)........................147
Identifying Unhelpful Behaviours 149
Acquiring Anti-obsessional Attitudes..149
Tolerating doubt and uncertainty 150
Trusting your judgement...150
Treating your thoughts as nothing more than thoughts..............151
Being flexible and not trying too hard...151
Using external and practical criteria 152
Allowing your mind and body to do their own things..................152
Normalising physical sensations and imperfections....................153
Facing Your Fears: Reducing (And Stopping) Rituals 153
Resist! Resist! Resist!..154
Delaying and modifying rituals 154
Being Realistic about Responsibility 155
Dividing up your responsibility pie...155
Retraining your attention 157

**Chapter 12: Overcoming Low Self-esteem
by Accepting Yourself** **159**

Identifying Issues of Self-Esteem 159
Developing Self-Acceptance...160
Understanding that you have worth because you're human 161
Appreciating that you're too complex to globally
measure or rate...161
Acknowledging your ever-changing nature 163
Accepting your fallible nature 165
Valuing your uniqueness 165
Using self-acceptance to aid self-improvement............................166
Understanding that acceptance doesn't mean giving up.............168

Being Inspired to Change 168
Actioning Self-Acceptance 170
    Self-talking your way to self-acceptance 170
    Following the best-friend argument 171
    Dealing with doubts and reservations...........................172
Selecting the Self-help Journey to Self-Acceptance 173

Chapter 13: Cooling Down Your Anger **175**
Discerning the Difference between Healthy and Unhealthy Anger 175
    Key characteristics of unhealthy anger...........................176
    Hallmarks of healthy anger 177
Assembling Attitudes That Underpin Healthy Anger 178
    Putting up with other people..179
    Forming flexible preferences 180
    Accepting other people as fallible human beings 181
    Accepting yourself 182
    Developing high frustration tolerance...........................182
    Pondering the pros and cons of your temper.................183
Imparting Your Indignation in a Healthy Way........................184
    Asserting yourself effectively 184
    Coping with criticism...185
    Using the disarming technique....................................186
Dealing with Difficulties in Overcoming Anger 187

Part IV: Looking Backwards and Moving Forwards........189

Chapter 14: Taking a Fresh Look at Your Past **191**
Exploring How Your Past Can Influence Your Present 191
Identifying Your Core Beliefs 192
    The three camps of core beliefs 194
    Seeing how your core beliefs interact 195
Detecting Your Core Beliefs 195
    Following a downward arrow.......................................195
    Picking up clues from your dreaming and screaming 196
    Tracking themes 197
    Filling in the blanks 197
Understanding the Impact of Core Beliefs 198
    Spotting when you are acting according to old rules
       and beliefs 198
    Understanding that unhealthy core beliefs make
       you prejudiced 199
Making a Formulation of Your Beliefs.................................200
Limiting the Damage: Being Aware of Core Beliefs 203
Developing Alternatives to Your Core Beliefs 204
    Revisiting history 205
    Starting from scratch 207

Chapter 15: Moving New Beliefs from Your Head to Your Heart . . . 209

Defining the Beliefs You Want to Strengthen 209
Acting As If You Already Believe 211
Building a Portfolio of Arguments..212
Generating arguments against an unhelpful belief......................212
Generating arguments to support your helpful
alternative belief 214
Understanding That Practice Makes Imperfect 215
Dealing with your doubts and reservations 215
Zigging and zagging through the zigzag technique.....................216
Putting your new beliefs to the test..218
Nurturing Your New Beliefs 220

Chapter 16: Heading for a Healthier and Happier Life 223

Planning to Prevent Relapse...223
Filling In the Gaps...224
Choosing absorbing activities 224
Matchmaking your pursuits 225
Putting personal pampering into practice 225
Overhauling Your Lifestyle..226
Walking the walk 227
Talking the talk 229
Getting intimate 229

Chapter 17: Overcoming Obstacles to Progress 233

Tackling Emotions That Get in the Way of Change 233
Shifting shame 233
Getting rid of guilt 234
Putting aside pride 235
Seeking support..236
Trying a little tenderness 236
Adopting Positive Principles That Promote Progress..........................237
Understanding that simple doesn't mean easy 237
Being optimistic about getting better...238
Staying focused on your goals 238
Persevering and repeating 239
Tackling Task-Interfering Thoughts 239

**Chapter 18: Psychological Gardening: Maintaining
Your CBT Gains 243**

Knowing Your Weeds from Your Flowers...243
Working on Weeds...244
Nipping weeds in the bud..244
Spotting where weeds may grow...246
Dealing with recurrent weeds 247

Tending Your Flowers 248
    Planting new varieties..249
    Being a compassionate gardener 251

Chapter 19: Working with the Professionals 253

Procuring Professional Help 253
    Thinking about the right therapy for you 255
    Meeting the experts 256
Tracking Down the Right CBT Therapist for You............257
    Asking yourself the right questions 257
    Speaking to the specialists 259
Making the Most of CBT 261
    Discussing issues during sessions 261
    Being active between sessions 263

Part V: The Part of Tens **265**

Chapter 20: Ten Healthy Attitudes for Living 267

Assuming Emotional Responsibility: You Feel the Way You Think........267
Thinking Flexibly...268
Valuing Your Individuality 269
Accepting That Life Can Be Unfair 269
Understanding That Approval from Others Isn't Necessary.................270
Realising Love's Desirable, Not Essential 270
Tolerating Short-Term Discomfort..............................271
Enacting Enlightened Self-Interest 272
Pursuing Interests and Acting Consistently with Your Values 273
Tolerating Uncertainty 273

Chapter 21: Ten Self-Esteem Boosters That Don't Work 275

Putting Others Down 275
Thinking You're Special 276
Trying to Get Everyone to Like You 276
Placing Yourself above Criticism 277
Avoiding Failure, Disapproval, Rejection, and Other Animals 278
Avoiding Your Emotions 278
Attempting to Feel More Significant by Controlling Others 278
Over-Defending Your Self-Worth 279
Feeling Superior 279
Blaming Nature or Nuture for Your Problems 280

Chapter 22: Ten Ways to Lighten Up 281

Accept That You Can – and Will – Make Mistakes 281
Try Something New..282

Stamp on Shame..282
Laugh at Yourself...283
Don't Take Offence So Easily 284
Make Good Use of Criticism..284
Settle into Social Situations 285
Encourage Your Creativity to Flow 286
Act Adventurously 286
Enjoy Yourself: It's Later than You Think..................287

Chapter 23: Ten Books to Add to Your Library **289**
Cognitive Therapy – Basics and Beyond.....................289
Cognitive Therapy and the Emotional Disorders..........289
Full Catastrophe Living..290
Overcoming 290
Overcoming Anger 290
Oxford Guide to Behavioural Experiments in Cognitive Therapy............290
Reason and Emotion in Psychotherapy........................291
Reinventing Your Life 291
Status Anxiety 291
A Woman in Your Own Right.......................................291

Appendix A: Resources.................................**293**
Organisations in the United Kingdom 293
Organisations in the United States 294
Other Organisations 296

Appendix B: Forms **297**
The 'Old Meaning–New Meaning' Sheet.....................297
The Cost–Benefit Analysis Form 299
The 'Tic-Toc' Sheet..301
The Zigzag Form 303
The Vicious Flower 305
The Task Concentration Sheet 306
The ABC Form I 307
The ABC Form II 308

Index **309**

Introduction

· ·

*C*ognitive behavioural therapy, or CBT, is growing in popularity as an effi-cient and long lasting treatment for many different types of psychologi-cal problem. If the word 'psychological' sends you running from the room screaming, try to consider the term referring to problems that affect your emotional rather than your physical sense of wellbeing. At some point in your life, something's going to go a bit wrong with your body. So why on earth do humans assume that their minds and emotions should be above the odd hiccup, upset, or even more serious difficulty?

This book gives you a comprehensive introduction to the theory and applica-tion of CBT techniques. Although we don't have the space to go into nitty-gritty specifics about how to use CBT to overcome every type of emotional or psychological problem, we do try to lead you in a helpful direction. We believe all the CBT principles and strategies outlined in this book can improve your life and help you to stay healthy, regardless of whether you are currently working with a psychotherapist or other mental health professional.

In addition, whether you think your problems are minimal, you're living the life of Riley, you feel mildly depressed, or you've had years of uncomfortable psychological symptoms, CBT can help you. We ask you to be open-minded and to use the stuff in this book to help you make your life better and fuller.

About This Book

If you're embarking on a journey of self-help or self-improvement, we hope that this book provides a useful introduction to CBT techniques and will be of benefit to you. Depending on the degree of disruption and distress that your personal difficulties are causing you, this book may or may not be enough treatment to help you recover. The book may spur you on to get further help (Chapter 19 has more on seeking professional help) to really knock your emo-tional demons on the head. This book covers the following:

✔ The basics of using CBT as a scientifically tested and verified psy-chotherapeutic method of overcoming common emotional problems.

✔ Ways in which you can identify your problems and set specific goals for how you would rather be living your life.

✔ Techniques to identify errors in the way you may be thinking and to adopt more helpful thoughts, attitudes, philosophies, and beliefs.

- ✔ Behavioural experiments and strategies you can incorporate into your life to improve your day-to-day functioning.

- ✔ Information that can help you to understand, normalise, and address some common human problems. You may think that you're the only person in the world who feels and thinks the way you do. This book shows you that many of the problems you may be experiencing such as depression, anxiety, anger, and obsessions are in fact very common. You are not alone.

We hope that the whole experience will be at least a little entertaining in the process. So read on, welcome new concepts, and consider trying some of the ideas we offer in the book.

Conventions Used in This Book

To make your reading experience easier and to alert you to key words or points, we use certain conventions.

- ✔ *Italics* introduce new terms, underscore key differences in meaning between words, and highlight the most important aspects of a sentence or example.

- ✔ We use the terms 'him' in even-numbered chapters and 'her' in odd-numbered chapters when writing, with a view to incorporate gender equality.

- ✔ The case studies in the book are illustrative of actual clients we have treated and are not direct representations of any particular clients.

- ✔ **Bold** text is used to show the action part of numbered lists.

What You're Not to Read

This book is written in a rough order to help you progress from the basics of CBT on to more complex techniques and ideas. However, you can read the chapters in any order you like or just hit on the ones that cover subjects you think you want to know more about.

To make your reading experience even easier, we identify 'skippable' material:

- ✔ **Sidebars:** Within most chapters, we include sidebars of shaded text. These sidebars contain interesting titbits of information or occasionally expand on a topic within the chapter. Read them if they sound interesting to you and skip them if they don't.

- ✔ **Our acknowledgements:** Probably pretty boring to the average reader.

Foolish Assumptions

In writing this little tome, we make the following assumptions about you, dear reader:

- ✔ You're human.

- ✔ As a human, you're likely at some stage in your life to experience some sort of emotional problem that you'd like to surmount.

- ✔ You've heard about CBT, or are intrigued by CBT, or have had CBT suggested to you by a doctor, friend, or mental health professional as a possible treatment for your specific difficulties.

- ✔ Even if you don't think you're particularly in need of CBT right now, you want to discover more about some of the principles outlined in this book.

- ✔ You think that your life is absolutely fine right now, but you want to find interesting and useful information in the book that will enhance your life further.

How This Book Is Organised

This book is divided into five parts and 23 chapters. The table of contents lists subheadings with more information about every chapter, but the following describes the major sections of the book.

Part 1: Introducing CBT Basics

This part gives you a pretty good idea about what CBT consists of and how the techniques differs from other forms of psychotherapy. 'You think how you feel' is a good way of summing up CBT, and the chapters in this part expand on this simple idea. We explain common thinking errors as well as ways to counteract skewed thinking. You discover the basic CBT model of emotional disturbance and find out more about how you can make positive changes, even when your circumstances and other people in your life are unlikely to change for the better.

Part II: Charting the Course: Defining Problems and Setting Goals

This part helps you to define your emotional problems more accurately, see where your problems are springing from, and develop solid goals for your emotional future. Some of your valiant attempts to deal with your worries, terrors, and ideas about yourself are frequently counterproductive in the long term. These chapters explore this notion and give you ideas about more productive alternative strategies to produce long-term benefits.

Part III: Putting CBT into Action

Actions speak louder than words, and believe us when we say that actions also produce better results than words alone. Correcting your thinking is an important endeavour, but all your efforts to think healthily can fall apart at the seams unless you translate new beliefs into new action. The chapters in this part set out some good ways to test your new ways of thinking, strengthen healthy new beliefs, and promote helpful emotional responses to life, the universe, and everything else. If you don't believe us, try out the ideas for yourself! We also explore some common human difficulties such as anxiety and obsessional problems.

Part IV: Looking Backwards and Moving Forwards

'But CBT ignores my past!' is an oft-heard complaint by individuals new to CBT. So we're here to tell you that CBT does not ignore your past. Yes, CBT concentrates on how your *current* thinking and behaviour cause your *current* difficulties. This part aids you in recognising experiences from your past that may have led you to form certain types of beliefs about yourself, other people, and the world around you. Assigning updated, helpful, and more accurate meanings to past events really can make a difference to the way you experience life today. So read on!

Part V: The Part of Tens

This section of the book is part fun and part solid CBT stuff. Looking here first can help you connect to other parts of the book and provide quick and easy tips for healthier living, boosting your self-esteem the right way, and lightening up your attitudes towards yourself and life in general.

Appendixes

Appendix A gives you a list of useful organisations and Web sites that you may wish to investigate.

Throughout the book, we refer to and explain various forms and CBT tools that may be helpful to you. Appendix B provides you with blank forms to photocopy at will and use to your heart's delight. You can also print out the forms from www.wiley.com/go/cbt.

Icons Used in This Book

We use the following icons in this book to alert you to certain types of information that you can choose to read, commit to memory (and possibly interject into dinner party conversation), or maybe just utterly ignore:

This icon highlights practical advice for putting CBT into practice.

This icon is a cheerful, if sometimes urgent, reminder of important points to take notice of.

This icon marks out specific things to avoid or possible traps to keep your eyes open for in your quest for better emotional health.

This icon highlights CBT terminology that may sound a bit like psychobabble but is commonly used by CBT practitioners.

This icon alerts you to stuff that has a bit of a philosophical basis and may need some mulling over in your spare time.

This icon indicates a CBT technique that you can try out in real life to see what results you get.

Where to Go from Here

We'd really like you to read everything in this book and then recommend it to all your friends and random people you meet on the street. Failing that, just use this book as your reference guide to CBT, dipping in and out of it as and when you need to.

Have a browse through the table of contents and turn to the chapters that look as if they may offer something helpful to you and your current difficulties.

When you've used the book in one way or another, you may decide that you want to get stuck into CBT treatment with a therapist. If so, consult Chapter 19 for more advice on getting treatment.

Part I
Introducing CBT Basics

The 5th Wave — By Rich Tennant

"Let's see if we can identify some of the stress triggers in your life. You mentioned something about a large wolf that periodically shows up and attempts to blow your house down..."

In this part . . .

You'll get to grips with what CBT stand for and why it's such a hot topic among mental health professionals. You'll get a good idea of how your thinking about events leads to how you feel. We'll get you started on recognising and tackling your negative thought patterns, and give you some tips about exerting control over your attention.

Chapter 1

You Feel the Way You Think

In This Chapter

▶ Defining CBT

▶ Exploring the power of meanings

▶ Understanding how your thoughts lead to emotions and behaviours

▶ Getting acquainted with the ABC formula

*C*ognitive behavioural therapy – more commonly referred to as *CBT* – focuses on the way people think and act in order to help them overcome their emotional and behavioural problems.

Many of the effective CBT practices we discuss in this book should seem like everyday good sense. In our opinion, CBT does have some very straightforward and clear principles and is a largely sensible and practical approach to helping people overcome problems. However, human beings don't always act according to sensible principles, and most people find that simple solutions can be very difficult to put into practice sometimes. CBT can maximise on your common sense and help you to do the healthy things that you may sometimes do naturally and unthinkingly in a deliberate and self-enhancing way on a regular basis.

In this chapter we take you through the basic principles of CBT and show you how to use these principles to better understand yourself and your problems.

Using Scientifically Tested Methods

The effectiveness of CBT for various psychological problems has been researched more extensively than any other psychotherapeutic approach. CBT's reputation as a highly effective treatment is growing. Several studies reveal that CBT is more effective than medication alone for the treatment of anxiety and depression. As a result of this research, briefer and more intense treatment methods have been developed for particular anxiety disorders such as panic, anxiety in social settings, or feeling worried all the time.

Scientific research of CBT continues. As a result, more is being discovered about which aspects of the treatment are most useful for different types of people and which therapeutic interventions work best with different types of problems.

Research shows that people who have CBT for various types of problems – in particular, for anxiety and depression – stay well for longer. This means that people who have CBT relapse less often than those who have other forms of psychotherapy or take medication only. This positive result is likely due in part to the *educational aspects* of CBT – people who have CBT receive a lot of information that they can use to become their own therapists.

CBT is growing in popularity. More and more physicians and psychiatrists refer their patients for CBT to help them overcome a wide range of problems with good results. These problems include:

- ✔ Addiction
- ✔ Anger problems
- ✔ Anxiety
- ✔ Body dysmorphic disorder
- ✔ Chronic fatigue syndrome
- ✔ Chronic pain
- ✔ Depression
- ✔ Eating disorders
- ✔ Obsessive-compulsive disorder
- ✔ Panic disorder
- ✔ Personality disorders
- ✔ Phobias
- ✔ Post-traumatic stress disorder
- ✔ Psychotic disorders
- ✔ Relationship problems
- ✔ Social phobia

We discuss many of the disorders in the preceding list in more depth throughout this book but it is very difficult to cover them all. Fortunately, the CBT skills and techniques in this book can be applied to most types of psychological difficulties, so give them a try whether or not your particular problem is specifically discussed.

Understanding CBT

Cognitive behavioural therapy is a school of *psychotherapy* that aims to help people overcome their emotional problems.

- ✔ **Cognitive** means mental processes like thinking. The word 'cognitive' refers to everything that goes on in your mind including dreams, memories, images, thoughts, and attention.

- ✔ **Behaviour** refers to everything that you do. This includes what you say, how you try to solve problems, how you act, and avoidance. Behaviour refers to both action and inaction, for example biting your tongue instead of speaking your mind is still a behaviour even though you are trying *not* to do something.

- ✔ **Therapy** is a word used to describe a systematic approach to combating a problem, illness, or irregular condition.

A central concept in CBT is that *you feel the way you think*. Therefore, CBT works on the principle that you can live more happily and productively if you're thinking in healthy ways. This principle is a very simple way of summing up CBT, and we have many more details to share with you later in the book.

Combining science, philosophy, and behaviour

CBT is a powerful treatment because it combines scientific, philosophical, and behavioural aspects into one comprehensive approach to understanding and overcoming common psychological problems.

- ✔ **Getting scientific.** CBT is scientific not only in the sense that it has been tested and developed through numerous scientific studies, but also in the sense that it encourages clients to become more like scientists. For example, during CBT, you may develop the ability to treat your thoughts as theories and hunches about reality to be tested (what scientists call *hypotheses*), rather than as facts.

- ✔ **Getting philosophical.** CBT recognises that people hold values and beliefs about themselves, the world, and other people. One of the aims of CBT is to help people develop flexible, non-extreme, and self-helping beliefs that help them adapt to reality and pursue their goals.

  Your problems are not all just in your mind. Although CBT places great emphasis on thoughts and behaviour as powerful areas to target for change and development, it also places your thoughts and behaviours within a *context*. CBT recognises that you're influenced by what's going on around you and that your *environment* makes a contribution towards the way you think, feel, and act. However, CBT maintains that you can make a difference to the way you feel by changing unhelpful ways of thinking and behaving – even if you can't change your environment. Incidentally, your environment in the context of CBT includes other people and the way they behave towards you.

✔ **Getting active.** As the name suggests, CBT also strongly emphasises behaviour. Many CBT techniques involve changing the way you think and feel by modifying the way you behave. Examples include gradually becoming more active if you're depressed and lethargic, or facing your fears step by step if you're anxious. CBT also places emphasis on *mental behaviours*, such as worrying and where you focus your attention.

Progressing from problems to goals

A defining characteristic of CBT is that it gives you the tools to develop a *focused* approach. CBT aims to help you move from defined emotional and behavioural problems towards your goals of how you'd like to feel and behave. Thus, CBT is a goal-directed, systematic, problem-solving approach to emotional problems.

Making the Thought–Feeling Link

Like many people, you may assume that if something happens to you, the event *makes* you feel a certain way. For example, if your partner treats you inconsiderately, you may conclude that she *makes* you angry. You may further deduce that her inconsiderate behaviour *makes* you behave in a particular manner, such as sulking or refusing to speak to her for hours (possibly even days; people can sulk for a very long time!).

CBT encourages you to understand that your thinking or *beliefs* lie between the event and your ultimate feelings and actions. Your thoughts, beliefs, and the meanings that you give to an event, produce your emotional and behavioural responses.

So in CBT terms, your partner does not *make* you angry and sulky. Rather, your partner behaves inconsiderately, and you assign a meaning to her behaviour such as 'she's doing this deliberately to upset me!' thus *making yourself* angry and sulky.

Emphasising the meanings you attach to events

The *meaning* you attach to any sort of event influences the emotional responses you have to that event. Positive events normally lead to positive feelings of happiness or excitement, whereas negative events typically lead to negative feelings like sadness or anxiety.

However, the meanings you attach to certain types of negative events may not be wholly accurate, realistic, or helpful. Sometimes, your thinking may lead you to assign extreme meanings to events, leaving you feeling disturbed.

Psychologists use the word 'disturbed' to describe emotional responses that are unhelpful and cause significant discomfort to you. In CBT terminology, 'disturbed' means that an emotional or behavioural response is hindering rather than helping you to adapt and cope with a negative event.

For example, if a potential girlfriend rejects you after the first date (event), you may think 'This proves I'm unlikeable and undesirable' (meaning), and feel depressed (emotion).

CBT involves identifying thoughts, beliefs, and meanings that are activated when you're feeling emotionally disturbed. If you assign less extreme, more helpful, more *accurate* meanings to negative events, you are likely to experience less extreme, less disturbing emotional and behavioural responses.

Thus, on being rejected after the first date (event), you could think 'I guess that person didn't like me that much; oh well – they're not the one for me' (meaning), and feel disappointment (emotion).

Acting out

The ways you think and feel also largely determine the way you *act*. If you feel depressed, you're likely to withdraw and isolate yourself. If you're anxious, you may avoid situations that you find threatening or dangerous. Your behaviours can be problematic for you in many ways, such as the following:

- ✔ **Self-destructive behaviours,** such as excessive drinking or using drugs to quell anxiety, can cause direct physical harm.

- ✔ **Isolating and mood-depressing behaviours,** such as staying in bed all day or not seeing your friends, increase your sense of isolation and maintain your low mood.

- ✔ **Avoidance behaviours,** such as avoiding situations you perceive as threatening (attending a social outing, using a lift, speaking in public), deprive you of the opportunity to confront and overcome your fears.

Consider the reactions of ten people

Different people can attach different meanings to a specific situation, resulting in the potential for a vast array of emotional reactions to one situation. For example, consider ten basically similar people who experience the same event, which is having their partner treat them inconsiderately. Potentially, they can have ten (or maybe more) different emotional responses to precisely the same event, depending on how they *think* about the event:

Person 1 attaches the meaning, 'That idiot has no right to treat me badly – who the hell do they think they are?' and feels angry.

Person 2 thinks, 'This lack of consideration means that my partner doesn't love me' and feels depressed.

Person 3 believes that 'This inconsideration must mean that my partner is about to leave me for someone else' and feels jealous.

Person 4 thinks, 'I don't deserve to be treated poorly because I always do my best to be considerate to my partner' and feels hurt.

Person 5 reckons the event means that 'I must have done something serious to upset my partner for them to treat me like this' and feels guilty.

Person 6 believes that 'This inconsideration is a sign that my partner is losing interest in me' and feels anxious.

Person 7 thinks, 'Aha! Now I have a good enough reason to break up with my partner, which I've been wanting to do for ages!' and feels happy.

Person 8 decides the event means that 'My partner has done a bad thing by treating me in this way, and I'm not prepared to put up with it' and feels annoyed.

Person 9 thinks, 'I really wish my partner had been more considerate because we're usually highly considerate of each other' and feels disappointed.

Person 10 believes that 'My partner must have found out something despicable about me to treat me in this way' and feels ashamed.

You can see from this example that very different meanings can be assigned to the same event and in turn produce very different emotional responses. Some emotional responses are healthier than others; we discuss this matter in depth in Chapter 6.

Learning Your ABCs

When you start to get an understanding of your emotional difficulties, CBT encourages you to break down a specific problem you have using the *ABC format*, in which:

- ✔ A is the *activating event*. An activating event means a real *external* event that has occurred, a future event that you anticipate occurring, or an *internal* event in your mind, such as an image, memory, or dream.

  The 'A' is often referred to as your 'trigger'.

✔ **B** is your *beliefs*. Your beliefs include your thoughts, your personal rules, the demands you make (on yourself, the world, and other people), and the meanings that you attach to external and internal events.

✔ **C** is the *consequences*. Consequences include your emotions, behaviours, and physical sensations that accompany different emotions.

Figure 1-1 shows the ABC parts of a problem in picture form.

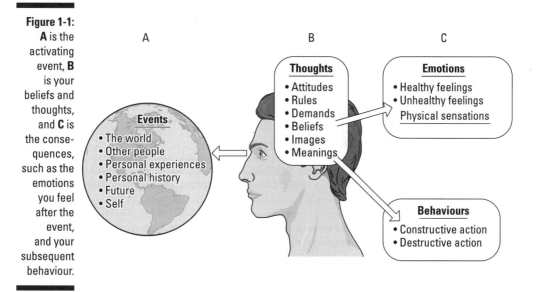

Figure 1-1: **A** is the activating event, **B** is your beliefs and thoughts, and **C** is the consequences, such as the emotions you feel after the event, and your subsequent behaviour.

Writing down your problem in *ABC form* – a central CBT technique – helps you differentiate between your thoughts, feelings, and behaviours, and the *trigger* event. We give more information about the ABC form in Chapter 3, and you can find a blank ABC form at the back of the book.

Consider the ABC formulations of two common emotional problems, anxiety and depression. The ABC of anxiety may look like this:

✔ **A:** You imagine failing a job interview.

✔ **B:** You believe: 'I've got to make sure that I don't mess up this interview, otherwise I'll prove that I'm a failure.'

✔ **C:** You experience anxiety (emotion), butterflies in your stomach (physical sensation), and drink alcohol to calm your nerves (behaviour).

The ABC of depression may look like this:

- ✔ **A:** You fail a job interview.
- ✔ **B:** You believe: 'I should've done better. This means that I'm a failure!'
- ✔ **C:** You experience depression (emotion), loss of appetite (physical sensation), and stay in bed avoiding the outside world (behaviour).

You can use these examples to guide you when you are filling in an ABC form on your own problems. Doing so will help ensure that you record the actual facts of the event under 'A', your thoughts about the event under 'B', and how you feel and act under 'C'. Developing a really clear ABC of your problem can make it much easier for you to realise how your thoughts at 'B' lead to your emotional/behavioural responses at 'C'. (Chapter 3 describes the ABC form more fully.)

Characterising CBT

We give a much fuller description of the principles and practical applications of CBT in the rest of this book. However, here's a quick reference list of key characteristics of CBT. CBT:

- ✔ Emphasises the role of the personal meanings that you give to events in determining your emotional responses.
- ✔ Was developed through extensive scientific evaluation.
- ✔ Focuses more on how your problems are being *maintained* rather than on searching for a single root cause of the problem.
- ✔ Offers practical advice and tools for overcoming common emotional problems (see Chapters 9, 10, and 11).
- ✔ Holds the view that you can change and develop by thinking things through and by trying out new ideas and strategies (head to Chapter 4).
- ✔ Can address material from your past if doing so can help you to understand and change the way you're thinking and acting now (Chapter 14 covers this in depth).
- ✔ Shows you that some of the strategies you're using to cope with your emotional problems are actually maintaining those problems (Chapter 7 is all about this).
- ✔ Strives to normalise your emotions, physical sensations, and thoughts rather than to persuade you that they're clues to 'hidden' problems.

✔ Recognises that you may develop emotional problems *about* your emotional problems, for example feeling ashamed about being depressed. (See Chapter 6 for more on this concept.)

✔ Highlights learning techniques and maximises self-help so that ultimately you can become your own therapist. (Head to Chapter 18.)

Getting complicated

Sticking to the simple ABC formulation in which A+B=C can serve you well. But if that seems a little simplistic, you can consider the more complicated formulations shown here:

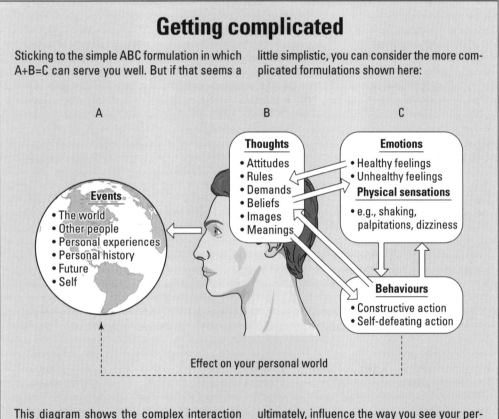

A B C

Events
• The world
• Other people
• Personal experiences
• Personal history
• Future
• Self

Thoughts
• Attitudes
• Rules
• Demands
• Beliefs
• Images
• Meanings

Emotions
• Healthy feelings
• Unhealthy feelings

Physical sensations
• e.g., shaking, palpitations, dizziness

Behaviours
• Constructive action
• Self-defeating action

Effect on your personal world

This diagram shows the complex interaction between your thoughts, feelings, and behaviours. Although your thoughts affect how you feel, your feelings also affect your thinking. So, if you're having depressed thoughts, your mood is likely to be low. The lower your mood, the more likely you are to act in a depressed manner and to think pessimistically. The combination of feeling depressed, thinking pessimistically, and acting in a depressed manner can, ultimately, influence the way you see your personal world. You may focus on negative events in your life and the world in general and therefore accumulate more negative As. This interaction between A, B, and C can become a vicious circle.

CBT pays a lot of attention to changing both unhealthy thinking patterns and unhealthy patterns of behaviour.

Chapter 2

Spotting Errors in Your Thinking

....

In This Chapter

▶ Identifying classic pitfalls in human thought

▶ Correcting your thinking

▶ Getting to know the thinking errors you make most

....

You probably don't spend a lot of time mulling over the pros and cons of the way you think. Most people don't – but to be frank, most people ideally ought to!

One of the messages of CBT is that the thoughts, attitudes, and beliefs you hold have a big effect on the way you interpret the world around you and on how you feel. So, if you're feeling excessively bad, chances are that you're thinking badly – or, at least, in an unhelpful way. Of course, you probably don't *intend* to think in an unhelpful way, and no doubt you're largely unaware that you do.

Thinking errors are slips in thinking that everyone makes from time to time. Just as a virus stops your computer from dealing with information effectively, so thinking errors prevent you from making accurate assessments of your experiences. Thinking errors lead you to get the wrong end of the stick, jump to conclusions, and assume the worst. Thinking errors get in the way of, or cause you to distort, the facts. However, you do have the ability to step back and take another look at the way you're thinking and set yourself straight.

Months or years after the event, you've probably recalled a painful or embarrassing experience and been struck by how differently you feel about it at this later stage. Perhaps you can even laugh about the situation now. Why didn't you laugh back then? Because of the way you were thinking at the time.

To err is most definitely human. Or, as American psychotherapist Albert Ellis is quoted as saying, 'If the Martians ever find out how human beings think, they'll kill themselves laughing.' By understanding the thinking errors we outline in this chapter, you can spot your unhelpful thoughts and put them straight more quickly. Get ready to identify and respond in healthier ways to some of the most common 'faulty' and unhelpful ways of thinking identified by researchers and clinicians.

Catastrophising: Turning Mountains Back Into Molehills

Catastrophising is taking a relatively minor negative event and imagining all sorts of disasters resulting from that one small event, as we sum up in Figure 2-1.

Figure 2-1: Catastrophising.

Consider these examples of catastrophising:

✔ You're at a party and you accidentally stumble headlong into a flower arrangement. After you extract yourself from the foliage, you scurry home and conclude that everyone at the party witnessed your little trip and laughed at you.

✔ You're waiting for your teenage daughter to return home after an evening at the cinema with friends. The clock strikes 10:00 p.m., and you hear no reassuring rattle of her key in the door. By 10:05 p.m., you start imagining her accepting a lift home from a friend who drives recklessly. At 10:10 p.m., you're convinced she's been involved in a head-on collision and paramedics are at the scene. By 10:15 p.m., you're weeping over her grave.

✔ Your new partner declines an invitation to have dinner with your parents. Before giving him a chance to explain his reasons, you put down the phone and decide that this is his way of telling you the relationship's over. Furthermore, you imagine that right now he's ringing friends and telling them what a mistake it was dating you. You decide you're never going to find another partner and will die old and lonely.

Catastrophising leads many an unfortunate soul to misinterpret a social faux pas as a social disaster, a late arrival as a car accident, or a minor disagreement as total rejection.

Nip catastrophic thinking in the bud by recognising it for what it is – just thoughts. When you find yourself thinking of the worst possible scenario, try the following strategies:

- ✔ **Put your thoughts in perspective.** Even if everyone at the party did see your flower-arranging act, are you sure no one was sympathetic? Surely you aren't the only person in the world to have tripped over in public. Chances are, people are far less interested in your embarrassing moment than you think. Falling over at a party isn't great, but in the grand scheme of things it's hardly society-page news.

- ✔ **Consider less terrifying explanations.** What other reasons are there for your daughter being late? Isn't being late for curfew a common feature of adolescence? Perhaps the movie ran over, or she got caught up chatting and forgot the time. Don't get so absorbed in extreme emotions that you're startled to find your daughter in the doorway apologising about missing the bus.

- ✔ **Weigh up the evidence.** Do you have enough information to conclude that your partner wants to leave you? Has he given you any reason to think this before? Look for evidence that contradicts your catastrophic assumption. For example, have you had more enjoyable times together than not?

- ✔ **Focus on what you can do to cope with the situation, and the people or resources that can come to your aid.** Engaging in a few more social encounters can help you put your party faux pas behind you. You can repair a damaged relationship – or find another. Even an injury following an accident can be fixed with medical care.

 No matter how great a travesty you create in your mind, the world's unlikely to end because of it even if the travesty comes to pass. You're probably far more capable of surviving embarrassing and painful events than you give yourself credit for – human beings can be very resilient.

All-or-Nothing Thinking: Finding Somewhere in Between

All-or-nothing or *black-or-white thinking* (see Figure 2-2) is extreme thinking that can lead to extreme emotions and behaviours. People either love you or hate you, right? Something's either perfect or a disaster. You're either responsibility-free or totally to blame? Sound sensible? We hope not!

Figure 2-2:
All-or-
nothing
thinking.

Unfortunately, humans fall into the all-or-nothing trap all too easily:

✔ Imagine you're trying to eat healthily in order to lose weight and you cave in to the temptation of a doughnut. All-or-nothing thinking may lead you to conclude that your plan is in ruins and then to go on to eat the other 11 doughnuts in the pack.

✔ You're studying a degree course and you fail one module. All-or-nothing thinking makes you decide that the whole endeavour is pointless. Either you get the course totally right or it's just a write-off.

Consider the humble thermometer as your guide to overcoming the tendency of all-or-nothing thinking. A thermometer reads degrees of temperature, not only 'hot' and 'cold'. Think like a thermometer – in degrees, not extremes. You can use the following pointers to help you change your thinking:

✔ **Be realistic.** You can't possibly get through life without making mistakes. One doughnut doesn't a diet ruin. Remind yourself of your goal, forgive yourself for the minor slip, and resume your diet.

✔ **Develop 'both–and' reasoning skills.** An alternative to all-or-nothing thinking is *both–and reasoning*. You need to mentally allow two seeming opposites to exist together. You can *both* succeed in your overall educational goals *and* fail a test or two. Life is not a case of being either a success or a failure. You can *both* assume that you're an OK person as you are *and* strive to change in specific ways.

All-or-nothing thinking can sabotage goal-directed behaviour. You're far more likely to throw in the towel at the first sign of something blocking your goal when you refuse to allow a margin for error. Beware of 'either/or' statements and global labels such as 'good' and 'bad' or 'success' and 'failure'. Neither people nor life situations are often that cut and dry.

Fortune-telling: Stepping Away from the Crystal Ball

Often, clients tell us after they've done something they were anxious about that the actual event wasn't half as bad as they'd predicted. Predictions are the problem here. You probably don't possess extrasensory perceptions that allow you to see into the future. You probably can't see into the future even with the aid of a crystal ball like the one in Figure 2-3. And yet, you may try to predict future events. Unfortunately, the predictions you make may be negative:

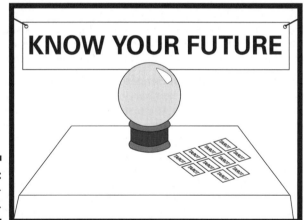

Figure 2-3: Fortune-telling.

KNOW YOUR FUTURE

✔ You've been feeling a bit depressed lately and you aren't enjoying your-self like you used to. Someone from work invites you to a party, but you decide that if you go you won't have a good time. The food will unpalat-able, the music will be irksome, and the other guests are sure to find you boring. So, you opt to stay in and bemoan the state of your social life.

✔ You fancy the bloke who sells you coffee every morning on the way to the office, and you'd like to go out with him on a date. You predict that if you ask him, you'll be so anxious that you'll say something stupid. Anyway, he's bound to say no thanks – someone that attractive must surely be in a relationship.

✔ You always thought that hang-gliding would be fun, but you've got an anxious disposition. If you try the sport, you're sure to lose your nerve at the last minute and just end up wasting your time and money.

You're better off letting the future unfold without trying to guess how it may turn out. Put the dustcover back on the crystal ball and leave the tarot cards alone, and try the following strategies instead:

✔ **Test out your predictions.** You really never know how much fun you might have at a party until you get there – and the food could be amazing. Maybe the chap at the coffee shop has got a partner, but you won't be sure until you ask. To find out more about testing out your predictions, have a read through Chapter 4.

✔ **Be prepared to take risks.** Isn't it worth possibly losing a bit of cash for the opportunity to try a sport you've always been interested in? And can't you bear the possibility of appearing a trifle nervous for the chance to get to know someone you really like? There's a saying 'a ship is safe in a harbour, but that's not what ships are built for'. Learning to live experimentally and taking calculated risks is a recipe for keeping life interesting.

✔ **Understand that your past experiences don't determine your future experiences.** Just because the last party you went to turned out to be a dreary homage to the seventies, the last person you asked out went a bit green, and that scuba-diving venture resulted in a severe case of the bends doesn't mean that you'll never have better luck again.

Typically, fortune-telling stops you from taking action. It can also become a bit of a self-fulfilling prophecy. If you keep telling yourself that you won't enjoy that party, you're liable to make that prediction come true. Same goes for meeting new people and trying new things. So, put on your party gear, ask him out for dinner, and book yourself in for some hang-gliding.

Mind-Reading: Taking Your Guesses with a Pinch of Salt

So, you think you know what other people are thinking, do you? With *mind-reading* (see Figure 2-4), the tendency is often to assume that others are thinking negative things about you or have negative motives and intentions.

Figure 2-4:
Mind-
reading.

Here are some examples of mind-reading tendencies:

✔ You're chatting with someone and they look over your shoulder as you're speaking, break eye contact, and (perish the thought) yawn. You conclude immediately that the other person thinks your conversation is mind-numbing and that he'd rather be talking to someone else.

✔ Your boss advises that you book some time off to use up your annual leave. You decide that he's saying this because he thinks your work is rubbish and wants the opportunity to interview for your replacement while you're on leave.

✔ You pass a neighbour on the street. He says a quick hello but doesn't look very friendly or pleased to see you. You think that he must be annoyed with you about your dog howling at the last full moon and is making plans to report you to environmental health.

You can never know for certain what another person is thinking, so you're wise to pour salt on your negative assumptions. Stand back and take a look at all the evidence to hand. Take control of your tendency to mind-read by trying the following:

✔ **Generate some alternative reasons for what you see.** The person you're chatting with may be tired, be preoccupied with his own thoughts, or just have spotted someone he knows.

✔ **Consider that your guesses may be wrong.** Are your fears really about your boss's motives, or do they concern your own insecurity about your abilities at work? Do you have enough information or hard evidence to conclude that your boss thinks your work is substandard? Does it follow logically that 'consider booking time off' means 'you're getting the sack'?

> ✔ **Get more information (if appropriate).** Ask your neighbour whether your dog kept him up all night, and think of some ways to muffle your pet next time the moon waxes.

You tend to mind-read what you fear most. Mind-reading is a bit like putting a slide in a slide projector. What you *project* or imagine is going on in other people's minds is very much based on what's already in yours.

Emotional Reasoning: Reminding Yourself That Feelings Aren't Facts

Surely we're wrong about this one. Surely your feelings are real hard evidence of the way things are? Actually, no! Often, relying too heavily on your feelings as a guide leads you off the reality path. Here are some examples of emotional reasoning:

> ✔ Your partner has been spending long nights at the office with a co-worker for the past month. You feel jealous and suspicious of your partner. Based on these feelings, you conclude that your partner's having an affair with his co-worker.
>
> ✔ You feel guilty out of the blue. You conclude that you must have done something wrong otherwise you wouldn't be feeling guilty.

When you feel emotional reasoning taking over your thoughts, take a step back and try the following:

1. **Take notice of your thoughts.** Note thoughts such as 'I'm feeling nervous, something must be wrong' and 'I'm so angry, and that really shows how badly you've behaved', and recognise that feelings are not always the best measure of reality, especially if you're not in the best emotional shape at the moment.

2. **Ask yourself how you'd view the situation if you were feeling calmer.** Look to see if there is any concrete evidence to support your interpretation of your feelings. For example, is there really any hard evidence that something bad is going to happen?

3. **Give yourself time to allow your feelings to subside.** When you're feeling calmer, review your conclusions and remember that it is quite possible that your feelings are the consequence of your present emotional state (or even just fatigue) rather than indicators of the state of reality.

The problem with viewing your feelings as factual is that you stop looking for contradictory information – or for any additional information at all. Balance your emotional reasoning with a little more looking at the facts that support and contradict your views, as we show in Figure 2-5.

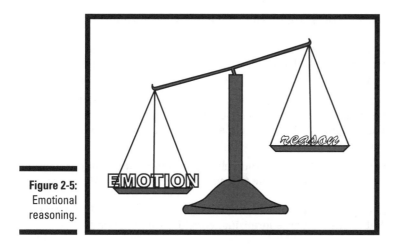

Figure 2-5:
Emotional
reasoning.

Overgeneralising: Avoiding the Part/Whole Error

Overgeneralising is the error of drawing global conclusions from one or more events. When you find yourself thinking 'always', 'never', 'people are . . .', or 'the world's . . .', you may well be overgeneralising. Take a look at Figure 2-6. Here, our stick man sees one black sheep in a flock and instantly assumes the whole flock of sheep is black. However, his overgeneralisation is inaccurate because the rest of the flock are white sheep.

Figure 2-6:
Overgener-
alising.

You might recognise overgeneralising in the following examples:

✓ You feel down. When you get into your car to go to work, it doesn't start. You think to yourself, 'Things like this are always happening to me. Nothing ever goes right', which makes you feel even more gloomy.

✓ You become angry easily. Travelling to see a friend, you're delayed by a fellow passenger who cannot find the money to pay her train fare. You think, 'This is typical! Other people are just so stupid', and you become tense and angry.

✓ You tend to feel guilty easily. You yell at your child for not understanding his homework and then decide that you're a thoroughly rotten parent.

Situations are rarely so stark or extreme that they merit terms like 'always' and 'never'. Rather than overgeneralising, consider the following:

✓ **Get a little perspective.** How true is the thought that nothing *ever* goes right for you? How many other people in the world may be having car trouble at this precise moment?

✓ **Suspend judgement.** When you judge all people as stupid, including the poor creature waiting in line for the train, you make yourself more outraged and are less able to deal effectively with a relatively minor hiccup.

✓ **Be specific.** Would you be a *totally* rotten parent for losing patience with your child? Can you legitimately conclude that one incident of poor parenting cancels out all the good things you do for your little one? Perhaps your impatience is simply an area you need to target for improvement.

Shouting at your child in a moment of stress no more makes you a rotten parent than singing him a great lullaby makes you a perfect parent. Condemning yourself on the basis of making a mistake does nothing to solve the problem, so be specific and steer clear of global conclusions.

Labelling: Giving Up the Rating Game

Labels, and the process of labelling people and events, are everywhere. For example, people who have low self-esteem may label themselves as 'worthless', 'inferior', or 'inadequate' (see Figure 2-7).

Figure 2-7:
Labelling.

If you label other people as 'no good' or 'useless', you're likely to become angry with them. Or perhaps you label the world as 'unsafe' or 'totally unfair'? The error here is that you're globally rating things that are too complex for a definitive label. The following are examples of labelling:

- ✔ You read a distressing article in the newspaper about a rise in crime in your city. The article activates your belief that you live in a thoroughly dangerous place, which contributes to you feeling anxious about going out.

- ✔ You receive a poor mark for an essay. You start to feel low and label yourself as a failure.

- ✔ You become angry when someone cuts in front of you in a traffic queue. You label the other driver as a total loser for his bad driving.

Strive to avoid labelling yourself, other people, and the world around you. Accept that they're complex and ever-changing (see Chapter 12 for more on this). Recognise evidence that doesn't fit your labels, in order to help you weaken your conviction in your global rating. For example:

- ✔ **Allow for varying degrees.** Think about it: The world isn't a dangerous place but rather a place that has many different aspects with varying degrees of safety.

- ✔ **Celebrate complexities.** All human beings – yourself included – are unique, multifaceted, and ever-changing. To label yourself as a failure on the strength of one failing is an extreme form of overgeneralising. Likewise, other people are just as complex and unique as you. One bad action doesn't equal a bad person.

When you label a person or aspect of the world in a global way, you exclude potential for change and improvement. Accepting yourself as you are is a powerful first step towards self-improvement.

Making Demands: Thinking Flexibly

Albert Ellis, founder of rational emotive behaviour therapy, one of the first cognitive-behavioural therapies, places demands at the very heart of emotional problems. Thoughts and beliefs that contain words like 'must', 'should', 'need', 'ought', 'got to', and 'have to' are often problematic because they're extreme and rigid (see Figure 2-8).

Figure 2-8: Demands.

The inflexibility of the demands you place on yourself, the world around you, and other people often means you don't adapt to reality as well as you could. Consider these possible examples:

- You believe that you *must* have the approval of your friends and colleagues. This leads you to feel anxious in many social situations and drives you to try and win everyone's approval.

- You think that because you try very hard to be kind and considerate to others, they really *ought* to be just as kind and considerate in return. Because your demand is not realistic – sadly, other people are governed by their own priorities – you often feel hurt about your friends not acting the way you do yourself.

✔ You believe that you *absolutely should* never let people down. Therefore, you rarely put your own welfare first. At work, you do more than your fair share because you don't assert yourself, and so you often end up feeling stressed and depressed.

Holding *flexible preferences* about yourself, other people, and the world in general is the healthy alternative to inflexible rules and demands. Rather than making demands on yourself, the world, and others, try the following techniques:

✔ **Pay attention to language.** Replace words like 'must', 'need', and 'should' with 'prefer', 'wish', and 'want'.

✔ **Limit approval seeking.** Can you manage to have a satisfying life even if you don't get the approval of everyone you seek it from? Specifically, you'll feel more confident in social situations if you hold a *preference* for approval rather than viewing approval as a dire need.

✔ **Understand that the world doesn't play to your rules.** In fact, other people tend to have their own rulebooks. So, no matter how much you value considerate behaviour, your friends may not give it the same value. If you can give others the right to not live up to your standards, you'll feel less hurt when they fail to do so.

✔ **Retain your standards, ideals, and preferences, and ditch your rigid demands about how you, others, and the world 'have to' be.** So keep acting consistently with how you *would like* things to be rather than becoming depressed or irate about things not being the way you believe they *must* be.

 When you hold rigid demands about the way things 'have got to be', you have no margin for deviation or error. You leave yourself vulnerable to experiencing exaggerated emotional disturbance when things in life just don't go your way.

Mental Filtering: Keeping an Open Mind

Mental filtering is a bias in the way you process information, in which you acknowledge only information that fits with a belief you hold. The process is much like a filter on a camera lens that allows in only certain kinds of light. Information that doesn't fit tends to be ignored. If you think any of the following, you're making the 'mental filtering' thinking error:

- ✔ You believe you're a failure, so you tend to focus on your mistakes at work and overlook successes and achievements. At the end of the week, you often feel disappointed about your lack of achievement – but this is probably largely the result of you not paying attention to your successes.

- ✔ You believe you're unlikeable, and *really* notice each time your friend is late to call back or seems too busy to see you. You tend to disregard the ways in which people act warmly towards you, which sustains your view that you're unlikeable.

To combat mental filtering, look more closely at situations you feel down about. Deliberately collecting evidence that contradicts your negative thoughts can help you to correct your information-processing bias. Try the following:

- ✔ **Examine your filters closely.** For example, are you sifting your achievements through an 'I'm a failure' filter? If so, then only failure-related information gets through. If you look for a friend's achievements over the same week without a filter, you'd be likely to find far more success.

- ✔ **Gather evidence.** Imagine you're collecting evidence for a court case to prove that your negative thought isn't true. What evidence do you cite? Would, for example, an assertion that you're unlikeable stand up in court against the proof of your friends behaving warmly towards you?

If you only ever take in information that fits with the way you think, you can very easily end up thinking the same way. The fact that you don't see the positive stuff about yourself, or your experiences, doesn't mean it isn't there (just bear in mind Figure 2-9!).

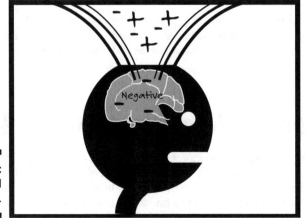

Figure 2-9:
Mental
filtering.

Disqualifying the Positive: Keeping the Baby When Throwing Out the Bathwater

Disqualifying the positive (see Figure 2-10) is related to the biased way that people can process information. Disqualifying the positive is a mental action that transforms a positive event into a neutral or negative event in your mind.

Figure 2-10:
Disqualifying
the positive.

The following are examples of disqualifying the positive:

✔ You believe that you're worthless and unlovable. You respond to a work promotion by thinking, 'This doesn't count, because anyone could get this sort of thing.' The result: Instead of feeling pleased, you feel quite disappointed.

✔ You think you're pathetic and feel low. A friend tells you you're a very good friend, but you disqualify this in your mind by thinking, 'She's only saying that because she feels sorry for me. I really am pathetic.'

Hone your skills for accepting compliments and acknowledging your good points. You can try the following strategies to improve your skills:

✔ **Become aware of your responses to positive 'data'.** Practice acknowledging and accepting positive feedback and acknowledging good points about yourself, others, and the world. For example, you could override your workplace disappointment by recognising that *you're* the one who

got the promotion. You can even consider that the promotion may well
have been a result of your hard work.

✔ **Practice accepting a compliment graciously with a simple thank you.**
Rejecting a sincerely delivered compliment is rather like turning down a
gift. Steer your thinking towards taking in positive experiences. When
others point out attributes you have, start deliberately making a note of
those good points.

If you frequently disqualify or distort your positive attributes or experiences,
you can easily sustain a negative belief about yourself, even in the face of
overwhelming positive evidence.

Low Frustration Tolerance: Realising You Can Bear the 'Unbearable'

Low frustration tolerance refers to the error of assuming that when something's difficult to tolerate, it's 'intolerable'. This thinking error means magni-
fying discomfort and not tolerating temporary discomfort when it's in your
interest to do so for longer-term benefit, as we show in Figure 2-11.

Figure 2-11:
Low
frustration
tolerance.

The following are examples of low frustration tolerance:

✔ You often procrastinate on college assignments, thinking, 'It's just too much hassle. I'll do it later when I feel more in the mood.' You tend to wait until the assignment's nearly due and it becomes too uncomfortable to put off any longer. Unfortunately, waiting until the last moment means that you can rarely put as much time and effort into your coursework as you need to in order to reach your potential.

✔ You want to overcome your anxiety of travelling away from home by facing your fear directly. And yet, each time you try to travel farther on the train, you become anxious, and think 'This is so horrible, I can't stand it', and quickly return home, which reinforces your fear rather than helping you experience travel as less threatening.

The best way to overcome low frustration tolerance is to foster an alternative attitude of *high frustration tolerance*. You can achieve this way of thinking by trying the following:

✔ **Pushing yourself to do things that are uncomfortable or unpleasant.** For example, you can train yourself to work on assignments even if you aren't in the mood, because the end result of finishing work in good time, and to a good standard, outweighs the hassle of doing something you find tedious.

✔ **Giving yourself messages that emphasise your ability to withstand pain.** To combat a fear of travel, you can remind yourself that feeling anxious is really unpleasant, but you *can* stand it. Ask yourself whether, in the past, you've ever withstood the feelings you're saying you presently 'can't stand'.

Telling yourself you can't stand something has two effects. First, it leads you to focus more on the discomfort you're experiencing. Second, it leads you to underestimate your ability to cope with discomfort. Many things can be difficult to tolerate, but rating them as 'intolerable' often makes situations seem more daunting than they really are.

Personalising: Removing Yourself from the Centre of the Universe

Personalising involves interpreting events as being related to you personally and overlooking other factors. This can lead to emotional difficulties, such as feeling hurt easily or feeling unnecessarily guilty (see Figure 2-12).

Figure 2-12:
Personal-
ising.

Here are some examples of personalising:

✔ You may tend to feel guilty if you know a friend is upset and you can't make him feel better. You think, 'If I was really a good friend, I'd be able to cheer him up. I'm obviously letting him down.'

✔ You feel hurt when a friend you meet in a shop leaves quickly after saying only a hurried 'hello'. You think, 'He was obviously trying to avoid talking to me. I must have offended him somehow.'

You can tackle personalising by considering alternative explanations that don't revolve around you. Think about the following examples:

✔ **Imagine what else may have contributed to the outcome you're assuming personal responsibility for.** Your friend may have lost his job or be suffering from depression. Despite your best efforts to cheer him up, these factors are outside your control.

✔ **Consider why people may be responding to you in a certain way.** Don't jump to the conclusion that someone's response relates directly to you. For example, your friend may be having a difficult day or be in a big hurry – he may even feel sorry for not stopping to talk to you.

Because you really aren't the centre of the universe, look for explanations of events that have little or nothing to do with you.

Getting intimate with your thinking

Figuring out which thinking errors you tend to make the most can be a useful way of making your CBT self-help more efficient and effective. The simplest way of doing this is to jot down your thoughts whenever you feel upset and note what was happening at the time. Remember the maxim: When you feel bad, put your thoughts on the pad! See Chapter 3 for more on managing unhelpful thoughts by writing them down.

You can then review your thoughts against the list of thinking errors in this chapter and write down next to each unhelpful thought which thinking error you may be making. With practice you can get better at spotting your thinking errors – and in all probability, you may notice that you're more prone to making some errors than others. You can then choose which alternative thinking styles to develop.

You may also become aware of patterns or themes in the kinds of situations or events that trigger your negative thoughts. These can also help you to focus on the areas in which your thoughts, beliefs, and attitudes need most work.

Chapter 3

Tackling Toxic Thoughts

• •

In This Chapter

▶ Identifying the thoughts underpinning the way you feel

▶ Questioning your negative thoughts and generating alternatives

▶ Using the ABC self-help forms to manage your emotions

• •

*I*n your endeavours to become your own CBT therapist, one of the key techniques you use is a tool known as an *ABC form*, which provides you with a structure for identifying, questioning, and replacing unhelpful thoughts using pen and paper.

CBT therapists can sometimes use similar tools to the ABC form we offer in this chapter, all of which help patients to identify and replace negative thoughts. Different therapists may refer to these forms as *thought records*, *thought diaries*, *daily records of dysfunctional thoughts*, or *dysfunctional thought records (DTRs)*. Fret not – in general, all of these forms are simply different ways of saying largely the same thing: Your thinking impacts on your feelings and actions.

The way you think affects the way you feel. Therefore, changing your unhelpful thoughts is a key to feeling better.

In this chapter, we give you two versions of the ABC form: one to get you started with identifying your triggers, thoughts, and feelings, and another that takes you right through to developing alternative thoughts so you can act differently in the future.

Catching NATs

Getting the hang of the ABC form is often easier if you break down the process into two steps. The first step is to fill out the first three columns (*Activating* event, *Beliefs* and thoughts, *Consequences*) of the form, which you can find further on in this chapter (ABC Form I). This gives you a chance to focus on catching your *negative automatic thoughts* (NATs) on paper and to see the connection between your thoughts and emotions.

Using the ABC form is great, but if you don't have one to hand when you feel an upsetting emotion, grab anything you can write on to scribble down your thoughts and feelings. You can always transfer your thoughts to a form later.

Making the thought–feeling link

A crucial step in CBT is to make the *thought–feeling link* or *B-to-C connection*; that is, seeing clearly for yourself the connection between what goes through your mind and your resulting emotions. When you see this connection, it can help you to make much more sense of why to challenge and change your thoughts.

Becoming more objective about your thoughts

One of the biggest advantages of writing down your thoughts is that the process can help you to regard these thoughts simply as hunches, theories, and ideas – rather than as absolute facts.

The more negative the meaning you give to an event, the more negative you'll feel, and the more likely you'll act in a way that maintains that feeling. Crucially, when you feel negative, you're more likely to generate negative thoughts. See how easily you can get caught in a vicious circle? Just one of the reasons to take your negative thoughts with a bucket of salt!

Stepping Through the ABC Form 1

So, time to embark on this major CBT self-help technique using Figure 3-1. The basic process for completing the ABC form is as follows:

1. **In the 'Consequences' box, point 1, write down the emotion you're feeling.**

   Therapy's about becoming emotionally healthier and acting in a more self-helping or productive way. So, when you're filling out the ABC form, the most logical place to start is with the emotion you're feeling.

   Emotions and behaviour are *consequences* (C) of the interaction between the *activating event or trigger* (A) and the *beliefs or meanings* (B) in the ABC model of emotion.

Examples of emotions you may choose to list in the 'Consequences' box include:

- Anger
- Anxiety
- Depression
- Envy
- Guilt
- Hurt
- Jealousy
- Shame

Fill out an ABC form when you feel emotionally upset, when you've acted in a way that you want to change, or when you feel like acting in a way that you wish to change. We give you more information on how to help you understand and identify emotions in Chapter 6.

2. In the 'Consequences' box, point 2, write down how you acted.

Write down how your behaviour changed when you felt your uncomfortable emotion. Examples of the behaviour that people often identify in this box include:

- Avoiding something
- Becoming withdrawn, isolated, or inactive
- Being aggressive
- Binge-eating or restricting food intake
- Escaping from a situation
- Putting off something (procrastination)
- Seeking reassurance
- Taking alcohol or drugs
- Using safety behaviours, such as holding on to something if you feel faint

3. In the 'Activating Event' box, write down what triggered your feelings.

As we discuss in Chapter 1, the A in ABC stands for *activating event or trigger*, which are the things that triggered your unhelpful thoughts and feelings. Activating events or triggers to put in this box can include:

- Something happening right now
- Something that occurred in the past
- Something that you're anticipating will happen in the future

- Something in the external world (an object, place, or person)

- Something in your mind (an image or memory)

- A physical sensation (increased heart rate, headache, feeling tired)

- Your own emotions or behaviour

An activating event can be pretty much anything. Use your feelings – rather than whether you think the event is important – as a guide to when you should fill out a form.

To keep your ABC form brief and accurate, focus on the specific aspect of the activating event that you're upset about. Use the table of emotions in Chapter 6 to help you detect the themes to look out for if you're unsure about what may have triggered your thoughts and feelings.

4. In the 'Beliefs' box, write down your thoughts, attitudes, and beliefs.

Describe what the event (whatever you've put in the 'Activating Event' box) meant to you when you felt the emotion (what you've written under point 1 in the 'Consequences' box).

The thoughts, attitudes, and beliefs you put in 'Beliefs' box often pop up reflexly. They may be extreme, distorted, and unhelpful – but they may *seem* like facts to you. Some examples of these NATs include:

- Here I go again, proving that I'm useless!

- I should've known better!

- Now everyone knows what an idiot I am!

- This proves that I can't cope like normal people do!

Thoughts are what count, so think of yourself as a detective and set out to capture suspect thoughts. If your thoughts are in the form of a picture, describe the image, or what the image means to you – write them down in the 'Beliefs' box.

We think not only in words but also in pictures. People who are feeling anxious frequently describe that they see *catastrophic images* going through their mind. For example, if you fear fainting in a restaurant, you may get an image of yourself on the restaurant floor with staff fussing over you.

5. In the 'Thinking Error' box, consider what your thinking errors may be.

One of the key ways to become more objective about your thoughts is to identify the *thinking errors* that may exist in the thoughts you list in this box. (Have a look at Chapter 2 for more details on common thinking errors.)

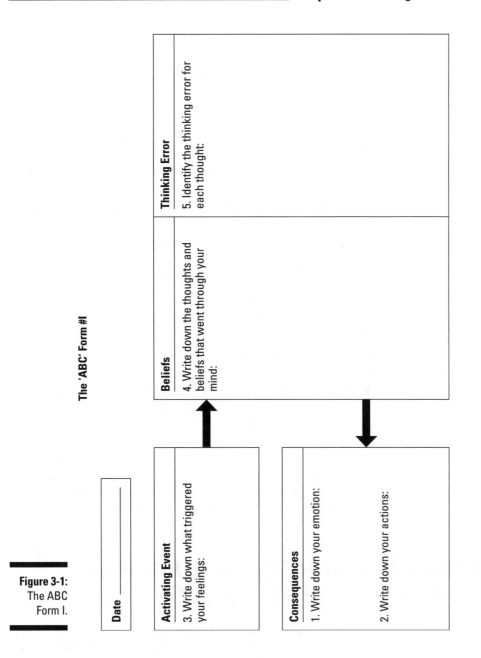

Figure 3-1:
The ABC
Form I.

The 'ABC' Form #I

Date

Activating Event

3. Write down what triggered your feelings:

Beliefs

4. Write down the thoughts and beliefs that went through your mind:

Thinking Error

5. Identify the thinking error for each thought:

Consequences

1. Write down your emotion:

2. Write down your actions:

Questions that you might ask yourself in order to identify your thinking errors include:

- Am I jumping to the worst possible conclusion? (Catastrophising)

- Am I thinking in extreme – all-or-nothing – terms? (Black-and-white thinking)

- Am I using words like 'always' and 'never' to draw generalised conclusions from a specific event? (Overgeneralising)

- Am I predicting the future instead of waiting to see what happens? (Fortune-telling)

- Am I jumping to conclusions about what other people are thinking of me? (Mind-reading)

- Am I focusing on the negative and overlooking the positive? (Mental filtering)

- Am I discounting positive information or twisting a positive into a negative? (Disqualifying the positive)

- Am I globally putting myself down as a failure, worthless, or useless? (Labelling)

- Am I listening too much to my negative gut feelings instead of looking at the objective facts? (Emotional reasoning)

- Am I taking an event or someone's behaviour too personally or blaming myself and overlooking other factors? (Personalising)

- Am I using words like 'should', 'must', 'ought', and 'have to' in order to make rigid rules about myself, the world, or other people? (Demanding)

- Am I telling myself that something is too difficult or unbearable or that 'I can't stand it' when actually it's hard to bear but it *is* bearable and worth tolerating? (Low frustration tolerance)

Creating Constructive Alternatives: Completing the ABC Form II

When you feel more confident about identifying your As, Bs, Cs, and thinking errors, you can move on to the ABC form II. This second form helps you question your unhelpful thoughts in order to reduce their intensity, generate and rate the effects of alternative thoughts, and focus on acting differently.

The first five steps for completing the ABC form II (see Figure 3-2) are the same as those for the ABC form I. Then come five more steps. You can find a blank version of the ABC form II in Appendix B. In the ABC form II, column A is the Activating Event, column B is Beliefs, column C is for Consequences, column D is Dispute, and column E is Effect.

6. **Examine your negative thoughts more closely.**

   Ask yourself the following questions in order to examine and weaken your unhelpful thoughts:

   - Can I prove that my thought is 100 per cent true?

   - What are the effects of thinking this way?

   - Is my thought wholly logical or sensible?

   - Would people whose opinions I respect agree that this thought's realistic?

   - What evidence exists against this thought?

   - Is my thought balanced, or extreme?

   - Is my thought rigid or flexible?

   - Am I thinking objectively and realistically, or are my thoughts being biased by how I feel?

Consider long and hard your negative or unhelpful thoughts in the light of the preceding questions. Don't simply give glib 'yes' or 'no' answers. Instead, think things through and perhaps write down your challenges to your unhelpful thoughts in column D. See the list of questions and prompters at the bottom of the ABC form II, which can help you further with this.

7. **Generate alternatives for each of your unhelpful thoughts, attitudes, and beliefs.**

   This step is critical as it's your alternative thoughts that will help you to feel better! In column D, write down a flexible, non-extreme, realistic, and helpful alternative for each thought, attitude, or belief that appears in column B. The following questions may help you to generate some alternatives:

   - What's a more helpful way of looking at the situation?

   - Do I encourage friends to think in this way?

   - When I'm feeling OK, how do I think differently?

   - Have any past experiences shown me that another possible outcome exists?

- What's a more flexible or less extreme way of thinking?

- What's a more realistic or balanced way of thinking that takes into account the evidence that does *not* support my thought?

- What do I need to think in order to feel and act differently?

Some thoughts are more stubborn than others, and you won't turn your thinking around completely in one go. Wrestling with NATs for a while before they weaken is typical and appropriate. Think of yourself as *training* your mind to think more flexibly and constructively over a period of time.

Some intrusive thoughts, images, and doubts can be made worse if you engage with them. If you have obsessive-compulsive disorder (OCD), health anxiety, body dysmorphic disorder (BDD), worry, or a jealousy problem, be sure to develop the capability to live with doubt, and allow catastrophic thoughts to pass through your mind rather than challenging them. We explain this in more depth in Chapter 5, Chapter 9, and Chapter 11. So if you think you need to learn to live with doubt, or to tolerate upsetting, intrusive thoughts in general, we suggest steering clear of using ABC forms for these problems.

8. **In column E, rate the effects of your alternatives on your feelings.**

Rate your original feelings 0–100 per cent. Also note whether you experience any alternative healthier emotions such as:

- Concern

- Annoyance

- Sadness

- Remorse

- Disappointment

- Sorrow

You won't always notice a great deal of change in how you feel at first, so keep persevering!

9. **Develop a plan to move forward.**

The final step on the ABC form II is to develop a plan to move forward. Your plan may be to conduct a behavioural experiment to help you gather more information about whether your thoughts are true or realistic, or to behave differently in a specific situation. Refer to Chapter 3 and Chapter 4 for more ideas.

The 'ABC' Form #II

Date March 18th

Activating Event (Trigger).	Beliefs, thoughts, and attitudes about A.	Consequences of A+B on your emotions and behaviours.	Dispute (question and examine) B and generate alternatives. The questions at the bottom of the form will help you with this.	Effect of alternative thoughts and beliefs (D).
2. Briefly write down what triggered your emotions. (e.g. event, situation, sensation, memory, image)	3. Write down what went through your mind, or what A meant to you. B's can be about you, others, the world, the past, or the future.	1. Write down what emotion you felt and how you acted when you felt this emotion.	4. Write an alternative for each B, using supporting arguments and evidence.	5. Write down how you feel and wish to act as consequence of your alternatives at D.
Returning to work for the first time after being off sick.	*Things will have changed and I won't know what to do* (Fortune Telling). *People will ask me awkward questions about why I've been off sick and I won't know what to say* (Catastrophising). *They'll think I'm crazy if they find out I've had depression* (Catastrophising, Mind Reading).	**Emotions** e.g. Depression, guilt, hurt, anger, shame, jealousy, envy, anxiety. Rate intensity 0–100. *Anxiety 70%* **Behaviour** e.g. Avoidance, withdrawing, escape, using alcohol or drugs, seeking reassurance, procrastination *Running over in my mind what I'll say to everyone.*	*I don't know whether things have changed. Even if they have I've coped with changes many times before. I'm sure my colleagues will help. Possibly one or two people will ask, and I can just keep my answers short. Mostly everyone will be glad to have me back.* *I've no reason to think they'll think I'm crazy. When Peter was off with stress people were mostly supportive and understanding. When Helen called last week she seemed to treat me just the same as normal.*	**Emotions** Re-rate 0–100. List any healthy alternative emotion e.g. Sadness, regret, concern. *Anxiety 40%* **Alternative Behaviour or Experiment** e.g. Facing situation, increased activity, assertion *Wait and deal with things when I get there, and stop trying to work it out in advance.*

Figure 3-2:
An example of a filled-in ABC Form II.

Disputing (Questioning and Examining) and Generating Alternative Thoughts, Attitudes, and Beliefs: 1. Identify your 'thinking errors' at **B** (e.g. Mind Reading, Catastrophising, Labelling, Demands etc.). Write them next to the appropriate 'B'. 2. Examine whether the evidence at hand supports that your thought at **B** is 100% true. Consider whether someone whose opinions you respect would totally agree with your conclusions. 3. Evaluate the helpfulness of each **B**. Write down what you think might be a more helpful, balanced and flexible way of looking at **A**. Consider what you would advise a friend to think, what a role model of yours might think, or how you might look at **A** if you were feeling OK. 4. Add evidence and arguments that support your alternative thoughts, attitudes and beliefs. Write as if you were trying to persuade someone you cared about.

An ABC a day keeps the doctor at bay!

If you want to master any skill, remember these three words: *Practice, practice, practice!* You may not need to fill out an ABC form everyday. Other days, you may need to complete more than one form. The point is, that practising ABC forms regularly is worthwhile because:

✔ Practice helps change disturbing feelings and the thoughts that underpin them.

✔ Sinking a new thought into your head and heart takes repetition.

✔ By completing forms on paper, you can become increasingly able to challenge unhelpful thoughts in your head – although you may still need to do it on paper sometimes.

As you progress in your ability to overcome difficulties and develop your CBT self-help skills, you may still find the ABC form useful when you're hit with a biggy. And remember: If you can't work out your unhelpful thinking on the hoof, do sit down and bash it out on paper.

10. **Set yourself some homework.**

When you've completed several ABC forms, you may well begin to notice recurring themes, thoughts, attitudes, or beliefs. Such repetitions may suggest that you need to add some other CBT techniques in order to overcome certain emotions or behaviours, for example:

- Facing a fear until it reduces (Chapter 9)

- Conducting a behavioural experiment to test out a thought (Chapter 4)

- Acting repeatedly 'as if' you believe an alternative thought, attitude, or belief (Chapter 15)

- Completing a Zig-Zag form to strengthen an alternative thought, attitude, or belief (Chapter 15)

Read on and set yourself some more therapy assignments using the CBT principles in this book.

Keeping your old ABC forms can be a rewarding record of your progress, and a useful reminder of how to fill them in if you need to use one again in the future. Many of our clients look back over their ABC forms after they feel better and tell us: 'I can't believe I used to feel and think like that!'

Chapter 4

Behaving like a Scientist: Designing and Conducting Behavioural Experiments

In This Chapter

▶ Testing out your thoughts and assumptions as predictions

▶ Exploring theories and gathering information

▶ Designing and recording your experiments

*O*ften, CBT can seem like common sense. *Behavioural experiments* are particularly good examples of the common-sense side of CBT. If you want to know whether your hunch about reality is accurate, or your way of looking at something is helpful, put it to a test in reality.

This chapter is an introduction to behavioural experiments, a key CBT strategy. We include in this chapter an overview of several behavioural experiments that you can try out for yourself. We also give you examples of these experiments in action. As with the other examples we use in this book, try to look for *anything* useful you can draw from them. Try not to home in too much on how the examples differ from your specific problem. Instead, focus on what you have in common with the examples and work from there to apply the techniques to your own problems.

Even in a 'talking treatment' like CBT, actions speak louder than words. Aaron Beck, founder of cognitive therapy, encourages a therapeutic perspective where client and therapist work on 'being scientific together'. Beck emphasises that testing your thoughts in reality, rather than simply talking about them, underpins effective therapy.

Seeing for Yourself: Reasons for Doing Behavioural Experiments

The proof of the pudding is in the eating. The same can be said of your assumptions, behaviours, beliefs, and predictions about yourself and the world around you. Use experiments to test out the *truth* about your beliefs and to assess the *usefulness* of your behaviours.

You can use behavioural experiments in the following ways:

- ✔ To test the validity of a thought or belief that you hold about yourself, other people, or the world.
- ✔ To test the validity of an alternative thought or belief.
- ✔ To discover the effects that mental or behavioural activities have on your difficulties.
- ✔ To gather evidence in order to clarify the nature of your problem.

Living according to a set of beliefs because you think they're true and helpful is both easy and common. You can also easily stick to familiar ways of behaving because you *think* that they keep you safe from feared events, or that they help you to achieve certain goals. An example of this may be holding a belief that other people are out to find fault with you – with this thought in mind, you then work hard to hide your mistakes and shortcomings.

The beauty of a behavioural experiment is that you often find that your worst imagined scenarios don't happen, or that you deal with such situations effectively when, or even if, they do occur.

We may be stating the obvious, but change can be less daunting if you keep in mind that you can always return to your old ways of thinking about things if the new ways don't seem any better. If your old ways seem to be the best option, nothing's stopping you from going back to them. The trick is to prepare yourself to try out new strategies and to give them a chance before returning to your former ways. Find out what works best for you and your particular situation.

Testing Out Predictions

When testing out your predictions, strive to get *unambiguous disconfirmation*, in so far as you can. Unambiguous disconfirmation means discovering *conclusively* that your fears *don't* come true, whether or not you actually do something to prevent them occurring. An example of unambiguous disconfirmation may be finding out that your dizziness is caused by anxiety, and that you won't collapse even if you don't sit down or hold on to something.

Go through the following four steps to devise a behavioural experiment:

1. **Describe your problem.**

   Write down the nature of your problem and include your *safety behaviours* (things you do to try to prevent your feared catastrophe – head to Chapter 7 for loads more on safety behaviour). Phrase the problem in your own words and make a note of how the problem negatively affects your life.

2. **Formulate your prediction.**

   Decide what you think will happen if you try out a new way of thinking or behaving in real life.

3. **Execute an experiment.**

   Think of a way of putting a new belief or behaviour to the test in a real-life situation. Try to devise more than one way to test out your prediction.

4. **Examine the results.**

   Look to see whether your prediction came true. If it didn't, check out what you've learned from the results of the experiment.

You can rate the degree to which you believe a prediction will come true on a percentage between 0 and 100 at the start of your experiment. After you've done the experiment and processed your results, re-rate your conviction in the original prediction.

Take care not to use subtle ways of keeping your feared catastrophe at bay, such as doing experiments only when you feel 'right', are with 'safe' people, have *safety objects* to hand (such as a mobile phone or a bottle of water), or are using safety behaviours (such as trying to control your anxiety with distraction or by gripping tightly to your steering wheel). Using these subtle safety measures during your exposure to a fear can leave you with the impression that you've had a narrow escape, rather than highlighting that your predicted fear didn't come true.

For example, consider the following experiment, which Nadine initiates to examine her fear of rejection and social anxiety:

- ✔ **Describe the problem.** Nadine's afraid of people thinking negatively of her and of being rejected by her friends. In social situations, Nadine monitors her body language and censors what she says, taking great care not to cause offence. She often plans in advance what she's going to say.

- ✔ **Formulate a prediction.** Nadine predicts 'If I express an opinion or disagree with my friends, they'll like me less.' She rates her conviction in this idea as 90 per cent.

✔ **Execute an experiment.** For the next six social gatherings Nadine attends, she decides that she'll speak up and try to offer an opinion. If at all possible, she'll find a point on which to disagree with someone.

✔ **Examine the results.** Nadine discovers that no one took exception to her saying more. In fact, two friends commented that it was nice to hear more about what she thought about things. Nadine re-rates her conviction in her original prediction as 40 per cent.

By conducting a behavioural experiment, Nadine observed that her feared prediction – 'Others will like me less if I express my opinions' – didn't happen. This result gives Nadine the opportunity to change her behaviour according to the results of her experiment; therefore, to speak up more often. It also helps to reduce how much she believes the original prediction. Nadine can now adjust her thinking based on evidence gathered through the experiment.

Nigel used a behavioural experiment to test out his prediction that he wouldn't enjoy engaging in social activities. Since self-isolating and disengaging from previously enjoyed activities promotes depression, Nigel really needs to understand the benefits of becoming more active. Nigel worked through an experiment as follows:

✔ **Describe the problem.** Nigel's depression typically leads to him having gloomy and pessimistic thoughts. He tends to avoid going out with his friends or doing any of his regular hobbies because he doesn't feel like it these days. He believes that he won't enjoy himself; therefore, there's no point in trying any of these activities. (As we note in Chapter 10, self-isolation is one of the key ways in which depression is maintained.)

✔ **Formulate a prediction.** Nigel chooses to experiment with the prediction 'Even if I do go out, I won't enjoy myself and I'll end up feeling even worse once I get home.' He rates his strength of conviction in this thought as 80 per cent.

✔ **Execute an experiment.** Nigel plans to structure his week and to schedule two occasions to see friends. He also plans to spend two half-hour sessions riding his bike, which he used to enjoy. He rates each day over the next seven days in terms of his mood and of how much he enjoys his activities.

✔ **Examine the results.** Nigel notices that he does get some enjoyment from seeing his friends, although less than he usually would. Although he doesn't particularly enjoy his cycling and feels more tired than usual, he notes that he at least felt glad he had done something. He re-rates his conviction in his original prediction as 40 per cent, and decides to conduct further experiments to see whether his mood and energy levels improve over the next two weeks if he continues to be more active.

> This experiment helped Nigel to see that he felt better for doing *something*, even if he didn't enjoy cycling or socialising as much as he would when he wasn't depressed. Noting these results can help Nigel to stick to a schedule of activity and ultimately help him to overcome his depression.

Seeking Evidence to See Which Theory Best Fits the Facts

The scientific principle known as *Occam's razor* states that all things considered, the simplest theory is usually the best. Whichever theory explains a phenomenon most simply is the one a scientist adopts. When you want to test out a theory or idea you hold about yourself, others, or the world, developing an *alternative theory* is a good idea. This gives you the chance to disprove your original theory and to endorse the healthier alternative.

Some emotional problems don't respond well to attempts to disprove a negative prediction. In such cases, you may be better off developing some *competing theories* about what the problem actually is. You then devise experiments to gather more evidence and see which theory reflects reality most accurately.

For example, imagine that your boss never says a cheerful 'good morning' to you. You develop the following two theories:

- ✔ Theory A: 'My boss doesn't like me at all.'
- ✔ Theory B: 'My boss isn't friendly in the mornings and is a bit rude, but he's like this to a lot of employees, not just me.'

You're now in a position to gather evidence for whether theory A or B best explains the phenomenon of your boss failing to be cheerful towards you in the mornings.

A *theory* is just an idea or assumption that you hold, which to your mind, explains why something happens – a technical word for a simple concept.

Often, developing one additional theory to compete with your original theory is enough. However, you can develop more alternative theories if you think they may help you get to the bottom of what you're experiencing. Taking the above example, you may have a third theory, such as 'My boss is cheerful only with employees that he knows very well', or even a fourth theory, such as 'My boss is cheerful only with employees of the same rank as him or above him'.

Developing competing theories can be particularly helpful in the followings situations:

- ✔ **Dealing with predictions that may be months or years away from being proven.** If you fear you'll go to hell for having an intrusive thought about causing harm to someone, then this outcome is likely to be sometime away. Similarly, if you have *health anxiety* and spend hours each day preoccupied with the idea that physical sensations in your body may be signs that you'll become ill and die, you're unlikely to know straightaway whether this will actually happen. With these kinds of catastrophic thoughts, you need to design experiments to help you gather evidence to support the theory that you have a worry or anxiety problem, rather than a damnation problem or terminal illness.

- ✔ **Dealing with beliefs that are impossible to prove or disprove conclusively.** Perhaps you're anxious about others having negative opinions of you. You cannot know for sure what other people think, but even if someone tells you that your fears are unfounded, you can never know with absolute certainty what he's thinking. Similarly, if you have jealous thoughts that your partner desires someone else, but he reassures you otherwise, you may remain uncertain of his true feelings.

For both of these situations, you can employ the theory A or theory B strategy:

- ✔ Design an experiment to gather evidence to support the idea that your jealous feelings are based on your jealous *thoughts* (theory B), rather than on reality (theory A).

- ✔ Similarly, devise an experiment to test out whether your original theory A that, 'People don't like me', or alternative theory B that, 'I often *think* that people don't like me because I'm so worried about others' opinions of me that I end up seeing a lot of their behaviour as signs of dislike', best explains your experiences in social situations.

Following is an example of how Alex used the competing theories approach to get a better understanding of his physical sensations. Originally, Alex assumed his theory that uncomfortable bodily sensations signalled the onset of a heart attack was correct. By testing this in practice, Alex was able to consider that an alternative theory – uncomfortable bodily sensations are a by-product of anxiety – may be more accurate.

- ✔ **Describe the problem.** Alex suffers from panic attacks. He feels hot and his heart races, sometimes out of the blue. When he feels these sensations, he fears he's having a heart attack. Alex sits down to try to reduce the strain on his heart (an example of a safety behaviour). He goes out of his way to avoid situations in which he has experienced these symptoms.

✔ **Develop competing theories.** Alex devises two theories about his raised heart rate:

- Theory A: 'My heart beating quickly means I'm vulnerable to having a heart attack.'

- Theory B: 'My heart beating quickly is a consequence of anxiety.'

✔ **Execute an experiment.** Alex decides to deliberately confront situations that tend to trigger off his raised heart rate and to stay in them, *without sitting down*, until his anxiety reduces. He predicts that if theory B is correct, then his heart rate will reduce after his anxiety subsides and he can leave the situation without having come to any harm.

✔ **Examine the results.** Alex finds that his heart rate does indeed reduce when he stays with his anxiety. He's struck by what a difference this knowledge makes to his confidence, and that he's not going to come to any harm from his raised heart rate when he resists the urge to sit down. He concludes that he can reasonably have about 70 per cent confidence in his new theory that his raised heart rate is a benign consequence of anxiety.

You can't always prove conclusively that something isn't so. However, you can experiment to see whether certain emotional states, and mental or behavioural activities, have a beneficial or detrimental effect on the kinds of thoughts that play on your mind.

Conducting Surveys

You can use the clipboard and pen of the survey-taker in your endeavours to tackle your problems, by designing and conducting your own survey. Surveys can be especially helpful in terms of getting more information about what the average person thinks, feels, or does.

We suggest you have more than one type of behavioural experiment in your repertoire. Surveys are very useful if you believe that your thoughts, physical sensations, or behaviours are out of the ordinary. If you have upsetting, intrusive thoughts and images, or experience urges to say socially unacceptable things (symptoms typical of obsessive-compulsive disorder, OCD), feel pulled to the edge of high places (as in vertigo), or get a sense of impending doom when you're not in a familiar place (symptoms associated with agoraphobia), you may think that you're the only person who ever feels this way. Use surveys to see whether other people have the same thoughts and urges. You'll probably discover that other people experience the same things as you do. You may also discover that the symptoms you experience are actually less of a problem than the way you currently deal with them.

Henry suffers from OCD. His particular obsessional problem is related to frequent intrusive images of harm coming to his family. Henry's convinced that he's the only person in the world who gets such unpleasant and unwanted images entering his mind. Henry concludes that there's something very different and wrong about him because he has such images. He tests his theory about his abnormality by conducting the following survey:

- ✔ **Describe the problem.** Henry's convinced that his intrusive thoughts about his family being hurt in a car accident are unusual, and mean that he has to protect his family by changing the image in his mind to them being happy at a party.

- ✔ **Formulate a prediction.** Henry comes up with the prediction 'No one will admit to having the kind of thoughts I have'. He rates his strength of belief as 70 per cent.

- ✔ **Execute an experiment.** Henry tests his perception that his images are abnormal by devising a checklist of intrusive thoughts and asking his friends and family members to tick any that they experience.

- ✔ **Examine the results.** Henry's surprised at the variety of thoughts that people report entering their minds. Henry concludes that perhaps his images aren't so abnormal after all. He re-rates his conviction in his original prediction as 15 per cent. Henry also learns that other people simply discount their unpleasant images and don't worry that they mean anything sinister.

Charlotte worries a lot about her health and the possibility of developing a life-threatening illness. Sometimes, Charlotte notices funny sensations in her body and instantly interprets them as signs of an undiagnosed disease. Charlotte assumes that no one else gets unusual bodily sensations from time to time.

- ✔ **Describe the problem.** Charlotte worries that the bodily sensations she experiences are a sign of disease. She's unsatisfied by frequent reassurance from her family doctor and husband. Charlotte's problems are based partly on two ideas:

  - Physical sensations must have a clear medical explanation.

  - Any sensible person would seek an immediate explanation for the physical sensations she's currently experiencing.

- ✔ **Formulate a prediction.** Charlotte makes the following prediction: 'Most people won't have many physical sensations, and if they do they go immediately to see their doctor.' She rates her strength of conviction in this idea as 80 per cent.

- ✔ **Execute an experiment.** Charlotte devises a list of physical sensations, including many of those that she worries about herself. Her checklist requires people to tick whether they've ever experienced the sensation and to indicate how long they might leave it before consulting their doctor about such sensations. She asks ten people to fill out her questionnaire.

✔ **Examine the results.** Charlotte's shocked that many people reported experiencing some of the bodily sensations she described and stated that they'd leave going to their doctor for several days, or even weeks. Some people reported that they probably wouldn't bother seeing their doctor at all regarding some sensations. Charlotte concludes that perhaps she's worrying too much about her health, and plans to delay consulting her doctor when she next has unexplained physical sensations. Her strength of belief in her original prediction reduces to 30 per cent.

Making Observations

Observations can be an easier way of getting started with doing experiments to test out the validity of your thoughts. Observations usually involve collecting evidence related to a specific thought by watching other people in action.

You may assume, for example, that no one in their right mind would admit to not understanding an important point about a work procedure. If they did, they'd no doubt be ridiculed and promptly sacked on the basis of highlighting their incompetence.

Test this assumption by observing what other people actually *do*. Behave like a scientist and gather evidence of others admitting lack of understanding, asking for clarification, or owning up to mistakes. Observe whether your predication that they'll be ridiculed or fired is accurate. Making observations to gather evidence both for and against your assumptions is another way of behaving like a scientist.

Ensuring Successful Behavioural Experiments

To get the highest level of benefit when designing and carrying out behavioural experiments, keep the following in mind:

✔ Ensure that the type of experiment you choose is appropriate. Make your experiments challenging enough for you to gain a sense of accomplishment from conducting them. Equally, take care to devise experiments that won't overwhelm you.

✔ Have a clear plan about how, when, and where (and with whom, if relevant) you plan to carry out your experiment.

✔ Be clear and specific about what you want to find out from your experiment – 'to see what happens' is too vague.

✔ Decide in advance how you'll know whether your prediction comes true. For example, what are the clues that someone's thinking critically of you?

✔ Plan what you'll do if your prediction comes true. For example, how do you respond assertively if someone is actually critical of you?

✔ Use the behavioural experiments record sheet in this chapter to plan and record your experiment.

✔ Consider what obstacles may interrupt your experiment and how you can overcome them.

✔ When evaluating the outcome of your experiment, check that you're not being biased (for example, discounting the positive or mind-reading, thinking errors we describe in Chapter 2) in the way you process your results.

✔ Consider whether you rely on any (including subtle) safety behaviours. Safety behaviours can affect the results of your experiment or determine how confident you feel about the outcome – for example, thinking that you avoided collapsing by concentrating hard, rather than discovering conclusively that your feelings of dizziness are a result of anxiety, not imminent fainting.

✔ Plan ways to consolidate what you discover from your experiment. For example, should you repeat the experiment, devise a new experiment, change your daily activities, or some other action?

Treating your negative and unhelpful thoughts with scepticism is a key to reducing their emotional impact. Experiments can help you to realise that many of your negative thoughts and predictions are not accurate in reality. Therefore, we suggest you take many of your negative thoughts with a pinch or more of salt.

Think about therapy as an experiment, rather than a lifelong commitment, especially at the beginning. By thinking in this manner, you can feel less under pressure and more able to approach therapy with an open mind.

Keeping Records of Your Experiments

All good scientists keep records of their experiments. If you do the same, you can look back over your results in order to:

✔ Draw conclusions.

✔ Decide what kind of experiment you may want to conduct next in order to gather more information.

✔ Remind yourself that many of your negative predictions won't come true.

To help you keep records of your experiments, photocopy Figure 4-1, and use it as often as you like, following the instructions in the figure.

Behavioural Experiment Record Sheet

Figure 4-1:
Photocopy
and fill in
your own
Behavioural
Experiment
Record
Sheet.

Date: _____

Prediction or Theory	Experiment	Results	Conclusion/Comments
Outline the the thought, belief, or theory you are testing. Rate your strength of conviction 1–100%	Plan what you will do (including where, when, how, with whom), being as specific as you can.	Record what actually happened including relevant thoughts, emotions, physical sensations, and other people's behaviour.	Write down what have you learned about your prediction or theory in light of the results. Re-rate your strength of conviction 0–100%.

Guidance on carrying out a behavioural experiment: 1. Be clear and specific about the negative and alternative predictions you are testing. Rate your strength of conviction in the prediction or theory you are testing or evaluating. 2 Decide upon your experiment, and be as clear as you can be as to how you will measure your results. 3. Record the results of your experiment, emphasizing clear, observable outcomes. 4. Evaluate the results of your experiment. Write down what these results suggest in terms of the accuracy of your predictions, or which theory the evidence supports. 5. Consider whether a further behavioural experiment might be helpful.

Don't take our word for it . . .

This book's full of suggestions on how to reduce and overcome emotional problems. If you're sceptical about whether CBT can work for you, you're in very good company. However, loads of scientific evidence shows that CBT is more effective than all other psychotherapies.

So, CBT may well work for you, but how can you tell? The answer is to consider applying a specific tool or technique for a period of time as an experiment to see how the technique works for you. Depending on the outcome, you can then choose to do more, modify your approach, or try something different.

Try to have a no-lose perspective on your experiments. If you do one experiment and it goes well, then great! However, if you plan an experiment but ultimately avoid doing it, you can at least identify the thoughts that blocked you. Even if your negative predictions turn out to be accurate, you have an opportunity to see how well you cope – and very probably that it isn't the end of the world – and then decide whether you need to take further action. The point is, you can always gather information that you can make into a useful experience.

Chapter 5

Pay Attention! Refocusing and Retraining Your Awareness

. . . .

In This Chapter

▶ The role of attention in overcoming emotional problems

▶ Concentrating on tasks

▶ Directing and redirecting your attention

▶ Practising mindfulness

. . . .

*T*raditionally, CBT has tended to concentrate many of its techniques on helping people change the *content* of their thinking – from a negative to a more realistic thought, for example. However, modern CBT has begun to incorporate another area of human psychology – how we focus our attention.

This chapter does not discuss *what* you think, but does discuss *how* you manage your thoughts and attention. We introduce *task concentration training* and *mindfulness*, two techniques for managing problematic thoughts and exerting some power over your attention. This chapter has two main messages:

✔ For the most part, your thoughts, no matter how distressing and negative, are not the real problem. Rather, the importance or meaning you attach to those thoughts is what causes you the problem. If you view the notion, 'I'm a hopeless case', as a thought rather than a fact, you can greatly lessen its impact.

✔ When you have an emotional problem, your mind tends to attach unhelpful meanings to aspects of yourself, the world around you, and other people. You can also tend to *overfocus* on particular aspects of these unhelpful meanings. Fortunately, you can develop the ability to steer your attention towards, and away from, any features of your experience you choose, which can help improve your mood and reduce anxiety.

Training in Task Concentration

Becoming adept at redirecting your attention away from yourself (this includes your bodily sensations, thoughts, and mental images), in certain situations, is the essence of *task concentration*. Rather than thinking about yourself, you focus your attention towards your external environment and what you're doing.

Task concentration involves paying less attention to what's going on *inside* of you and more attention to what's happening *outside* of you.

Task concentration can be particularly useful in situations that trigger anxiety. Task concentration can help you to counterbalance your tendency to focus on threats and on yourself when you feel anxious.

As you begin to practise task concentration, break down the process into two rehearsal arenas – just as when learning to drive you begin on quiet roads and eventually advance on to busier roads.

The two rehearsal arenas are as follows:

- ✔ **Non-threatening situations:** Here, you typically experience little or no anxiety. For example, if you have social phobia, you may feel little anxiety walking through a park, travelling on a very quiet train, or socialising with family members and close friends.

- ✔ **More challenging situations:** Here, you tend to experience moderate to severe anxiety. More challenging situations may include shopping in a busy grocery store, travelling on a train during rush hour, or attending a party with many guests whom you do not know.

Typically, you gradually progress from moderately threatening situations to more challenging situations as you practise and develop greater skill.

First, practise redirecting your attention in situations you regard as relatively non-threatening, then you can move on to using the techniques in increasingly challenging situations.

Choosing to concentrate

The point of task-concentration exercises is not to lessen your overall concentration, but to concentrate harder on different aspects of the external environment. Some tasks require you to focus your attention on certain behaviours – such as listening to what another person is saying during a conversation, or attempting to balance a tray of drinks as you walk through a crowded room.

In other situations, you may feel anxious but you don't have a specific task to attend to. In such a situation, for example, while sitting in a crowded waiting room, you can direct your attention to your surroundings, noticing other people, the features of the room, sounds, and smells.

With practice, you can be both task- and environment-focused rather than self-focused, even in situations that you regard as highly threatening.

The following exercises aim to increase your understanding of how paying attention to sensations and images limits your ability to process information around you. The exercises will also help you realise that you can attend to external task-related behaviours. In other words, you can master *choosing* what you pay attention to in situations when your anxiety is triggered.

Intentionally directing your attention away from yourself does not mean *distracting* yourself from your physical sensations or suppressing your thoughts. Sometimes, people try to use thought suppression as a means of alleviating uncomfortable sensations and anxiety. However, suppression usually works only briefly, if at all.

Concentration exercise: Listening

For this exercise, sit back-to-back with someone else, perhaps a friend or your therapist. Ask the person to tell you a story for about two minutes. Concentrate on the story. Then, summarise the story: Note how much of your attention you directed towards the task of listening to the other person, towards yourself, and towards your environment during the exercise – try using percentages to do this. Your partner can give you feedback on your summary to give you some idea of how accurate your summary is.

Now do the exercise again, but this time round sit face-to-face with the storyteller and make eye contact. Ask the person to tell you a story, but on this occasion deliberately distract yourself by focusing on your thoughts and sensations, and then redirect your attention towards the storyteller. Summarise the story, and note (using percentages again) how you divided your attention between yourself, listening to the other person, and your environment.

Repeat the storytelling activities, sitting back-to-back and thenface-to-face, several times until you become readily able to redirect your attention to the task of listening after deliberate distraction through self-focusing. Doing so helps you to develop your ability to control where you focus your attention.

Concentration exercise: Speaking

Follow the same steps for this speaking exercise as you do for the listening exercise, as we describe in the preceding section. Starting with your back to the back of the other person, tell a two-minute story, focusing your attention on making your story clear to the listener.

Next, position yourself face-to-face with the listener, making eye contact. Deliberately distract yourself from the task of storytelling by focusing on your feelings, sensations, and thoughts. Then, refocus your attention towards what you're saying and towards the listener, being aware of her reactions and whether she understands you.

Again, using percentages, monitor how you divide your attention among yourself, the task, and your environment.

Concentration exercise: Graded practice

For this exercise, prepare two lists of situations. For your first list, write down five or so examples of situations you find non-threatening. Practise distracting yourself (by focusing on your internal sensations and thoughts) and then refocus your attention onto external things in these non-threatening situations. For your second list, write down ten or so examples of situations you find threatening. Arrange the situations in a hierarchy, starting from the least anxiety-provoking and graduating up to the most anxiety-provoking. Now work through your hierarchy by deliberately entering situations, while practising task concentration until you reach the top of your list. This means you start to practice mastering your anxiety in real-life situations.

Concentration exercise: Taking a walk

For this exercise, walk through a park, paying attention to what you hear, see, feel, and smell. Focus your attention for a few minutes on different aspects of the world around you. First, focus your attention mainly on what you can hear. Then shift your attention to focus on smells, and then on to the feel of your feet on the ground, and so on. You can move your attention around to different sensations, which can help you tune your attention into the outside world.

After you've practised directing most of your attention to individual senses, try to integrate your attention to include all aspects of the park. Try to do this for at least 20 minutes. Really let yourself drink in the detail of your surroundings. Discover what hooks your attention. You may be drawn to water or have a keen interest in birds, plants, or perhaps even woodland smells. Notice how you feel much more relaxed and less self-conscious as you train your attention on the world around you.

Tuning in to tasks and the world around you

If you're suffering from anxiety, you're probably self-focused in social situations and fail to notice the rest of the world. On top of feeling unnecessarily uncomfortable, your self-focus means that you're likely to miss out on a lot of interesting stuff. Luckily, you can change your attention bias and overcome much of your anxiety.

You can also use your re-training attention to help prevent yourself from engaging with the stream of negative thoughts that accompanies depression, which will in turn help you lift your mood.

Here's an example of how you can use task-concentration techniques to overcome anxiety, specifically social phobia (see Chapter 9 for more on social phobia).

Harold was particularly worried that people would notice that he blushed and sweated in social situations. He believed that people would think he was odd or a nervous wreck. Harold constantly self-monitored for blushing and sweating and tried very hard to mask these symptoms of his anxiety.

Here's Harold's list of non-threatening situations, in which he practises task concentration techniques:

1 Having dinner with his parents and brother.

2 Socialising with his three closest mates at a local pub.

3 Using public transport during quiet periods.

4 Eating lunch with colleagues at work.

5 Going to the cinema with a friend.

Next is Harold's list of threatening situations, with each situation becoming gradually more challenging.

1 Walking alone down a busy street.

2 Socialising with strangers at a party.

3 Going to the grocery shop alone.

4 Going to the gym alone.

5 Initiating conversation with strangers.

6 Using public transport during busy periods.

7 Eating alone in a restaurant.

8 Going for an interview.

9 Offering his opinion during work meetings.

10 Giving a presentation for work.

Harold used the principles of task concentration to increase his ability to focus deliberately on chosen external factors in non-threatening situations. When Harold was at the pub with his mates, he focused his attention on what his friends were saying, other people in the pub, the music, and the general surroundings. Harold also deliberately distracted himself by focusing on whether he was blushing and sweating, and then he refocused his attention again.

Harold then used the same techniques in more-threatening situations. In the grocery store, Harold found that the more he focused on his blushing and sweating, the more anxious he felt and the less able he was to pack up his shopping. When he paid attention to the task of packing his groceries, made eye contact with the cashier, and even made a bit of small talk, Harold's anxiety symptoms reduced, and he became more aware of what he was doing and what was going on around him.

Harold worked diligently through his hierarchy of feared situations and now feels much more confident and relaxed in social situations.

Imagine that you're going to be called on by the police to act as an eyewitness. For a few minutes, try to take in as much information as you can about the environment and the people around you. Notice how much more detail you can recount when you *choose* to focus outwards, compared with when you're concentrating on your thoughts and physical sensations.

Tackling the task concentration record sheet

You can keep an account of your task-concentration practice, and note the results, by using the task-concentration record sheet in Table 5-1. The brief instructions at the top of the sheet are there to remind you how to do your concentration exercises. You can find a blank copy of the form in Appendix B.

Table 5-1	Harold's Task-Concentration Record Sheet			
Who were you with? Where were you? What were you doing?	Record your focus of attention. Note what you focused on most. 1. Self % 2. Task % 3. Environment and other people % (Total = 100%)	Use task concentration to direct your attention outwards. Remember to focus on your task or environment. Note what you did.	Record how you felt.	Record anything you learned from the exercise. Note how the situation turned out, changes in your anxiety level, and your ability to complete the task.
Eating by myself in restaurant. *Lunchtime.*	*1. Self 40 %* *2. Task 35 %* *3. Environment and other people 25 %*	*Took my time to eat rather than rushing.* *Made eye contact with waiter.* *Tried to eat my meal mindfully and enjoy it.* *Observed other diners.* *Kept my head up and didn't hide away at a corner table.*	*Anxious.* *Scared at first.*	*My anxiety lessened as I ate.* *No one seemed to think I was odd for eating alone.* *I felt less awkward than I expected to feel.* *It took a lot of effort at first to keep my attention on the task of eating but it got easier.*

Becoming More Mindful

Mindfulness meditation, commonly associated with Zen Buddhism, has become popular in the past few years as a technique for dealing with depression, and managing stress and chronic pain. Evidence shows that mindfulness meditation can help reduce the chance of problems such as depression returning, and adds another weapon into your armoury against emotional problems.

Being present in the moment

Mindfulness is the art of being present in the moment, without passing judgement about your experience. The mindfulness process is so simple – and yet so challenging. Keep your attention focused on the moment that you're experiencing *right now*. Suspend your judgement about what you're feeling, thinking, and absorbing through your senses. Simply observe what's going on around you, in your mind, and in your body without doing anything. Just allow yourself to be aware of what's happening.

Mindfulness literature talks about the way your mind almost mechanically forms judgements about each of your experiences, labelling them as good, bad, or neutral depending on how you value them. Things that generate good and bad feelings within you get most of your attention, but you may ignore neutral things or deem them to be boring. Mindfulness meditation encourages awareness of the present moment with an uncultured mind, observing even the seemingly mundane without judgement. The whole experience is a bit like looking at the world for the first time.

When you meet someone you know, try to see her through fresh eyes. Suspend your prior knowledge, thoughts, experiences, and opinions about her. You can try this with acquaintances or people you know very well, such as family members and close friends.

Try mindfulness exercises when you're in the countryside or walking down the street. Whether the surroundings are familiar to you or not, try to see the details of the world around you through fresh eyes.

Letting your thoughts pass by

You can develop your mindfulness skills and use them to help you deal with unpleasant thoughts or physical symptoms. If you have social anxiety for example, you can develop the ability to *focus away* from your anxious thoughts.

Watching the train pass by

Imagine a train passing through a station. The train represents your thoughts and sensations (your 'train of thought'). Each carriage may represent one or more specific thoughts or feelings. Visualise yourself watching the train pass by without hopping onto any carriage. Accept your fears about what other people may be thinking about you without trying to suppress them or engaging with them. Simply watch them pass by like a train through a station.

Standing by the side of the road

Another version of the exercise is to imagine that you're standing on the side of a reasonably busy road. Each passing vehicle represents your thoughts and sensations. Just watch the cars go by. Observe and accept them passing. Don't try to hitch-hike, redirect the flow of traffic, or influence the cars in any way.

Discerning when not to listen to yourself

One of the real benefits of understanding the way that your emotions influence the way you think, is to know when what you're thinking isn't likely to be helpful or very realistic. Being mindful means learning to experience your thoughts without passing judgement as to whether they are true or not.

Given that many of the negative thoughts you experience when you're emotionally distressed are distorted and unhelpful, you're much better off letting some thoughts pass you by, recognising them as *symptoms* or *output* of a given emotional state or psychological problem. Chapter 6 covers the *cognitive consequences* of emotions, giving you an idea of the types of thoughts that can occur as a consequence of how you're feeling.

Becoming more familiar with the thoughts that tend to pop into your head when you feel down, anxious, or guilty makes it easier for you to recognise them as thoughts and let them come and go, rather than treating them as facts. This familiarity gives you another skill to help manage your negative thoughts in addition to challenging or testing them out in reality.

Incorporating mindful daily tasks

Becoming more mindful about little everyday tasks can help you to strengthen your attention muscles. Essentially, everything you do throughout the day can be done with increased awareness. For example, think about the following:

- Washing-up mindfully can help you experience the process more fully. Notice the smell of the washing-up liquid, the temperature of the water, and the movement of your hands.

- Eating mindfully can give you a more enjoyable eating experience. Slow down the speed you eat, and pay attention to the texture of the food, the subtlety of the flavours, and the appearance of the dish.

Part II

Charting the Course: Defining Problems and Setting Goals

The 5th Wave   By Rich Tennant

"I've tried Ayurveda, meditation, and aromatherapy but nothing seems to work. I'm still feeling nauseous and disoriented all day."

In this part . . .

More than a feeling . . . we help you to clearly name your emotions and also help you to work out the difference between helpful and unhelpful emotions. In this part you discover what you want to change in your life, and realise how some of your current solutions to problems may not be benefiting you in the long run. We also offer alternatives to current solutions that may not actually be working for you!

Chapter 6

Exploring Emotions

. . . .

In This Chapter

▶ Identifying healthy and unhealthy negative emotions

▶ Understanding the thinking, behaving, and attention components of emotions

▶ Defining the emotional problems you want to solve

. . . .

*T*his chapter aims to introduce you to some of the key differences between the unhealthy negative emotions you may experience and their healthy counterparts. The information we offer also helps you to discover ways to identify whether you're experiencing a healthy or an unhealthy emotional response.

You may be wondering why we're focusing on *negative* emotions in this chapter and neglecting positive feelings such as happiness. You may be asking: 'What *is* it with these two? They're so bleak!' The reason for dealing with the negative is that few people pitch up for therapy because they're having problems with positive emotions. Not a lot of people come to us looking for a way to overcome their relentless feelings of contentment. The emotions that give people trouble typically include guilt, anger, depression, and shame.

Although feeling bad when bad things happen is natural, you don't need to make things worse for yourself by giving yourself unhealthy negative emotions. Healthy negative emotions are generally less profoundly uncomfortable and less problematic than their unhealthy counterparts. For example, feeling intensely *sad* (a healthy negative emotion) is less uncomfortable than feeling intensely *depressed* (an unhealthy emotion). Likewise, feeling intense sadness can prompt you to do things to improve your situation, but depression's more likely to lead to your inaction and resignation.

Fortunately, you can *think* what to *feel*, to a greater or lesser extent, which can reduce your emotional discomfort. By choosing to think in healthy and helpful ways, you're more likely to experience healthy emotions.

Naming Your Feelings

If someone asks you how you feel, you may have difficulty describing exactly which emotion you're feeling. You may not be sure what name to give to your internal experience, or perhaps you're feeling more than one emotion at the same time.

Don't get caught up on words! When you start to make a distinction between healthy and unhealthy feelings, what you call them isn't terribly important. The main point is to be able to analyse your thoughts and behaviours, and to take notice of where your attention is focused (CBT refers to this as *attention focus*). These three areas are ultimately your most reliable guides as to which type of emotion you're experiencing.

For the sake of clarity, therapists can often encourage people to use different words for unhealthy and healthy alternatives to common feelings. For example, you could use the word 'anger' to describe an unhealthy emotion and 'annoyance' to describe the healthy counterpart.

Some people find it simpler to choose a descriptive word for their emotion and to add the term 'healthy' or 'unhealthy' to that word. Whatever way you prefer to describe your emotions is okay – the important bit's understanding the category each emotion falls into. Different people have different ways of describing things. Think about how you'd describe an oil painting compared with the way a friend or art critic may talk about it. Similarly, people describe emotional states in diverse ways. You, a friend, and a psychotherapist (someone highly skilled in discussing emotions) may all use very different words to describe the same type of feeling.

If you're not used to talking about the way you feel, you may have a hard time finding the words to reflect your feelings.

The following is a reference list of common human emotions and their synonyms, which you can use to increase your vocabulary of *emotive* (relating to emotions) terminology. This list is not broken down into healthy and unhealthy emotions.

> ✔ **Angry:** aggressive, annoyed, bad-tempered, complaining, confounded, cross, displeased, enraged, fractious, fuming, furious, hostile, ill-tempered, incensed, irritated, livid, miffed, peevish, prickly, resentful, testy, touchy, truculent.

✔ **Anxious:** agitated, apprehensive, bothered, concerned, edgy, fearful, fretful, frightened, jumpy, nervous, nervy, panicky, restless, tense, troubled, uneasy, vexed, worried.

✔ **Ashamed:** belittled, debased, defamed, degraded, discredited, disgraced, dishonoured, humiliated, mortified, scorned, smeared, sullied, tarnished, undignified, vilified.

✔ **Disappointed:** crestfallen, deflated, dejected, discouraged, disenchanted, disheartened, disillusioned, dismayed, gutted, let down, thwarted.

✔ **Embarrassed:** awkward, diminished, discomfited, humiliated, ill at ease, insecure, self-conscious, small, timid, uncomfortable, unconfident, unsure of oneself.

✔ **Envious:** green with envy, malevolent, malicious, Schadenfreude, sour, spiteful.

✔ **Guilty:** answerable, at fault, blameworthy, condemned, culpable, deplorable, indefensible, inexcusable, in the wrong, liable, reprehensible, unforgivable, unpardonable.

✔ **Hurt:** aggrieved, broken-hearted, cut to the quick, cut up, damaged, devastated, gutted, hard done by, harmed, horrified, injured, marred, offended, pained, wounded.

✔ **Jealous:** bitter and twisted, distrustful, doubtful, green-eyed, sceptical, suspicious, wary.

✔ **LOVE:** (we threw this one in just to lighten the mood) admiring, adoring, affectionate, besotted, blissful, crazed, devoted, enamoured, esteemed, fond, head over heels, infatuated, keen, loved-up, love-struck, mad about, on cloud nine, smitten, struck by cupid's arrow, worshipping.

✔ **Sad:** bereft, blue, depressed, distraught, distressed, down, downcast, downhearted, grief-stricken, heartsick, inconsolable, melancholic, mournful, shattered, sorrowful, tearful.

Thinking What to Feel

One benefit of understanding the difference between healthy and unhealthy emotions is that you give yourself a better chance to check out what you're thinking. If you recognise that you're experiencing an unhealthy emotion, you're then in a position to challenge any faulty thinking that may be leading to your unhealthy emotional response. Disputing and correcting thinking errors can help you to experience a healthy, negative emotion instead of an unhealthy feeling (see Chapter 2 for more on thinking errors and how to correct them).

A common axiom is 'I think therefore I am'; a CBT version is 'I think; therefore I feel.'

Feelings aren't as one-dimensional as they may seem. How you feel is more than just the emotion itself, because feelings don't just come out of thin air – they have a context. When you begin to make a distinction between your healthy and unhealthy emotions, look at the *interaction* between your thinking, your actions, your attention focus, your memory, your themes or triggers, and the way you feel. Take a look at Table 6.1 in the section that covers comparing healthy and unhealthy emotions further on in this chapter, which gives a clear breakdown of the characteristics of healthy and unhealthy emotions.

Understanding the Anatomy of Emotions

Figure 6-1 shows the complex processes involved in human emotion. Whenever you feel a certain emotion, a whole system is activated. This system includes the thoughts and images that enter your mind, the memories you access, the aspects of yourself or the surrounding world that you focus on, the bodily and mental sensations you experience, physical changes such as appetite, your behaviour, and the things you *feel like* doing.

As the diagram shows, these different dimensions interact in complex ways. For example, training your attention on possible threats is likely to increase the chance of anxious thoughts popping into your mind, and vice versa. Not sleeping well may increase the chances of you being inactive; continued inactivity can further disrupt your usual sleeping pattern. The advantage of understanding this system of emotion as presented in Figure 6.-1, is that it gives you plenty of opportunity to make changes. Changing even one aspect of the system can make changing other parts easier.

An example of change is becoming more active if you've been inactive, which may alleviate your feelings of depression and make it easier for you to challenge your depressive, pessimistic thinking. Being prescribed antidepressant medication, which works by effecting brain chemistry, can take the edge off your depression. Use of antidepressants can make it easier for you to train your attention *away* from your negative thoughts and uncomfortable symptoms and *towards* possible solutions to some of your practical problems. (See Chapter 10 for more about overcoming depression.)

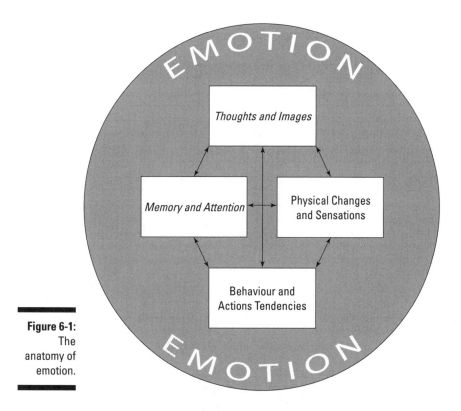

Figure 6-1:
The
anatomy of
emotion.

Comparing Healthy and Unhealthy Emotions

Deciphering between healthy and unhealthy versions of negative emotions can be challenging, especially when the process is new to you. Think of Table 6-1 as your emotional ready reckoner for the characteristics of both healthy and unhealthy emotions. Everything you may need to identify the emotion you're experiencing is in this table. Plus, if you do identify that an emotion you're experiencing is unhealthy, you can implement the thoughts, attention focuses, and behaviours of the healthy version to aid you in feeling better.

Table 6-1 **Healthy and Unhealthy Emotions**

Emotion	Theme	Thoughts	Attention Focus	Behaviour/Action Tendencies
Anxiety (unhealthy)	Threat or danger	Has rigid or extreme attitudes	Monitors threat or danger excessively	Withdraws physically and mentally from threats
		Overestimates degree of threat		Uses superstitious behaviour to ward off threat
		Underestimates ability to cope with threat		Numbs anxiety with drugs or alcohol
		Increases threat-related thoughts		Seeks reassurance
Concern (healthy)	Threat or danger	Has flexible and preferential attitudes	Doesn't see threat where no threat exists	Faces up to threat
		Views threat realistically		Deals with threat constructively
		Realistically assesses ability to cope with threat		Doesn't seek unneeded reassurance
		Doesn't increase threat-related thoughts		
Depression (unhealthy)	Loss or failure	Has rigid and extreme attitudes	Dwells on past loss/failure	Withdraws from others
		Sees only negative aspects of loss/failure	Ruminates on unsolvable problems	Neglects self and living environment
		Feels helpless	Focuses on personal flaws and failings	Attempts to end feelings of depression in self-destructive ways
		Thinks future is bleak and hopeless	Focuses on negative world events	

Emotion	Theme	Thoughts	Attention Focus	Behaviour/Action Tendencies
Sadness (healthy)	Loss or failure	Has flexible and preferential attitudes	Doesn't dwell on past loss/failure	Talks to significant others about feelings about loss/failure
		Sees both negative and positive aspects of loss/failure	Focuses on problems that one can change	Continues to care for self and living environment
		Is able to help self	Focuses on personal strengths and skills	Avoids self-destructive behaviours
		Is able to think about future with hope	Balances focus between positive and negative world events	
Anger (unhealthy)	Personal rule is broken or self-esteem is threatened	Has rigid and extreme attitudes	Looks for evidence of malicious intent in other person	Seeks revenge
		Assumes other person acted deliberately	Looks for evidence of offensive behaviour being repeated by other people	Attacks other person physically or verbally
		Thinks of self as right and other person as wrong		Takes anger out on innocent person, animal, or object
		Cannot see other person's point of view		Withdraws aggressively/sulks
				Recruits allies against other person
Annoyance (healthy)	Personal rule is broken or self-esteem is threatened	Has flexible and preferential attitudes	Looks for evidence that other person may not have malicious intent	Doesn't seek revenge

(continued)

Table 6-1 (continued)

Emotion	Theme	Thoughts	Attention Focus	Behaviour/Action Tendencies
Annoyance (healthy) (continued)		Considers other person may not have acted deliberately	Doesn't see further offence where it may not exist	Asserts self without physical/verbal violence
		Considers that both self and other person may be right to some degree		Doesn't take out feelings on innocent parties
		Is able to see other person's point of view		Remains in situation, striving for resolution (doesn't sulk)
				Requests other person to change their offensive behaviour
Shame (unhealthy)	Shameful personal information has been publicly revealed by self or others	Overestimates shameful-ness of information revealed	Sees disapproval from others where it doesn't exist	Hides from others to avoid disapproval
		Overestimates degree of disapproval from others		May attack others who have shamed self, in attempt to save face
		Overestimates how long disapproval will last		May try to repair self-esteem in self-destructive ways
				Ignores attempts from social group to return to normal
Regret (healthy)	Shameful personal information has been publicly revealed by self or others	Is compassionately self-accepting about information revealed	Focuses on evidence that self is accepted by social group despite information revealed	Continues to participate in social interaction

Emotion	Theme	Thoughts	Attention Focus	Behaviour/Action Tendencies
		Is realistic about degree of disapproval from others		Responds to attempts from social group to return to normal
		Is realistic about how long disapproval will last		
Hurt (unhealthy)	Other person treats one badly (self is undeserving)	Has rigid and extreme attitudes	Looks for evidence of other person not caring or being indifferent	Stops communicating with other person/sulks
		Overestimates unfairness of other's behaviour		Punishes other person through silence or criticism, without stating what one feels hurt about
		Thinks other person doesn't care		
		Thinks of self as alone and uncared for		
		Dwells on past hurts		
		Thinks other person must make first move towards resolution		
Disappointment (healthy)	Other person treats one badly (self is undeserving)	Has flexible and preferential attitudes	Focuses on evidence that other person does care and isn't indifferent	Communicates with other person about feelings
		Is realistic about degree of unfairness of other's behaviour		Tries to influence other person to act in fairer manner
		Thinks other person acted badly but doesn't think that they don't care		

(continued)

Table 6-1 (continued)

Emotion	Theme	Thoughts	Attention Focus	Behaviour/Action Tendencies
Disappointment (healthy) (continued)		Doesn't think of self as alone or uncaring		
		Doesn't dwell on past hurts		
		Doesn't wait for other person to make first move		
Jealousy (unhealthy)	Threat to relation-ship with partner from another person	Has rigid and extreme attitudes	Looks for sexual/romantic connotations in partner's conversat-ions with others	Seeks constant reassurance that partner is faithful and loving
		Overestimates threat to the relationship	Creates visual images of partner being unfaithful	Monitors and/or restricts partner's move-ments and actions
		Thinks partner is always on verge of leaving for another	Looks for evidence that partner is having an affair	Retaliates for partner's imagined infidelity
		Thinks partner will leave for another person who he has admitted to finding attractive		Sets tests/traps for partner
				Sulks
Concern for relationship (healthy)	Threat to relationship with partner from another person	Has flexible and preferential attitudes	Doesn't look for evidence that partner is having an affair	Allows partner to express love without needing excessive reassurance
		Is realistic about degree of threat to relationship	Doesn't create images of partner being unfaithful	Allows partner freedom without monitoring them

Emotion	Theme	Thoughts	Attention Focus	Behaviour/Action Tendencies
		Thinks partner finding others attractive is normal	Views partner's conversation with other as normal	Allows partner to express natural interest in opposite sex without imagining infidelity
Envy (unhealthy)	Another person possesses something desirable (self lacks desired thing)	Has rigid and extreme attitudes	Focuses on how to get the desired possession without regard for any consequences	Criticises the person with desired possession
		Thinks about the desired possession in a negative way to try and reduce its desirability	Focuses on how to deprive other person of the desired possession	Criticises the desired possession
		Pretends to self that one is happy without desired possession even though this is untrue		Attempts to steal/destroy the desired possession in order to deprive others
Guilt (unhealthy)	Broken moral code (by failing to do something or by committing a sin), hurting or offending significant other	Has rigid and extreme attitudes	Looks for evidence of others blaming one for the sin	Desires to escape from guilt feelings in self-defeating ways
		Thinks one has definitely sinned	Looks for evidence of punishment or retribution	Begs for forgiveness
		Thinks that one deserves punishment		Promises that a sin will never be committed again

(continued)

Table 6-1 (continued)

Emotion	Theme	Thoughts	Attention Focus	Behaviour/Action Tendencies
Guilt (unhealthy) (continued)		Ignores mitigating factors		Punishes self either physically or through deprivation
		Ignores other people's potential responsibility for sin		Attempts to disclaim any legitimate responsibility for the wrongdoing as an attempt to alleviate feelings of guilt
Remorse (healthy)	Broken moral code (by failing to do something or by committing a sin), hurting or offending significant other	Has flexible and preferential attitudes	Doesn't look for evidence of others blaming oneself for the sin	Faces up to healthy pain that comes with knowing that one has sinned
		Considers actions in context and with understanding before making a judgement about whether one has sinned	Doesn't look for evidence of punishment or retribution	Asks for forgiveness
		Takes appropriate level of responsibility for the sin		Atones for the sin by taking a penalty and/or make appropriate amends
		Considers mitigating factors		Doesn't have tendency to be defensive or to make excuses for the poor behaviour
		Doesn't believe that punishment is deserved and/or imminent		

Themes refer to situational aspects linked to emotion. Themes are the same for both healthy and unhealthy negative emotions. For example, when you feel *guilty* (an unhealthy negative emotion), the theme for that emotion is that you've 'sinned' by either *doing* or *failing to do* something. Another way of saying that you're guilty is that you've transgressed or failed to live up to your moral code. *Remorse*, the healthy alternative to guilt, results from the same theme as guilt. However, your thoughts, behaviours, and focus of attention, are different when you are remorseful and when you are guilty.

Themes can be useful in helping you to put your finger on the nature of the emotion you're experiencing. However, themes are not enough to help you decide whether your emotion is a healthy or unhealthy one. Consider the following situation:

> Imagine that you have an elderly aunt who needs your help to continue living independently. You usually visit your aunt at the weekend and do jobs that she's too frail to do for herself, like changing light bulbs and cleaning windows. Last weekend you went skiing with friends instead of checking in on your aunt. Your aunt got impatient waiting for the light bulb in her hallway to be changed and tried to do it herself. Unfortunately, your aunt fell off the chair she was standing on and broke her hip.

Thematically, this situation is one in which you broke or failed to fulfil a personal moral code, resulting in hurting or offending someone else.

If you feel guilty (an unhealthy negative emotion), you are very likely to experience the following:

- ✔ **Type of thinking:** Your thinking becomes rigid and demand-based. You conclude that you've definitely done a bad thing (sinned). You assume more personal responsibility than may actually be legitimate, discounting or not considering mitigating factors. You may believe that some form of punishment is deserved and/or imminent.

- ✔ **Focus of attention:** You look for more evidence that you've sinned, or you look for evidence that others hold you responsible for the sin.

- ✔ **Behaviour (action tendency):** You may desire to escape from guilty feelings in self-defeating ways – for example, begging for forgiveness, promising that you'll never commit a sin again, punishing yourself, physically or through deprivation, or by attempting to disclaim any legitimate responsibility for the wrongdoing.

By contrast, you can think about the situation differently and feel remorse (a healthy negative emotion). Although the same theme (a broken or failed moral code, causing hurt or offence to a significant other) still applies, you experience the following:

- **Type of thinking:** Your thinking is more flexible and preference-based. You look at actions in context and with understanding before making a judgement about whether you sinned. You consider mitigating factors of the situation and do not believe that punishment is deserved and/or imminent.

- **Focus of attention:** You don't look for further evidence that you sinned. Neither do you look for evidence that others hold you responsible for the sin.

- **Behaviour (action tendency):** You face up to the healthy pain that comes with knowing that you've sinned. You may ask for, but not beg for, forgiveness. You understand the reasons for your wrongdoing and act on that understanding. You may atone for the sin by taking a penalty and/or making appropriate amends. You avoid defensiveness and excuse-making.

The theme involving both guilt and remorse is the same, but your thinking, action tendencies, and focus of attention are very different.

Action tendency refers to an urge to behave in a certain way that you may or may not actually act upon. Different emotions produce an urge within you to do certain things. In some cases, you may actually do or say something, and in others you may just be aware that you *want* to do or say something. Maybe *wanting* to run out of a room and hide when feeling ashamed, or feeling unhealthily angry and *wanting* to punch someone's lights out, without actually doing so.

Spot the difference in thinking

As the example in the preceding section illustrates unhealthy emotions can spring from rigid, *demand-based thinking*. Thoughts or beliefs like 'other people must behave respectfully towards me at all times' and 'I should always get what I want without hassle' can lead to unhealthy anger when other people and the world don't meet these demands.

Healthy emotions spring from flexible, *preference-based thinking*. So, thoughts and beliefs like 'I prefer others to treat me respectfully, but they're not bound to do so' and 'I prefer to get what I want without hassle, but no reason exists that this should always be the case' can lead to healthy annoyance when other people and the world don't meet your preferences.

Rigid thinking is a reliable indicator that you're having an unhealthy feeling. When you think rigidly, you're more likely to underestimate your ability to cope with and overcome the negative event in question. The more adept you become at identifying your thoughts, beliefs, and attitudes as either rigid and demanding or flexible and preferential, the easier you can work out whether your feelings are healthy or unhealthy.

When you feel *guilty*, you think in an unhealthy, rigid, demand-based manner and may say things like the following:

- ✔ 'I absolutely shouldn't have left my aunt alone.'
- ✔ 'Leaving my aunt alone was a bad thing and means I'm a bad person.'
- ✔ 'I can't bear the pain of knowing that I've done this bad thing of leaving my aunt alone.'

You may then continue to think in the following guilt-enhancing ways:

- ✔ You fail to acknowledge that your aunt ultimately chose to try to change the light bulb herself. You fail to acknowledge that other members of your family can also check in on your aunt.
- ✔ You ignore the fact that you had no way of knowing that the light bulb needed changing, and that you had not foreseen your aunt taking such a risk.
- ✔ You expect that your aunt will blame your entirely. You think about the punishment that you believe you deserve.

By contrast, if you feel *remorseful*, you think in a healthy, flexible, preference-based manner and may say things such as:

- ✔ 'I wish I hadn't left my aunt alone, but regrettably I did.'
- ✔ 'Leaving my aunt alone may mean that I've done a bad thing but not that I'm a bad person.'
- ✔ 'I can bear the pain of knowing that I've done this bad thing of leaving my aunt alone.'

You can then continue to think in helpful ways:

- ✔ You can acknowledge your part in the accident occurring, but you can also consider that other members of the family failed to check in on your aunt.
- ✔ You can acknowledge that you didn't foresee your aunt taking the risk of changing a light bulb. Nor did you know that the bulb would burn out.
- ✔ You can expect that your aunt may be upset with you, but you believe that you don't deserve a severe punishment.

Taking legitimate responsibility for what happens in a situation enables you to think about the event in a holistic way. You don't need to prolong uncomfortable feelings of remorse beyond what is reasonable and appropriate to the situation. Your ability to solve problems isn't impeded by feelings of guilt.

Spot the difference in behaving, and ways you want to behave

Another way of figuring out whether your emotion is in the healthy or unhealthy camp, is to have a look at your actual behaviour or the way in which you feel inclined to behave.

Healthy negative emotions are accompanied by largely constructive behaviours, whereas unhealthy feelings usually go hand-in-hand with self-defeating behaviours. Problem-solving is still possible when you're healthily sad, annoyed, remorseful, or regretful, but you have much greater difficulty planning clear ways to surmount your problems when you're unhealthily depressed, enraged, guilty, or ashamed.

For example, if you respond to your aunt's falling over with *guilt-based action tendencies*, you may do one or more of the following:

- Go out and get quite drunk, trying to block out your guilty feelings.

- Visit your aunt in hospital and plead for her forgiveness.

- Promise that you'll never again let down your aunt, or anyone else dear to you, for as long as you live.

- Decide that you won't go on any other trips while your aunt is alive.

The preceding behaviours are problematic because they're extreme and unrealistic. These actions focus on self-punishment rather than look at the reality of the situation and how you can, in this example, best meet your aunt's needs.

On the other hand, if you're feeling healthy remorse your *action tendencies*, you may include some of the following:

- Endure the discomfort of knowing that your aunt has been hurt (rather than getting drunk to avoid it).

- Visit your aunt in hospital regularly and apologise for having left her alone.

- Understand that your aunt needs continuous support but that you have the right to go away with friends.

✔ Plan to stay with your aunt for a week or so after she's discharged from hospital.

✔ Resolve to plan your trips away more carefully and to arrange for nursing staff to be with your aunt when you're unavailable.

The preceding behaviours are geared towards making sure that your aunt doesn't hurt herself again during your absence. By taking an appropriate amount of responsibility for the accident, you can still look for ways to provide comfort for your aunt rather than concentrate on punishing yourself.

Spot the difference in what you focus on

In addition to differences in types of thinking and behaving, you can distinguish healthy from unhealthy emotions by checking out the focus of your attention. If you're having an unhealthy emotion, your mind is likely to focus on catastrophic possibilities in the future based on the primary event.

If you're responding to the injured auntie situation from a place of *guilt*, you may focus your attention on the following:

✔ Blaming yourself for abandoning your aunt and for the accident happening.

✔ Feeling the pain of your guilt whilst neglecting to consider potential solutions to the problem of your aunt needing continuous care.

✔ Looking for evidence that your aunt blames you entirely for the accident.

✔ Looking for blame from other people, such as hospital staff and family members.

You continue to give yourself an unduly rough ride, thereby prolonging your distressing, guilt feelings by focusing on the bleakest possible aspects of your aunt's accident.

If you respond to the situation from a place of remorse, you are likely to focus your attention on the following:

✔ Accepting that leaving your aunt alone may have been a bad decision but that you had no intention of putting her at risk.

✔ Feeling the pain of remorse over the accident but also trying to find ways to improve the situation.

✔ Not seeking out evidence of blame from your aunt.

✔ Acknowledging evidence that hospital staff or family members do not blame you for the accident.

Thus, your attention focus when you respond from a place of remorse enables you to take some responsibility for your aunt's broken hip, but you don't dwell on the potential for blame and punishment.

Spotting Similarities in Your Physical Sensations

Butterflies in your stomach, blood racing through your veins, light-headedness, sweaty palms, heart pounding. Sound familiar? We expect so. If someone described these physical symptoms to you, you may try to guess what emotion they were experiencing. However, it would be difficult to confidently determine the specific emotion, because these sensations can accompany several different positive and negative emotional states. For example, you may get butterflies in your stomach when you're excited, angry, anxious, or in love, as illustrated in Figure 6-2.

Figure 6-2:
Spot the similarities in your physical sensations.

The sensations that you feel in your body also tend to overlap in both healthy and unhealthy negative emotions. For example, you may get butterflies in your stomach when you're unhealthily anxious *and* when you're healthily concerned. Therefore, using your physical symptoms as a guide to judging the healthiness of your negative feelings isn't very reliable.

The main way in which your physical responses are likely to vary between the healthy and unhealthy categories is in their intensity. You probably find that sensations are more intense, uncomfortable, and debilitating when you're having unhealthy emotions, such as anxiety and anger. You may also notice that uncomfortable physical sensations last longer when you are experiencing unhealthy negative emotions.

Incidentally, we believe that if you're experiencing butterflies, sweaty palms, racing blood, light-headedness, and a pounding heart all at once, then you really *are* in love!

Identifying Feelings about Feelings

Getting two emotions for the price of one is not such a great deal when two unhealthy negatives emotions are on offer.

CBT professionals call feelings about feelings *meta-emotions*. The prefix *meta* comes from Greek and means 'beside' or 'after'.

Sometimes, you can give yourself a second helping of unhealthy emotion by holding rigid demands about which emotions you believe are acceptable for you to experience in the first place.

A common example of feelings about feelings is found in depression. Many people have guilty feelings about their depression. This guilt often comes from the demands people make of themselves, for example that they mustn't let other people down or put undue strain on loved ones. Here are some typical guilt-producing thoughts that are common in depressed people:

- ✔ 'I should be contributing more to the running of the home.'
- ✔ 'I must be able to demonstrate love and care to my children.'
- ✔ 'My partner and children are worried about me, and I'm making them suffer.'
- ✔ 'I shouldn't be neglecting my friends in this way.'

Recognising your meta-emotions is important, because meta-emotions can prevent you from dealing with your primary emotional problems. For example, you may be feeling guilty about having depression. If you can stop feeling guilty, you'll almost certainly find that you can work on overcoming your depression more effectively.

If you find that the concept of feeling guilty about being depressed really does strikes a chord with you, go to Chapter 10, where we discuss it in more detail.

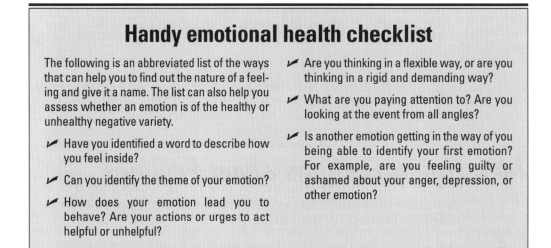

Defining Your Emotional Problems

The aim of CBT is to help you overcome your emotional problems and move you towards your goals. As with all kinds of problem-solving, *defining* your emotional problems is the first step in solving those problems.

Making a statement

Writing down a problem statement has three main components – the emotion, the theme or event (what you feel your emotion about), and what you do in response to that emotion. You can effectively describe an emotional problem by filling in the blanks of the following statement:

Feeling_____ (emotion) about _____
(theme or event), leading me
to_____(response).

For example:

Feeling *anxious* about *my face turning red in social situations*, leading me to *avoid going out to bars and clubs and to splash my face with water if I feel hot.*

Feeling *depressed* about *the end of my relationship with my girlfriend*, leading me to *spend too much time in bed, avoid seeing people, and take less care of myself.*

When positives are negatives

Although this chapter deals with unhealthy negative emotions because these are the most common factors in emotional disturbance, you can't forget that negative positive emotions do also exist.

An example of a negative positive emotion is holding a *rigid demand,* such as 'I must get approval from my boss' and then feeling a surge of delight when the demand is met. You may feel good about the approval and your confidence may soar for a time, but you're still vulnerable to unhealthy negative feelings if you later fail to get your boss's approval. If you hold a *flexible preference* for your boss's approval, you can feel healthily pleased if you get approval and healthily disappointed if you don't.

Another example of unhealthy positive emotions is the feeling of euphoria associated with *hypomanic* (excessively happy or 'high') states. People who suffer from bipolar affective disorder (formerly known as manic depression) can experience alternating periods of extreme low-mood and extreme high-mood. During high periods, people with bipolar affective disorder are often prone to making rash decisions and behaving in erratic, sometimes risky ways. People with bipolar affective disorder may seem to be very happy when in fact they're hypomanic and suffering from a genuine psychiatric condition. Bipolar affective disorder can be treated effectively with medication and CBT. Many of the tips for overcoming *unipolar* (or general depression) that you can find in Chapter 10 are also be very helpful for people with bipolar disorder. Appendix A lists organisations that you may find helpful.

If you think that you, or someone close to you, may have bipolar affective disorder, we strongly recommend seeing a psychiatrist to get a comprehensive assessment. Prescribed medication is an important part of managing the distressing symptoms of this disorder. Psychiatrists generally have more specialised knowledge about the disorder and appropriate medications than general physicians.

One key CBT strategy for helping people to manage bipolar depression involves making an activity schedule (see Chapter 10). Write down a plan of your daily activities and stick to doing them regardless of your mood. The crucial point is to establish a *consistent* level of activity in your daily life. Sticking to a daily schedule of activities can help you avoid being under-stimulated during lows (thereby combating a downward spiral into depression) and help you avoid becoming over-stimulated during highs (thereby preventing an upward spiral into hypomania).

Rating your emotional problem

Human nature leads you to focus on how bad you feel, rather than how much better you feel. As you reduce the intensity of any emotional disturbance, you can find motivation in being able to see a difference. After you describe a problematic emotion, rate it on a scale of 0–10, based on how much distress the emotion causes you and how much it interferes with your life.

As you work on resolving your emotional problem by making changes to your thinking and behaviour, continue to rate the distress and interference it is causing you. Your ratings are likely to go down over time as you make efforts to overcome your unhealthy negative emotions. Review your ratings regularly, once a week or so. Doing this review helps remind you of your progress and replenishes your motivation to keep up the good work!

Share your ratings with your CBT therapist if you have one. Your therapist can haul out your rating records and show you the progress you've made if your motivation begins to flag.

Chapter 7

Identifying Solutions That Cause You Problems

In This Chapter

▶ Understanding how common strategies can maintain (and worsen) your problems

▶ Examining and eliminating safety behaviours

▶ Understanding why doing the opposite of your current strategies can help you

*T*he first step in any kind of problem-solving is to *define* the problem. This chapter is about assessing your problems and putting your finger on the ways in which your current coping strategies are part of your specific problem.

Often, the problematic behaviours that maintain or worsen emotional problems are the very behaviours that people use to help themselves cope – hence the common CBT expression 'your solution is the problem'.

The reality is that you probably weren't taught how to best tackle emotional problems such as anxiety, depression, and obsessions. We confess that even though we have been trained in the art of emotional problem-solving, when it comes to dealing with our own emotions, we can still manage to get it wrong.

In this chapter, we guide you towards identifying the fact that your coping strategies may make you feel better in the short-term but that they are actually counterproductive – and that they can make things worse in the long-term.

When Feeling Better Can Make Your Problems Worse

Aaron Beck, founder of CBT and Dennis Greenberger, a well-known CBT therapist, note that, if you can turn a counterproductive strategy on its head, you're well on the way to a real solution. This concept basically means that by doing the polar opposite of your established coping strategies you can recover from your problems. Exposing yourself to feared situations rather than avoiding them is a good example of turning a counterproductive strategy on its head. The more you avoid situations that you fear, the more afraid you become of ever encountering feared situations. Avoidance also undermines your sense of being able to cope with unpleasant or uncomfortable events. For example, never using a lift may temporarily stop your anxious feelings about being in an enclosed space, but avoiding lifts does not help you to overcome your fear of enclosed spaces once and for all.

Windy Dryden, who trained us in CBT, coined the phrase 'Feel better, get worse. Feel worse, get better' when referring to people overcoming emotional problems. Many of the things that you may be doing that actually maintain your current problems, are driven by a highly understandable goal to reduce your distress. However, when you aim to get short-term relief, you often end up reinforcing the very beliefs and behaviours that underpin your problems.

One of the most powerful ways of changing your emotions in a lasting way, is to act against your unhelpful beliefs and to act on your alternative helpful beliefs (Chapters 3 and 14 contain more information about forming alternative healthy beliefs).

Here are some further examples of what we mean by *problem-maintaining solutions*:

- ✔ **Avoiding situations that you fear or that provoke anxiety.** Avoidance tends to erode rather than boost your confidence. You remain afraid of the situations you avoid, thus you don't give yourself a chance to confront and overcome your fears.

- ✔ **Drinking alcohol or taking drugs to block out uncomfortable feelings.** Often, those bad feelings persist in the long term, and you end up with the added problem of the effect of the alcohol or drugs (hangover, comedown). Also, you have the potential to develop a newproblem – substance dependence.

- ✔ **Concealing aspects of yourself that cause you shame.** Hiding things about yourself – such as imperfections in your appearance, childhood experiences, mistakes from the past, or current psychological difficulties – can make you feel chronically insecure that someone may 'find you out'. Hiding shameful aspects of your experiences also denies you the opportunity to find out that other people have similar experiences, and that they won't think any less of you for revealing your secrets.

- ✔ **Putting off dealing with problems or tasks until you're in the mood.** If you wait to take action until 'the right time', until you 'feel like it', or when you feel sufficiently inspired, you may wait a very long time. Putting off essential tasks may save you some discomfort in the short term, but undone tasks also tend to weigh heavily on your mind.

The following sections deal with common counterproductive strategies for coping with common psychological problems. We explain that doing what makes you feel briefly better may be perpetuating your problem.

Getting Over Depression Without Getting Yourself Down

If you're feeling depressed, you're likely to be less active and may withdraw from social contact. Inactivity and social withdrawal are often attempts to cope with depressed feelings, but they can reduce the positive reinforcement you get from life, increase isolation, increase fatigue, lead to the build-up of problems or chores, and leave you feeling guilty.

For example, if you've been feeling depressed for some time, you may use a number of ultimately negative strategies to relieve your depression:

- ✔ To avoid feeling ashamed about being depressed, you may avoid seeing friends. This coping strategy leaves you feeling more isolated and means you don't get the support you need.

- ✔ To avoid being irritable around your partner or children, you may try to minimise contact with them. Your children may become unruly, your relationship with your partner may suffer, and you may end up feeling guilty about not spending time with any of them.

- ✔ To avoid the embarrassment of making mistakes at work, you may stop going to work on a regular basis.

- ✔ To cope with feeling tired and to get some relief from your depression, you may take naps during the day. Unfortunately, napping can disrupt your sleeping pattern, leading to even more fatigue.

To see how your depression is affecting your activity levels, record a typical week on the *activity schedule* in Chapter 10 (and Appendix B). Then, as we explain in Chapter 10, combat depression by scheduling your activities and rest periods (but not naps because napping during the day can disrupt night time sleeping) for each day, and gradually build up your activity levels over time.

Loosening Your Grip on Control

Letting go of control is an especially relevant skill if you have any sort of anxiety problems, including obsessive-compulsive disorder (OCD), panic disorder, and post-traumatic stress disorder (PTSD). But, it also applies to other types of emotional problems, such as anger and jealousy.

Here are some common examples of how you may be gripping too hard on to the controls:

- Trying to limit your body's physical sensations because you believe that certain bodily symptoms will result in harm to yourself. For example, 'If I don't stop feeling dizzy, I'll pass out.'

- Trying to control and monitor your thoughts because you think that if they get out of control, you'll go crazy.

- Suppressing upsetting thoughts, doubts, or images because you believe that allowing them to enter your mind will cause harm to yourself or others. (This characteristic is very typical of OCD – check out Chapter 11 for more info.)

- Trying to control your body's physical reactions to anxiety, such as trembling hands, blushing, or sweating, because you think that others will judge you harshly if they notice your symptoms.

Trying to control the uncontrollable is destined to leave you feeling powerless and ineffective. Instead of striving for control, look to change your attitude about needing control by accepting the discomfort of certain types of thoughts or bodily sensations (head to Chapter 9 for more information).

If you try too hard to gain immediate control, you often end up:

- Focusing more on feeling out of control, thus making yourself feel even more powerless than you did to start with.

- Putting pressure on yourself to control symptoms and thoughts that aren't within your control, thus making yourself feel more anxious.

- Concluding that something must be deeply wrong with you because you can't keep symptoms under control, thus making yourself feel more anxious, and experience more racing thoughts and unpleasant physical sensations.

The next time you feel anxious in a public place or find yourself blushing, sweating, or having disturbing thoughts, put the concepts in this section to the test by trying harder to stop yourself from having those thoughts, blushing, or sweating. Chances are that you'll find your efforts produce even more of the thoughts and sensations you're trying so hard to control.

Feeling Secure in an Uncertain World

The need for certainty is a common contributing factor in anxiety, obsessional problems, and jealousy.

Unfortunately, the only things you can be 100 per cent sure of, as the saying goes, are birth, death, and taxes. Over and above that, humans live in a pretty uncertain universe. Of course, many things are predictable and pretty sure bets, like the sun rising in the morning and setting in the evening. However, other things in life are much more uncertain. 'Will I be pretty?' 'Will I be rich?' 'Will I live to a ripe old age surrounded by grandchildren and a few cats?' *Qué será, será.* Whatever will be, will be.

Trying to get rid of doubt by seeking unattainable certainty is like trying to put out a fire by throwing more wood on it. If you're intolerant of uncertainty, as soon as you quell one doubt another one's sure to pop up. The trick is to find ways to tolerate doubt and uncertainty – they exist whether you like it or not.

Here are some examples of how your demands for certainty may be reflected in your behaviour:

- **Frequent requests for reassurance.** Constantly asking yourself and other people questions, such as 'Is it safe to touch the door handle without washing my hands?', 'Do you find that person more attractive than me?', 'Do you think I'll pass the exam?', or 'Are you sure I won't get mugged if I go out?' are all efforts to find some reassurance in an uncertain world. Unfortunately, excessive reassurance-seeking can reduce your confidence in your own judgement.

- **Repeated checking behaviours.** Checking behaviours are actions you perform in an effort to create more certainty in your world. Such actions include checking several times that your doors and windows are locked, frequently asking your partner where they've been, seeing lots of different doctors to ensure that a physical sensation isn't a sign of serious illness, and going over conversations in your mind to be sure that you haven't said anything offensive. The irony is that the more you check, the more uncertain you feel. Excessive checking can be very time consuming, tiring, and can lower your mood.

- **Superstitious rituals.** Superstitious rituals are things that you do to try to keep yourself safe or to prevent bad things from happening. Typically, superstitious rituals are not directly related to whatever it is that you fear most. Examples of rituals include touching wood, repeating phrases in your mind, wearing lucky clothes or jewellery, and avoiding unlucky numbers, out of a faulty belief that these rituals will stop unfortunate or tragic events befalling yourself or your loved ones. Engaging in superstitious behaviours can lead you to conclude that the ritual has prevented bad things from happening, rather than help you understand that many bad events are unlikely to occur regardless of whether you perform a ritual or not.

✔ **Avoiding risk.** Risks – such as global tragedies, becoming ill, having an accident, making poor decisions, or committing a social faux pas – are unavoidable and are ever-present. You may be trying to eliminate risk by staying home or in 'safe' places, eating only certain foods, never deviating from set routines, overplanning for trips away, or overpreparing for unlikely events such as war, plague, or famine. In fact, risk is a part of life and can only be avoided to a limited extent. The more you try to eliminate all risk from your life, the more you're likely to focus on all the possible things that could go wrong. You're fighting a losing battle and are likely to undermine your sense of security even further. Focusing too much on the risks inherent in every day life will leave you chronically worried and cause you to overestimate the probability of bad things happening to you.

✔ **Trying to influence others.** Examples of influencing others' behaviour include, encouraging your partner to socialise only with members of the same sex, persuading your children to stay at home rather than go out with their friends, and asking your doctor to send you for another test. Demanding that other people act in ways to minimise your intolerance of uncertainty and risk can seriously damage your relationships. People close to you are likely to perceive you as controlling or suspicious.

Try to understand that uncertainty has always been a major feature of the world, and that people still manage to keep themselves safe and secure. You don't need to change the world to feel secure. You simply need to accept uncertainty and live with it. You *can* happily coexist with uncertainty – it's always been that way. Remind yourself that ordinary people cope with bad events every day and that you are likely to cope as well as others do if something wicked your way comes.

The next section deals with accepting uncertainty and letting go of unhelpful coping strategies.

Surmounting the Side Effects of Excessive Safety-Seeking

One of the main ways in which you maintain emotional problems is by rescuing yourself from your imagined catastrophes. Often, these anticipated disasters are products of your worried mind, rather than real or probable events. People with specific anxiety problems, such as the ones listed in this section, often take measures to reduce their anxiety and increase their sense of safety, but in effect make themselves even more intolerant of the inevitable uncertainty of everyday life.

The actions that people take to prevent their feared catastrophes from occurring are called *safety behaviours*.

Avoiding, escaping, or trying too hard to stop a feared catastrophe prevents you from realising three key things:

- ✔ Your feared event may never happen.

- ✔ If your feared event *does* happen, most likely you'll find ways to cope. For example, other people or organisations may be available to help you out.

- ✔ The feared event may well be inconvenient, uncomfortable, upsetting, and deeply unpleasant, but rarely is it terrible or unbearable.

Anxiety affects your thinking in two key ways, it leads you to overestimate the probability and gravity of danger, and leads you to underestimate your ability to overcome adversity. Of course you want to keep yourself as safe as possible. But sometimes you may try to keep yourself safe from events that really aren't that dangerous.

Additionally, some of the things that you do to eliminate risk and safeguard yourself may actually result in more discomfort and disturbance than necessary – using ultimately unhelpful strategies to avoid feared outcomes is very prevalent in anxiety disorders. Here are some examples of counterproductive safety behaviours that you might be using to cope with specific anxiety problems:

- ✔ **Panic attacks:** Michael's panic attacks are maintained by his fear that feeling dizzy will make him collapse. Whenever he feels dizzy, he takes a sip of water, sits down, or holds on to something. In this way, he prevents himself from finding out that he won't collapse simply because he feels dizzy.

- ✔ **Social anxiety:** Sally tends to overprepare what she's going to say before she actually says it. She monitors her speech and body language and reviews in her mind what she did and said when she gets home. In this way, she maintains her excessive self-consciousness.

- ✔ **Post-traumatic stress:** Since she had a car accident, Nina avoids motorways, grips tightly on to the steering wheel when driving in her car, repeatedly checks the rear-view mirror, and avoids being a car passenger. Because she's being so careful, her anxiety about having another accident remains at the forefront of her mind.

- ✔ **Agoraphobia:** Georgina's afraid of travelling far from her home or familiar places for fear of losing control of her bowels and soiling herself. She has become almost housebound, and she relies heavily on her husband to drive her around. This means that she doesn't go out on her own and never discovers that her fears are unfounded.

✔ **Fear of heights:** James is afraid of heights because he believes that the 'pulling' sensation he experiences in high places means that he's at risk of unintentionally throwing himself to his death. To cope with this sensation, he digs his heels firmly into the ground and leans slightly backwards to resist his feelings. He also tries to avoid high places as much as he can. These behaviours fuel his fear and leave him believing that somehow he's more at risk than other people in high places.

After you've drawn up a list of your avoidance and safety behaviours, you can have a better understanding of what areas you need to target for change. In essence, the real solution to your problem lies in exposing yourself to feared situations without using any safety behaviours. You can then see that you are able to cope with anxiety-provoking events and that you need not rely on distractions or spurious attempts to keep yourself safe. Give yourself the chance to see that your anxiety is not harmful in itself and that anxious feelings diminish if you let them do so of their own accord. (Chapter 9 contains more information about dealing with safety behaviours and devising exposures.)

Wending Your Way Out of Worry

One of the dilemmas faced by people who worry too much is how to reduce that worry. Some degree of worry is entirely normal – of course problems and responsibilities will cross your mind from time to time. Yet, you may be someone who worries all of the time. Being a true worrywart is intensely uncomfortable. Understandably, you may want to stop worrying quite so much.

Two reasons may account for your excessive worrying:

✔ You may think that by worrying about unpleasant events, you can prevent those events from happening. Or, you may believe that your worry can give you clues as to how to prevent negative events from coming to fruition.

✔ You may think that worry protects you by preparing you for negative events. You may believe that if you worry about bad things enough, they won't catch you off guard and you'll be better fixed to deal with them.

If you can convince yourself that excessive worry really doesn't prevent feared events from happening or prepare you for dealing with bad things, you may be in a better position to interrupt your repetitive cycle of worries.

Ironically, many people worry about things in a vain attempt to get all possible worries out of the way so they can then relax. Of course, this never happens – worry's a moveable feast, and something else always comes along for you to worry about.

If you worry excessively about everyday events, you may try to solve every possible upcoming problem in advance of it happening. You may hope that your worry will solve potential problems, and thus you won't have to worry about them any more.

Unfortunately, trying too hard to put your mind at rest can lead to increased mental activity and yet more worry. All too often, people then worry that worrying so much is harmful, and they end up worrying about worrying!

Try to see your worrying as a bad habit. Instead of focusing on the *content* of your worries, try to interrupt the worry *process* by engaging your mind and body in activities outside of yourself. Chapter 5 has some helpful hints on refocusing your attention away from you actively worrying.

Preventing the Perpetuation of Your Problems

Sometimes, the things you do to cope with your problems can bring about the very things that you're trying to avoid. An example of this is when you try to push upsetting thoughts out of your mind. Pushing away unpleasant thoughts is called *thought suppression,* and can generally make unwanted thoughts intrude more often. Research shows that when people try to suppress an unwanted thought, it can intrude into their mind twice as often than if they accept the thought and let it pass.

Close your eyes and try really hard not to think of a pink elephant. Just for a minute, really push any images of pink elephants out of your mind. What happened? Most people notice that all they can think of are pink elephants. This demonstrates that trying to get rid of thoughts by pushing them out of your mind usually results in them hanging around more persistently.

Trying too hard not to do, feel, or think specific things, and attempting to prevent certain events, can actually bring about what you most fear and wish to avoid. For example:

✔ Trying too hard not to make a fool of yourself in social situations can make you seem aloof and uninterested.

✔ Trying too hard to make sure a piece of work is perfect can lead you to overrunning a deadline, or you get so nervous that you produce poor work.

✔ Insisting that you must succeed at a task, like passing an exam or learning a skill, makes you concentrate too much on *how well* you're doing and not enough on *what* you're doing. This misplaced attention focus can lead to poor results.

> ✔ Feeling jealous and repeatedly checking up on your partner, testing them or demanding reassurance that they're not about to leave you, can potentially drive your partner away.
>
> ✔ Lying in bed, trying to deal with fatigue when you're depressed, can lower your mood further and may lead to feelings of shame and guilt about your inactivity.

Helping Yourself: Putting the Petals on Your Vicious Flower

The *vicious flower exercise* is a way of putting together different elements of your problem to aid your understanding of how your problem is maintained. Look at the example in Figure 7-1, and turn to Appendix B for a blank flower to photocopy and fill in. Follow these steps to fill in your own vicious flower:

1. **In the Trigger box, write down the trigger that makes you feel anxious or upset.**

2. **In the central circle, write down the key thoughts and meanings you attach to the trigger.**

3. **In the flower petals, write down the emotions, behaviours, and sensations you experience when your uncomfortable feeling is triggered. In the top petal, write down what you tend to focus on.**

Key negative thoughts, attitudes, or beliefs are at the heart of your vicious flower. The petals are your attentional, emotional, physical, and behavioural responses to the meaning you have attached to the trigger.

This chapter (and Chapter 6) gives you the kinds of emotions, behaviours, attention focus, and thoughts that you can fill in your petals with. If you suffer from anxiety, read Chapter 9; Chapter 10 for depression; Chapter 11 if you have an obsessional problem; and Chapter 13 for an anger problem.

One of the most important aspects of building a vicious flower is to think through how the petals affect the thought or 'meaning' that underpins your emotional problem. For example, the effect of anxiety on your thinking is to make you more likely to interpret experiences as more dangerous than they really are. The effect of depression is to make your thinking more gloomy and negative (refer to Chapter 6 for more on these and other emotions).

Focussing your attention on a sensation usually makes the sensation feel more intense. Acting upon an unhelpful thought or meaning usually makes the meaning seem more real. Unpleasant physical sensations accompanying your reaction can make upsetting thoughts seem even more real. You can design behavioural experiments to test out the effect of increasing or lessening a behaviour on your problems (refer to Chapter 4).

When you understand the mechanisms that maintain your problems, it will seem far more practical and sensible to target your petals for change.

The 'physical sensations' petal is the aspect of your problem that you're least able to change directly because physical sensations are outside your immediate conscious control. However, you can minimise the impact of physical sensations by learning to tolerate them whilst you overcome your problem, and to interpret them as no more dangerous than they really are.

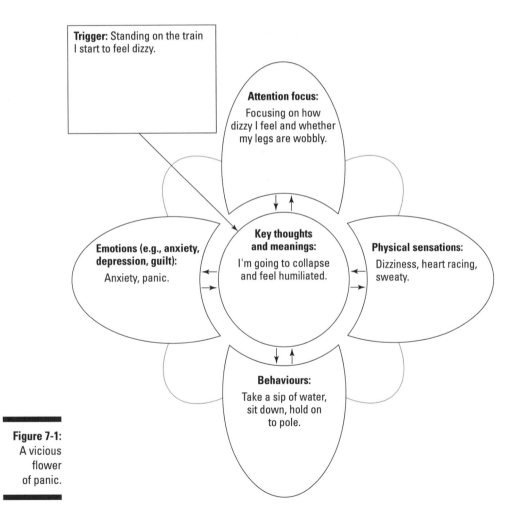

Figure 7-1:
A vicious
flower
of panic.

Put down that shovel and empty out your pockets!

One of the best metaphors for the kinds of behaviour we discuss in this chapter is the idea that some of your coping strategies may be like unwittingly trying to dig your way out of a hole. Naturally, the first step to overcoming your problems is to put down the shovel – to stop your self-defeating strategies, and gradually work out more productive ways of overcoming your emotional problems.

Over time, you may seek out bigger and better shovels in the guise of bigger and better avoidance and safety behaviours. We regularly invite those of our clients who suffer with agoraphobia, panic attacks, obsessive-compulsive disorder, and body dysmorphic disorder, to share with us the contents of their pockets or handbags, which is often very illuminating. Examples of *safety props* that people carry 'just in case' include, over-the-counter drugs, packets of tissues, antiseptic wipes, glucose sweets, handheld fans, make-up, plastic bags, paper bags, deodorant sprays, laxatives, and alcohol.

To help clients eliminate safety behaviours, we often encourage them to throw out or hand over these seemingly innocent everyday items in the spirit of getting rid of problematic solutions. Go through your pockets and handbag and collect all of your safety props. Throw them in the bin or hand them over to someone who knows about your problems and has an interest in helping you (this person can be anyone in your life if you are not currently seeing a CBT therapist). Be wary of purchasing or accumulating items to replace what you've already handed over or tossed away. Work on the basis that you only need essentials in your purse and pockets such as money, keys, and travel cards.

Chapter 8

Setting Your Sights on Goals

In This Chapter

▶ Defining your goals for emotional and behavioural change

▶ Motivating yourself

▶ Recording your progress

*I*f we had to define the purpose of therapy, its purpose would *not* be to make you a straighter-thinking, more rational person. Rather, the purpose of therapy is to help you achieve your goals. Thinking differently is one way of achieving those goals. CBT can help you change the way you feel and behave. This chapter helps you define your goals and suggests some sources of inspiration for change.

Aaron Beck, founder of cognitive therapy, says that CBT is whatever helps you move from your problems to your goals. This definition emphasises the pragmatic and flexible nature of CBT, and encourages clients and therapists to select from a wide range of psychological techniques to help achieve goals in therapy. The crucial message though, is that effective therapy is a constructive process, helping you to achieve your goals.

Putting SPORT Into Your Goals

Many people struggle to overcome their problems because their goals are too vague. To help you develop goals that are clearer and easier to set your sights on, we developed the acronym SPORT, which stands for:

> ✔ **Specific:** Be precise about where, when, and/or with whom you want to feel or behave differently. For example, you may want to feel concerned rather than anxious about making a presentation at work, and during the presentation you may want to concentrate on the audience rather than on yourself.

✔ **Positive:** State your goals in positive terms, encouraging yourself to develop more, rather than less, of something. For example, you may want to gain more confidence (rather than become less anxious) or to hone a skill (rather than make fewer mistakes).

Think of therapy as a journey. You're more likely to end up where you want to be if you focus on getting to your destination rather than on what you're trying to get away from.

✔ **Observable:** Try to include in your goal a description of a behavioural change that you can observe. Then, you can tell when you've achieved your goal because you can see a specific change.

If you're finding it hard to describe an observable change, think to yourself: 'How would the Martians, looking down from Mars, know I felt better simply by watching me?'

✔ **Realistic:** Make your goals clear, concrete, realistic, and achievable. Focus on goals that are within your reach, and that depend on change from you rather than from other people. Try to visualise yourself achieving your goals. Realistic goals help you to stay motivated and focused.

✔ **Time:** Set a timeframe to keep you focused and efficient in your pursuit of a goal. For example, if you've been avoiding something for a while, decide when you plan to tackle it. Specify how long and how often you wish to carry out a new behaviour, such as going to the gym three times a week for an hour at a time.

Some goals, such as recovering from severe depression, can vary a lot in terms of how long they take to achieve. Setting schedules too rigidly can lead you to become depressed or angry at your lack of progress. So, set your deadlines firmly but flexibly, accept yourself if you don't achieve them on time, and persevere!

Homing In on How You Want to Be Different

Defining your goals and writing them down on paper forms the foundation of your CBT programme. This section helps you identify how you may want to feel and act differently.

Setting goals in relation to your current problems

To set a goal concerned with overcoming an emotional problem, you first need to define the problem, which we talk about in Chapter 6 (where we explore unhealthy emotions and behaviours and their healthy counterparts). Also refer to Chapter 7, in which we explore how attempts to make yourself feel better can sometimes make problems worse.

A *problem statement* contains the following components:

- Feelings/emotions
- A situation or theme that triggered your emotion
- The way you tend to act in the situation when you feel your problem emotion

Defining how you want to feel as an alternative

CBT can help you attain changes in the way you feel emotionally. For example, you may decide that you want to feel sad and disappointed, rather than depressed and hurt, about the end of your marriage.

Aiming to feel 'okay', 'fine', or 'relaxed' may not fit the bill if you're dealing with a tough situation. Feeling negative emotions about negative events is realistic and appropriate. Keep your goals realistic and helpful by aiming to have healthy emotions. Try to maintain an appropriate level of emotional intensity when faced with difficult events (take a look at Chapter 6 for more on healthy emotions).

Defining how you want to act

The second area of change that CBT can help you with is your behaviour. For example, after going through a divorce, you may decide that you want to begin seeing your friends and return to work, instead of staying in bed and watching TV all day.

You can also include changes to your mental activities within your goal, such as refocusing your attention on the outside world or allowing *catastrophic* (upsetting or worst-case scenario) thoughts to simply pass through your mind (refer to Chapter 5 for more on this).

Making a statement

A *goal statement* is very similar to a problem statement – they have the same components, but the emotions and behaviours are different. A good goal statement involves the following:

To feel_____(emotion)
about_____(theme or situation) and
to_____(behaviour).

So, for example, you may want to feel *concerned* (emotion) about *saying something foolish at a dinner party* (situation) and to *stay at the table in order to make further conversation* (behaviour).

Maximising Your Motivation

Motivation has a funny way of waxing and waning, just like the moon. Luckily, you don't necessarily have to feel motivated about changing before you can take steps forward. Motivation often follows rather than precedes positive action – often people find they 'get into' something once they've started. This section suggests some ways to generate motivation and encourages you to carry on working towards goals in the temporary absence of motivation.

Identifying inspiration for change

Lots of people find change difficult. Your motivation may flag sometimes, or you may not ever be able to imagine overcoming your difficulties. If either of these situations sounds familiar to you, you're in good company. Many people draw on sources of inspiration when starting with, and persevering through, the process of overcoming emotional problems. Sources of encouragement worth considering include the following:

- ✔ **Role models who have characteristics you aspire to adopt yourself.** For example, you may know someone who stays calm, expresses feelings to others, is open-minded to new experiences, or is assertive and determined. Whether real-life or fictional, alive or dead, known to you or someone you've never met, choose someone who inspires you and can give you a model for a new way of being.

- ✔ **Inspirational stories of people overcoming adversity.** Ordinary people regularly survive the most extraordinary experiences. Stories of their personal experiences can lead you to make powerful personal changes.

Focus on taking a leaf out of an inspirational individual's book, not on comparing yourself negatively with someone's 'superior' coping skills.

  ✔ **Images and metaphors.** Thinking of yourself as, for example, a sturdy tree withstanding a strong wind blowing against you, which can be an inspiring metaphor to represent you withstanding unreasonable criticism.

  ✔ **Proverbs, quotes, and icons.** Use ideas you've heard expressed in novels, religious literature, films, songs, or quotes from well-respected people, to keep you reaching for your goals.

Focusing on the benefits of change

People often maintain unhelpful patterns of behaviour (such as, consistently arriving late for work) because they focus on the short-term benefit (in this case, avoiding the anxiety of being on a crowded bus or train) at the time of carrying out that behaviour. However, away from the immediate discomfort, these same people may focus on wishing they were free from the restrictions of their emotional problem (being able to travel carefree on public transport).

Completing a cost–benefit analysis

Carrying out a *cost–benefit analysis* (CBA) to examine the pros and cons of something can help galvanise your commitment to change. You can use a CBA to examine the advantages and disadvantages of a number of things, such as:

  ✔ **Behaviours:** How helpful is this action to you? Does it bring short-term or long-term benefits?

  ✔ **Emotions:** How helpful is this feeling? For example, does feeling guilty or angry really help you?

  ✔ **Thoughts, attitudes, or beliefs:** Where does thinking this way get you? How does this belief help you?

  ✔ **Options for solving a practical problem:** How can this solution work out? Is this really the best possible answer to the problem?

When using a CBA form such as the one shown in Table 8-1, remember to evaluate the pros and cons:

  ✔ In the short-term

  ✔ In the long-term

  ✔ For yourself

  ✔ For other people

Table 8-1	The Cost–Benefit Analysis Form
Costs and Benefits of:	
Costs (Disadvantages)	*Benefits (Advantages)*

Try to write CBA statements in pairs, particularly when you're considering changing the way you feel, act, or think. What are the *advantages* of feeling anxiety? And the *disadvantages*? Write down pairs of statements for what you feel, do, or think *currently,* and for other, healthier alternatives. Tables 8-2 and 8-3 show a completed CBA form. You can find a larger, blank cost–benefit analysis form in Appendix B, which you can photocopy and fill in.

Table 8-2	Cost–Benefit Analysis: 'Costs and Benefits of Saying What Comes Into My Mind and Paying Attention to the Conversation'
Costs	*Benefits*
I may end up saying something stupid.	I won't have to think so much and I might be able to relax.
I may not come up with the best thing to say.	I can be more spontaneous.
I may end up running off at the mouth and people might not like me.	I'll be able to concentrate on what's being said and I won't seem so distracted.

Table 8-3	Second Cost–Benefit Analysis: 'Costs and Benefits of Preparing in My Head What I'm Going to Say Before Speaking'
Costs	*Benefits*
I end up feeling very tired after going out.	I can make sure I don't say something foolish.

Costs	Benefits
I can't relax into the conversation.	I may think of something funny or entertaining to say.
Sometimes, I feel like the conversation moves on before I've had the chance to think of the right thing to say.	I can take more care not to offend people.

After you've done a CBA, review it with a critical eye on the 'benefits' of staying the same and the 'costs' of change. You may decide that these costs and benefits are not strictly accurate. The more you can boost your sense that change can benefit you, the more motivated you can feel in working towards your goals.

Write out a motivational flashcard that states the *benefits of change* and *costs of staying the same*, drawn from your cost–benefit analysis. You can then refer to this to give yourself a motivational boost when you need it.

A large aspect of achieving a goal, whether learning to play the guitar or building up a business, is about accepting temporary discomfort in order to bring long-term benefit.

Recording your progress

Keeping records of your progress can help you stay motivated. If your motivation flags, spur yourself on towards your goal by reviewing how far you've come. Use a problem-and-goal sheet like that in Figure 8-1, to specify your problem and rate its intensity. Then define your goal, and rate your progress towards achieving it. Do this at regular intervals, such as every one or two weeks.

1. **Identify the problem you're tackling.** Include information about the emotions and behaviours related to a specific event. Remember, you're feeling an *emotion* about a *situation*, leading you to *behave* in a certain way.

2. **At regular intervals, evaluate the intensity of your emotional problem and how much it interferes with your life.** 0 equals no emotional distress, and no interference in your life, and 10 equals maximum possible emotional distress, at great frequency, with great interference in your life.

3. **Fill in the goal section, keeping the theme or situation the same, but specifying how you wish to feel and act differently.**

4. **Rate how close you are to achieving your goal.** 0 equals no progress whatsoever, at any time, and 10 means that the change in your emotion and behaviour is completely and consistently achieved.

Figure 8-1:
The
Problem-
and-Goal
Sheet.

Using the form below, identify one of the main problems you wish to work on in therapy. A problem statement includes information about the emotions and behaviour related to a specific situation or event. For example: 'Feeling depressed about the end of my marriage leading me to become withdrawn and spend until around 6pm each day in bed'. or 'Feeling anxious about social situations leading me to avoid going to pubs, restaurants, and meetings, or to be extremely careful about what I say if I do socialise'. Think of writing your problem statement as filling in blanks: Feeling _____ (emotion) about _____ (situation), leading me to _____ (behaviour).

Use the same format to identify the goal you would like to achieve, but this time specify how you would like things to be different in terms of your emotions and behaviour.

PROBLEM No. ☐	DATE:	DATE:	DATE:	DATE:
	RATING:	RATING:	RATING:	RATING:
	DATE:	DATE:	DATE:	DATE:
	RATING:	RATING:	RATING:	RATING:

Rate the severity of your emotional problem 0 - 10. **0 = No distress/No impairment in ability to function 10 = Extreme distress/Virtuality unable to function in any area of life**

GOAL RELATED TO PROBLEM	DATE:	DATE:	DATE:	DATE:
	RATING:	RATING:	RATING:	RATING:
	DATE:	DATE:	DATE:	DATE:
	RATING:	RATING:	RATING:	RATING:

Rate how close you are to achieving your goal. **0 = No progress whatsoever 10 = Goal achieved and sustained consistently**

Change doesn't happen overnight, so don't rate your progress any more frequently than weekly. Look for *overall* changes in the *frequency*, *intensity*, and *duration* of your problematic feelings and behaviours.

Mercurial desires

People often find that they want to change their goals on a whim or a fancy. For example, you may have a goal of being more productive and advancing your position at work. Then, after going to a Summer Solstice rave, you decide that really your goal is to be free and to travel the world, communing with the essence of life. What you choose as your definitive goal is up to you. But be wary of being influenced too easily by whatever's foremost in your mind. Constantly abandoning former goals and adopting new ones can be a mask for avoidance and procrastination. Use the SPORT acronym, as described at the start of this chapter, to assess the durability and functionality of each of your chosen goals.

Part III
Putting CBT into Action

The 5th Wave   By Rich Tennant

"I sense that you're becoming more defensive and unapproachable lately."

In this part . . .

Sometimes it can seem as if no one understands your problem, but we do! These chapters give you CBT ammunition to surmount depression, obsessions, anxiety, and even unbridled rage. Read on to gain more control over your problems and really begin to realise recovery.

Chapter 9

Standing Up to Anxiety and Facing Fear

In This Chapter

▶ Understanding the nature of anxiety

▶ Developing attitudes that help overcome anxiety

▶ Designing a programme to face your fears

nxiety is a bully. And like most bullies, the more you let it shove you around, the pushier it gets. This chapter helps you get to know the nature of anxiety and to identify the ways in which it pushes you about. Fundamentally, you can beat anxiety, like any bully, by standing up to it.

Acquiring Anti-Anxiety Attitudes

Your thoughts are what count, because your feelings are influenced greatly by how you think. Feeling anxious increases the chance of you experiencing anxiety-provoking thoughts (refer to Chapter 6). Anxious thoughts can increase anxious feelings, and so a vicious circle can develop. You can help yourself to face your fears by adopting the attitudes we outline in this section.

Thinking realistically about the probability of bad events

If you have any kind of anxiety problem, you probably spend a lot of time worrying about bad things that *may* happen to you or your loved ones. The more you focus your attention on negative events and worry about bad things being just around the corner, the more likely you are to believe that they'll actually happen.

Proving for sure that bad events won't happen isn't that easy without a crystal ball or two, but you can acknowledge that you tend to *overestimate* the probability of bad things happening. Adjust your thinking appropriately to *counterbalance* for this tendency. Counterbalancing your attitude is a lot like riding a bike with the handlebars offset to the left – to steer straight, you need to turn the handlebars to the right, otherwise you keep veering off to the left. If you tend to always imagine the worst, straighten out your thinking by deliberately assuming that things are going to be okay.

Avoiding extreme thinking

Telling yourself that things are 'awful', 'horrible', 'terrible', or 'the end of the world' only turns up the anxiety heat. Remind yourself that few things are really that dreadful, and instead rate events more accurately as 'bad', 'unfortunate', or 'unpleasant but not the end of the world'.

Extreme thinking leads to extreme emotional reactions. When you mislabel a negative event as 'horrible', you make yourself overly anxious about unpleasant but relatively non-extreme events, such as minor public embarrassment.

Taking the fear out of fear

When people say things like 'Don't worry, it's *just* anxiety', the word 'just' implies – wrongly – that anxiety's a mild experience. Anxiety can, in fact, be a very profound experience, with strong bodily and mental sensations. Some anxious people misinterpret these intense physical symptoms as dangerous or as signs of impending peril. Common misreadings include, assuming that a nauseous feeling means that you're about to be sick, or thinking that you're going crazy because your surroundings feel 'unreal'.

If you have concerns about your physical sensations you may consider seeing your family doctor prior to deliberately confronting your fears. Your doctor may then be able to advise you as to whether deliberately increasing your anxiety in the short-term, in order to be free of it in the long-term, is safe enough for you. It is rare for people to be advised against facing their fears.

Understanding and accepting common sensations of anxiety can help you stop adding to your anxiety by misinterpreting normal sensations as dangerous. Figure 9-1 outlines some of the more common physical aspects of anxiety.

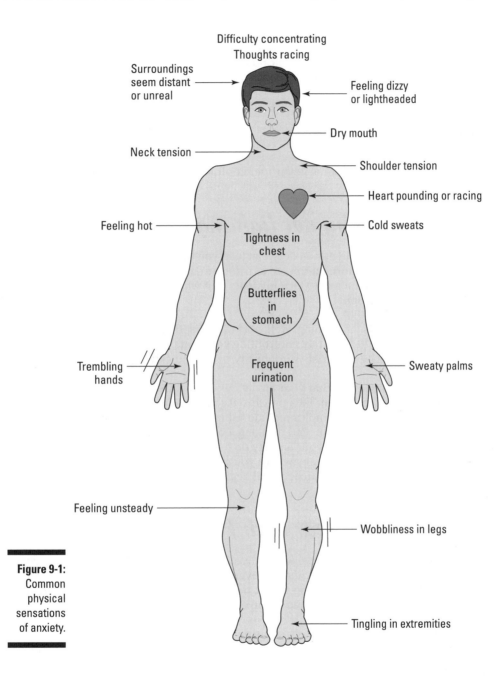

Difficulty concentrating
Thoughts racing

Surroundings seem distant or unreal

Feeling dizzy or lightheaded

Dry mouth

Neck tension

Shoulder tension

Heart pounding or racing

Feeling hot

Cold sweats

Tightness in chest

Butterflies in stomach

Trembling hands

Frequent urination

Sweaty palms

Feeling unsteady

Wobbliness in legs

Tingling in extremities

Figure 9-1:
Common physical sensations of anxiety.

Undoubtedly, anxiety is an unpleasant, sometimes extremely disturbing experience. However, evaluating your anxiety as 'unbearable' or saying 'I can't stand it' only turns up the emotional heat. Remind yourself that anxiety is hard to bear but not unbearable.

Attacking Anxiety

The following are some key principles for targeting and destroying anxiety.

Winning by not fighting

Trying to control your anxiety can lead you to feeling more intensely anxious for longer (for more on this, read through Chapter 7). Many of our clients say to us: 'It makes sense to face my fears, but what am I supposed to do while I'm feeling anxious?'

The answer is . . . nothing. Well, sort of. Accepting and tolerating your anxiety when you're deliberately confronting your fears is usually the most effective way of making sure that your anxiety passes quickly.

If you're convinced that your anxiety won't diminish by itself, even when you do nothing, test it out. Pick one anxiety-provoking situation that you normally withdraw from – examples include using a lift, travelling on a busy bus, standing in a crowded room, and drinking alone in a bar. Make yourself stay in the situation and just let your anxiety do its thing. Don't do anything to try and stop the anxiety. Just stay where you are and *do nothing* other than feel anxious. Eventually, your anxiety will begin to ebb away.

Defeating fear with FEAR

Perhaps the most reliable way of overcoming anxiety is the following maxim: FEAR – Face Everything And Recover. Supported by numerous clinical trials, and used daily all over the world, the principle of facing up to your fears until your anxiety reduces is one of the cornerstones of CBT.

The process of deliberately confronting your fear and staying within the feared situation until your anxiety subsides is known as *exposure* or *desensitisation*. The process of getting used to something, like cold water in a swimming pool, is called *habituation*. The principle is to wait until your anxiety reduces by at least half before ending your session of exposure – usually between twenty minutes and one hour, but sometimes more.

Repeatedly confronting your fears

As Figure 9-2 shows that if you deliberately confront your fears, your anxiety becomes less severe and reduces more quickly with each exposure. The more exposures you experience, the better. When you first confront your fears, aim to repeat your exposures at least daily.

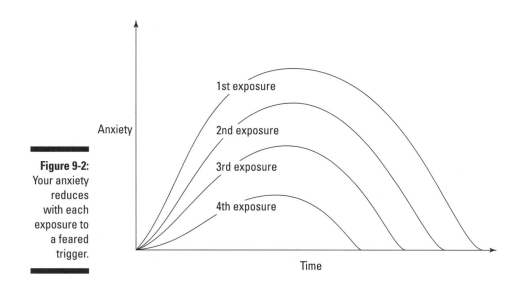

Figure 9-2: Your anxiety reduces with each exposure to a feared trigger.

Keeping your exposure challenging but not overwhelming

When confronting your fears, aim for *manageable exposure*, so that you can successfully experience facing your fears and mastering them. If your exposures are overwhelming, you may end up resorting to escape, avoidance, or safety behaviours. The flipside of choosing overwhelming exposures is taking things too gently, which can make your progress slow and demoralising. Strive to strike a balance between the two extremes.

If you set yourself only easy, gentle exposures, you risk reinforcing the erroneous idea that anxiety is unbearable and must be avoided. The point of exposure work is to prove to yourself that you *can* bear the discomfort associated with anxious feelings.

Taking it step by step

Avoid overwhelming or underchallenging yourself by using a *graded hierarchy* of feared or avoided situations. A graded hierarchy is a way of listing your fears from the mildest to the most severe.

If you want to kill your fear, let it die of its own accord.

You can use Table 9-1 to list people, places, situations, objects, animals, sensations, or whatever triggers your fear. Be sure to include situations that you tend to avoid. Rank these triggers in rough order of difficulty. Alongside each trigger, rate your anticipated level of anxiety on the good old 0–10 scale. *Voila!* You have a graded hierarchy.

After you have confronted your fear, rate the *actual* level of anxiety or discomfort you experienced. Then, tailor your next exposure session accordingly. Most situations are not as bad as you expect them to be. In the unlikely event that the reality is worse than your expectations, you may need to devise more manageable exposures for the next few steps and work your way up the hierarchy more gradually.

Table 9-1	Graded Hierarchy of Anxiety	
Feared or Avoided Trigger	*Anticipated Anxiety or Discomfort 0–10*	*Actual Anxiety or Discomfort 0–10*

Jumping in at the deep end

Although we caution about striking a balance between under- and overchallenging yourself, jumping in with both feet does have its benefits. The sooner you can face your biggest fears, the sooner you can master them. Consider whether you can climb to the top of your hierarchy straight away.

Graded exposure is a means to an end. Going straight to your worst-feared situation without resorting to safety behaviours (which we talk about in the next section) can help you get rapid results, as long as you stick with the exposure long enough to discover that nothing terrible happens.

Shedding safety behaviours

You can overcome anxiety by turning your anxiety upside-down. The best way to make your anxiety go away is to invite it to do its own thing. As we explain in a bit more detail in Chapter 7, the things you do to reduce your fear in the short-term are very often the very things that keep you feeling anxious in the long term. (Check out Chapter 7 for some common examples of safety behaviours.)

Recording your fear-fighting

Keep a record of your work against fear so you can check out your progress and make further plans. Your record can include:

- ✔ The length of your exposure session
- ✔ Ratings of your anxiety at the beginning, middle, and end of your exposure session.

A record helps you see whether you're sticking with your programme long enough for your fear to subside. If your fear doesn't seem to be reducing, make sure that you're still trying hard enough to reduce your fear by getting rid of those safety behaviours.

You can use the behavioural experiment record sheet in Chapter 4 to record your exposure and to compare your predicted outcome of confronting your fears with the actual outcome.

Overriding Common Anxieties

The following sections outline the application of CBT for some common anxiety problems. A full discussion of all of the specific types of anxiety problems lies outside of the scope of this book. However, the CBT principles that we introduce you to here are the very best bet for overcoming most anxiety problems.

First, define what you're doing to keep your anxiety alive in your thinking (see Chapters 2 and 6), and alive in your behaviour (see Chapters 6 and 7). Then, start to catch your unhelpful thoughts and generate alternatives (Chapter 3), and test them out in reality (Chapter 4). Understanding where you focus your attention, and re-training your attention, can also be hugely helpful (see Chapter 5). We discuss anxiety about health, fears of being ugly, and obsessions in Chapter 11.

Socking it to social anxiety

Attack *social anxiety* (excessive fear of negative evaluation by other people) by drawing up a list of your feared and avoided social situations and the safety behaviours you tend to carry out (check out Chapter 7 for more on safety behaviours).

Hang on to the idea that you can accept yourself even if other people don't like you. Be more flexible about how witty, novel, and entertaining you 'have' to be. Systematically test out your predictions about people thinking negatively about you – how do people act when you don't try so hard to perform? Refocus your attention on the world around you and the people you interact with, rather than on yourself. For more help on retraining your attention, refer to Chapter 5. Once you've left the social situation, resist the tendency to play your social encounters back in your mind.

Waging war on worry

To wage war on your excessive worry, resist the temptation to try to solve every problem in advance of it happening. Try to live with doubt and realise that the most important thing is not what you specifically worry about but *how* you manage your worrying thoughts. Overcoming worry is the art of allowing thoughts to enter your mind without trying to 'sort them out' or push them away.

Pounding on panic

Panic attacks are intense bursts of anxiety in the absence of real danger, and can often seem to come out the blue. Panic attacks often have very strong physical sensations such as nausea, heart palpitations, a feeling of shortness of breath, choking, dizziness, and hot sweats. Panic sets in when people mistake these physical sensations as dangerous and get into a vicious circle because these misinterpretations lead to more anxiety, leading to more physical sensations.

Put panic out of your life by deliberately triggering off panic sensations. Enter situations you've been avoiding and resist using safety behaviours. Realise, for example, that feeling dizzy does not cause you to collapse, so you don't need to sit down, and that other uncomfortable sensations of anxiety will pass without harming you. Carry out a behavioural experiment (see Chapter 4) to specifically test out whether your own feared catastrophes come true as a consequence of a panic attack.

Assaulting agoraphobia

Being afraid to travel far from home, or to venture away from safe or familiar places are common characteristics of *agoraphobia*.

To gain confidence and overcome agoraphobia, develop a hierarchy of your avoided situations and begin to face them, and stay in them until your anxiety reduces. This may include driving progressively longer distances alone, using public transport, and walking around in unfamiliar places. At the same time, work hard to drop your safety behaviours so you can discover that nothing terrible happens if you do become anxious or panicky, and ride it out.

Dealing with post-traumatic stress disorder

Post-traumatic stress disorder (PTSD) can develop after being involved in (or witnessing) an accident, assault, or other extremely threatening or distressing event. The symptoms of PTSD include being easily startled, feeling irritable and anxious, memories of the event intruding into your waking day, nightmares about the event, or feeling emotionally numb. If you have PTSD you may be sustaining your distress by misunderstanding your normal feelings of distress in response to the event, trying to avoid triggers that activate memories of the event, or trying too hard to keep yourself safe.

To combat PTSD, remind yourself that memories of a traumatic event intruding into your mind, and feelings of distress are normal reactions to trauma. Allowing memories to enter your mind and spending time thinking about them is part of processing traumatic events, and a crucial part of recovery. Many people find that deliberately confronting triggers or writing out a detailed first person account can be helpful. At the same time it's important to reduce any excessive safety precautions you may have begun to take.

Hitting back at fear of heights

Begin to attack a fear of heights by carrying out a survey among your friends about the kinds of feelings that they have when standing at the edge of a cliff or at the top of a tall building (see Chapter 4 for more on conducting surveys). You'll probably discover that your sensation of being unwillingly drawn over the edge is very common. Most people, however, just interpret this feeling as a normal reaction.

Put this new understanding into action to gain more confidence about being in high places. Work through a hierarchy of entering increasingly tall buildings, looking over bridges, and climbing to the top of high cliffs.

Fascinating phobias

One of the interesting things about anxiety problems is the wide variety of things that human beings fear. In our practise, we still encounter people with fears we've never heard of before. Crucially, what matters is not what you're afraid of but how negatively your fear is affecting your life.

Sometimes people are embarrassed by their phobias because they think others may find them silly or trivial. But extreme fear is never trivial – terror and fear can be very disabling, even if your fear is of something as simple as buttons. We suggest you seek out health professionals who take you seriously so you can get help for your phobia.

Common phobias include:

- **Acrophobia:** fear of heights or high levels
- **Agoraphobia:** fear of open spaces, crowded public places, or being away from a place of safety
- **Aichmophobia:** fear of pins, needles, and pointed objects
- **Arachnophobia:** fear of spiders
- **Claustrophobia:** fear of confined or small spaces

- **Emetophobia:** fear of vomiting
- **Haemophobia:** fear of blood and blood injury
- **Lockiophobia:** fear of childbirth
- **Noctiphobia:** fear of the night and the dark
- **Trypanophobia:** fear of injections

Less common phobias include:

- **Arachibutyrophobia:** fear of peanut butter sticking to the roof of one's mouth
- **Automatonophobia:** fear of ventriloquists' dummies, dolls, animatronic creatures, or wax statues
- **Barophobia:** fear of gravity
- **Bibliophobia:** fear of books (if you've got this one, stick with us – you're doing well!)
- **Blennophobia:** fear of slime
- **Lutraphobia:** fear of otters
- **Lyssophobia:** fear of going insane
- **Necrophobia:** fear of death or dead things
- **Ombrophobia:** fear of rain or being rained on
- **Soceraphobia:** fear of parents-in-law

Chapter 10

Deconstructing and Demolishing Depression

- -

In This Chapter

▶ Understanding depression

▶ Identifying thinking and behaviour patterns that keep your depression going

▶ Recognising and reducing ruminative thinking

▶ Confronting and solving practical problems

▶ Using activity as an antidepressant

▶ Getting your sleeping pattern back on track

- -

Statistics show that as many as one in two people are estimated to experience depression at some point in their lives. Luckily, the problem is well-recognised and treatable.

If for the past month, you've felt down, lacked energy, been pessimistic or hopeless about the future, and lost interest or enjoyment in doing things, then you may be suffering from depression. If you've also had difficulty concentrating, had a poor appetite, been waking early, and experienced a low mood, anxious thoughts or feelings of dread in the morning, then you're even more likely to be diagnosed with depression. If you have three or more of these symptoms, your symptoms have been present for two weeks or more, and are intense enough to interrupt your usual day-to-day activities, then we recommend that you visit your physician and investigate the possibility that you are suffering from depression.

Antidepressant medication can help to alleviate some of your depressive symptoms, although not every person diagnosed with depression needs to take medication. Depending on the severity of your depression, a course of CBT treatment may be enough to help you get better. CBT for the treatment of depression is well researched and the results show that it produces good outcomes. CBT and antidepressant medication are often used in conjunction to treat depression. Ask your doctor or psychiatrist to explain your medication and any possible side effects.

This chapter provides you with a guide to assess yourself for possible depression and offers some classic CBT strategies for defeating depression.

Understanding the Nature of Depression

The sort of depression we're talking about in this chapter is different to feeling down or blue in response to a bad event. We're talking about an illness now ranked as one of the most common reasons for people having to have time off work.

Specifically, depression has the following symptoms, usually lasting for at least two weeks:

- ✔ Appetite variation, such as eating far less or more ('comfort eating') than usual

- ✔ Sleep disturbance, including having difficulty sleeping, wanting to sleep too much, or experiencing early-morning wakefulness

- ✔ Lack of concentration and poor memory

- ✔ Irritability

- ✔ Loss of libido

- ✔ Loss of interest in activities previously enjoyed. Engaging in these activities no longer produces pleasure

- ✔ Social isolation and withdrawal from others

- ✔ Self-neglect with respect to feeding or grooming

- ✔ Neglecting to take care of your living environment

- ✔ Decreased motivation and activity levels, often described as a feeling of lethargy

- ✔ Feelings of hopelessness about the future and thinking bleak thoughts, such as 'What's the point?'

- ✔ Strong and enduring negative thoughts about yourself

- ✔ Feelings of guilt

- ✔ Inability to experience feelings of love, often described as a flattening of emotions or feeling numb

- ✔ Suicidal thoughts, such as feeling that you no longer care whether you live or die

Another common form of depression is *bipolar affective disorder,* formerly called 'manic depression'. People who have bipolar disorder experience periods of severe depression alternating with periods of *hypomania* (feelings of euphoria accompanied by impulsive and often risky behaviour). If you think that have this disorder we advise you to seek an assessment from a psychiatrist. A psychiatrist will be able to prescribe appropriate medication and can refer you to a CBT therapist.

The techniques covered in this chapter for overcoming *unipolar depression* (depression that is not accompanied by periods of hypomania) are also useful for bipolar sufferers. Keeping up a consistent day-to-day level of activity is one of the main CBT strategies for managing bipolar affective disorder. You can use the techniques in the following sections, which cover improving the quality of your sleep, solving problems, scheduling your activities, and interrupting rumination, to stabilise your mood and help you to minimise or avoid excessive highs and lows.

Looking at What Fuels Depression

Unfortunately, certain things that you do, in an attempt to alleviate your feelings of depression, may actually be making your symptoms worse. When people are depressed, they often make the mistake of doing what their mood dictates.

CBT helps depressed individuals learn to override their depressed mood and to do the *opposite* of what their depression makes them *feel like doing*. Here are some of the main actions and thoughts that actually stoke depression:

- **Rumination:** Getting hooked into a repetitive, cyclical process of negative thinking, repeatedly going over problems in the past, or asking yourself unanswerable questions. (We discuss rumination in detail in the next section.)

- **Negative thinking:** In depression, your negative thoughts about yourself are often based on beliefs that you're helpless and worthless. Thoughts about the world being an unsafe and undesirable place to live in are also a common feature of depression.

- **Inactivity:** Feeling that you can't be bothered to do day-to-day tasks, not participating in activities that previously you enjoyed, and staying in bed because you don't believe you can face the day.

- **Social withdrawal:** Avoiding seeing other people and not interacting with the people around you.

- **Procrastination:** Avoiding specific tasks, such as paying bills, booking appointments, and making phone calls, because you think they're too difficult or scary to confront.

✔ **Shame:** Feeling ashamed about your depression, and telling yourself that other people would judge you harshly if they knew how much your effectiveness and productivity had decreased.

✔ **Guilt:** Feeling guilty about your depression, and overestimating the degree to which your low mood causes inconvenience and suffering to your loved ones.

✔ **Hopelessness:** Thinking that you'll never feel better or that your situation will never improve.

Doing only what you feel like doing when you are depressed is likely to maintain or worsen your symptoms. Instead, try doing the opposite of what your depression directs you towards doing. For example, if you feel depressed and want to stay in bed all day avoiding phone calls and seeing friends, do the opposite. Try to make the colossal effort (and it can really feel colossal!) of getting up and dressed, answering the phone, and going out of the house to meet friends. Doing this limits you ruminating on your bad feelings and thoughts, and forces your attention onto external things, such as other people and your environment.

Most people find that they feel better for having done *something,* even if they do not experience enjoyment from social interaction like they did before they became depressed.

Depression typically dulls your ability to glean enjoyment from previously enjoyed activities. Be patient with yourself and trust that your feelings of enjoyment can return over time. In the first instance, it is enough to simply do the things that you have been avoiding *for the sake of it.* Doing something is better than doing nothing. Don't put pressure on yourself to 'have a good time' at this early stage in your recovery.

Going Round and Round in Your Head: Ruminative Thinking

Rumination is an integral process in maintaining your depression. Most people with depression are likely to engage in some rumination, even if they're not aware that they do.

Rumination is a circular thought process in which you go over the same things again and again. Often, the focus is on how bad you feel or doubting that you can ever feel differently or better. Your rumination may also focus on trying to work out the root cause of your depression, or on the events that have contributed to you being depressed. You may ask yourself questions like the following, over and over again:

- ✔ Why is this happening to me?
- ✔ What could I have done to stop this happening?
- ✔ If only *x*, *y* or *z* hadn't happened, I'd be okay.

Depression makes people feel compelled to ruminate. In a sense, rumination is like a faulty attempt to solve problems. Rumination is compelling because your depressed mood tells you that you must try to get to the bottom of why you feel bad. But rumination simply doesn't work: You end up trying to solve your depression by going over the same old ground and looking for answers inside the problem. You focus your attention on how depressed you feel, which leads to you feeling more depressed.

Fortunately, you can catch yourself going into a ruminative state by using the techniques we discuss in the following sections to interrupt the process.

Catching yourself in the act

Rumination is all-consuming. It will typically absorb you quite totally. You may look like you're simply staring blankly into space, but in your head your thoughts are going ten to the dozen. The key is to knowing when you're going *into* rumination, so you can take steps towards *getting out* of rumination.

Early warning signs of rumination taking hold include the following:

- ✔ **Getting stuck.** You may be in the middle of doing something and find that you've stopped moving and are deep in thought. For example, you may be perching on the side of the bed for several minutes (or even much longer!) when actually you intended going for a shower.

- ✔ **Feeling low.** Beware of times when your mood's at its lowest ebb: This is when you're most likely to engage in rumination. Most people ruminate at particular times of the day, more often than other times (although rumination can happen at any time).

- ✔ **Slowing down.** You may be doing something and then start to move more slowly, like pausing in the aisle at the supermarket. You start to slow down because your concentration's heading elsewhere.

- ✔ **Getting repetitive.** The same old thoughts and questions drift into your head, time and time again. You get a familiar niggling feeling that these vague questions must be answered.

The content of your ruminations is not the problem – the process of rumination itself is. You don't need to do anything with your thoughts other than disengage from them, as we explain in the following section.

Arresting ruminations before they arrest you

Several different tricks can help you stop the rumination process. Try some of the following:

- ✓ **Get busy.** Perhaps one of the most effective strategies you can adopt is to make your body and mind busy with something outside yourself. If you're vitally absorbed in an activity, you may find it harder to engage in rumination. These types of activities may include doing the housework with the radio on to hold your attention away from your internal thoughts, making a phone call, surfing the Internet, running errands, taking the dogs for a walk, and so on.

- ✓ **Work out.** Hard aerobic exercise can exorcise those toxic thought processes. Be sure to exercise during the day or in the early morning, because exercising too near bedtime can disturb your sleep.

- ✓ **Get up and out.** Rumination's more difficult when you're outside of your home or in the company of others. If you know that you're most vulnerable to ruminating at certain hours of the day, make sure that you schedule activities for these times.

- ✓ **Let your thoughts go.** Practice letting your negative thoughts pass by and simply observe them like pictures across a television screen. Don't engage with your negative thoughts, judge them, or try to answer any questions – just accept their existence and let them slip by. (Check out Chapter 5 for more on this technique.)

- ✓ **Get good at redirecting your attention.** You can strengthen your attention muscles and deliberately focus on less depressing things. Try using *task concentration training*, a method of attending to external aspects of your environment, as it can successfully interrupt rumination. (See Chapter 5 for more on task concentration training.)

- ✓ **Be sceptical.** Your depressed thoughts are a symptom of your depression, so try to take them with a sizable pinch of salt. You can resist the urge to ruminate about your depressed thoughts by deciding that they're neither true nor important.

Keeping busy is a great technique for interrupting ruminative thinking. However, you can still end up ruminating while you're engaged in an activity. Be aware of paying attention to whatever you're doing. Be mindful of your actions when you're ironing, cleaning, stringing beads, weeding the garden, or whatever. Rumination can take hold during activities if you're acting *mindlessly* rather than *mindfully* (refer to Chapter 5 for more on this distinction).

Activating Yourself as an Antidepressant

Withdrawal and inactivity are the two most fundamental *maintaining factors* in depression – they keep you in a vicious circle of isolation and low mood. For example, to counteract feelings of fatigue, you may be tempted (very tempted) to spend more time in bed. Unfortunately, remaining in bed means more inactivity and less energy.

If you feel ashamed of being 'flat', about having nothing to say, or feel guilty about burdening your friends, then keeping to yourself may seem sensible. The problem is that the less you do and the fewer people you see, the less pleasure and satisfaction you'll get out of life, the less support you'll receive, and the more your problems will pile up and weigh heavy on your mind.

Tackling inactivity

One of the best ways of starting to overcome depression is to gradually become more active, to steadily re-engage with other people, and to start tackling daily chores and other problems.

Use the activity schedule in Table 10-1 to start to plan each day with a realistic balance of activities and rest. Build up your activities gradually. If you've been in bed for days, getting out of the bedroom and sitting in a chair is a big move in the right direction. Remember: Take it step by step. Using the activity is incredibly simple; it merely involves allocating a specific time to do a specific activity. You can photocopy the blank schedule in Table 10-1 and fill it in.

Don't overload your activity schedule, otherwise you may feel overwhelmed, sink back into inactivity, and probably berate yourself for being ineffective. It's crucial to *realistically* plan a gradual increase in activities, starting from where you are *now*, not from where you think you *should* be.

Table 10-1				Activity Schedule			
	Monday	**Tuesday**	**Wednesday**	**Thursday**	**Friday**	**Saturday**	**Sunday**
6–8 a.m.							
8–10							
10–12							
12–2							
2–4							
4–6							
6–8							
8–10 p.m.							

Dealing with the here and now: Solving problems

As with other aspects of your daily or weekly activities, you need to be steady and systematic in your attempts to deal with practical problems, such as paying bills, writing letters, and completing other tasks that can pile up when you're less active.

To get started, set aside a specific amount of time each day for dealing with neglected chores. Allocating your time can help things seem more manageable. Try the following problem-solving process:

1. Define your problem.

At the top of a sheet of paper, write down the problems you're struggling with. For example, you might consider problems with the following:

- Relationships

- Isolation

- Interests and hobbies

- Employment and education

- Financial issues

- Legal issues

- Housing

- Health

Apply the following steps to each of your identified problems. You may need to do Steps 2 through 5 on each of your different problems.

2. Brainstorm solutions to your problem.

Write down all the possible solutions you can think of. Consider the following questions to help you generate some solutions:

- How did you deal with similar problems in the past?

- How have other people coped with similar problems?

- How do you imagine you'd tackle the problem if you weren't feeling depressed?

- How do you think someone else would approach the problem?

- What resources (such as professionals and voluntary services) can you access for help with your problems?

3. Evaluate your solutions.

Review your 'brainstormed' list. Select some of your most realistic seeming solutions, and list the pros and cons of each.

4. Try out a solution.

On the basis of your evaluation of pros and cons, choose a solution to try out.

You can easily feel overwhelmed when your mood is low. Even the best of solutions can seem too difficult. To deal with this, break down your solution into a series of smaller, more manageable steps. For example, if you're dealing with financial problems, your first step may be to ask friends for a recommended accountant, or to visit a financial consultant in your area. A second step may be to get your tax returns, proof of income, and so on, together. A third step may be selecting an accountant, and contacting them for information about their fees and the services they provide.

5. **Review.**

   After trying out a solution, review how much it has helped you to resolve your problem. Consider whether you need to take further steps, to try another solution, or move on to tackling another problem.

Taking care of yourself and your environment

One of the hallmarks of depression is neglecting yourself and your living environment, which in turn leaves you feeling more depressed.

Instead of allowing your depression to be mirrored in your appearance and your home, make an extra effort to spruce things up. Your environment can have an astounding affect on your mood, both positive and negative.

Include bathing, laundry, tidying, and cleaning as part of your weekly activity schedule.

Getting a Good Night's Sleep

Good night, sleep tight, and don't let the bedbugs bite!

Sleep disturbance, in one form or another, can often accompanydepression. Here are some tips you can use to improve your chances of greeting the sandman.

   ✔ **Get some exercise.** We cannot overstate the benefits of taking regular exercise. Exercise is good for your mood and good for your sleeping. You can take vigorous exercise during the day or even first thing in the morning to get your *endorphins* ('feel good' chemicals in your brain) charging. If you want to take some exercise in the evenings to help you wind down and de-stress, keep it gentle and not too close to your bedtime. A stroll, or an easy cycle ride, is an ideal choice.

✔ **Establish a schedule.** Getting up at the same time everyday and avoiding daytime naps can help you get your sleeping back on track. Catnapping may be very tempting, but ultimately it interferes with your bedtime and can actually lower your mood. If you know that you get the urge for a siesta around the same time everyday, make plans to be out of the house at this time. Make yourself busy to keep yourself awake.

✔ **Avoid lying in bed awake.** If you find dropping off to sleep difficult, don't lie in bed tossing and turning. Get out of bed and do something – ideally, something boring like sorting laundry or reading a book on something you find dull, drinking something warm and low-in-caffeine, such as milk or cocoa – until you feel ready for sleep. Try to stay up until your eyelids start to feel heavy. The same applies, if you wake in the middle of the night and can't get back to sleep easily. Don't stay in bed for longer than ten minutes trying to get back to sleep. Get up and do something like the above ideas, then get back into bed only when you feel sleepy.

✔ **Watch your caffeine and stimulant intake.** Avoid caffeinated drinks from mid- to late-afternoon. Caffeine can stay in your system for a long time. Remember that as well as tea and coffee, many soft drinks, chocolate (although not so much), and various energy drinks contain caffeine. Even some herbal teas contain stimulants, such as matte and guarana.

✔ **Establish a bedtime routine.** Going through the same pre-bedtime procedures each night can help your mind realise that it's getting near to shutdown time. Your routine may include having a warm bath, listening to a soothing radio programme, or having a warm, milky drink, or whatever works for you. Sometimes, having a very light, easily digestible snack before bedtime is a good idea to prevent sleep disturbance associated with going to bed hungry.

Setting realistic sleep expectations

During the day and while you try to fall asleep, you may well have thoughts like 'I'll never be able to get to sleep', or 'I'm in for another night of waking up every two hours'. Understandably, you may have these expectations if your sleep has been disturbed for some time, but such thinking is likely to perpetuate your sleep disturbance. Be aware of your worrying thoughts about sleep problems, such as 'I'll never be able to cope on such little sleep', or 'I've got to get some sleep tonight'. Trying to force yourself to go to sleep is rarely successful, and doing so contradicts the concept of *relaxation*, because you're making an *effort* to sleep.

Although it may sound like a tall order, try to take the attitude that you *can* cope with very little, or poor-quality, sleep. Also, answer back your sleep expectations by briefly telling yourself that you don't know for definite how you may sleep tonight and that you're just going to see how it goes.

Making your bedroom oh so cosy

Your bedroom should be used for sleeping and nothing else, apart from sex. When you're trying to settle your sleep pattern, you should avoid even reading in bed. The idea is to help your fatigued mind build helpful, sleep-inducing associations with your boudoir. So, you definitely don't want to be watching telly in bed, working on your laptop, talking on the phone, eating in bed, or any other activity, apart from slumbering or making sweet lurve.

Take care to make your bed and bedroom a relaxing, soothing place to be. Get yourself some very nice bed linen, remove clutter from the room, maybe put out some candles, hang some relaxing pictures on the walls, and make the temperature right for you. Smells can carry strong associations, so consider using a pleasant fabric softener on your linen or a special-purpose pillow spray. Just the smell of a soothing fabric softener on your linen can be enough for you to associate your bed with sleeping.

You can buy several natural essential oils from herbalists and health food shops that are thought to have relaxing properties. Try having an aromatherapy massage, or add essential oils to your bath, heat them in a burner to fragrance your room, or sprinkle them diluted on your bedclothes. You might want to try some of the following oils:

- Chamomile
- Clary sage
- Geranium and rose geranium
- Lavender (always popular)
- Palma rosa (also said to be good for depression)
- Ylang ylang (also claimed to have an aphrodisiac effect)

Always get advice from a qualified herbalist about how to use essential oils correctly and safely. Most good quality health food shops may either have some qualified staff or be able to recommend an herbalist or aromatherapist. Undiluted essential oils are very strong, and you shouldn't apply them directly to your skin. If you're taking medication, are pregnant, or have any allergies or medical conditions, you should always consult your doctor before using any aromatherapy or herbal remedies.

Managing Suicidal Thoughts

The most dangerous element of depression is that the feelings of hopelessness you can experience may become so strong that you try to take your own life. Don't panic about having suicidal thoughts if you're depressed. Such thoughts are very common and having them doesn't necessarily mean that you'll act on them.

If you've been feeling very hopeless about the future and have started to make plans about how to kill yourself, *you must immediately seek medical assistance*. Go to see your regular doctor as a first point of call, or attend Accident and Emergency (Casualty) if you feel at risk of suicide outside of surgery hours.

Famous and depressed

One of the most crucial aspects of recovering from depression is shedding any feelings of shame that you have about the problem. Something that can help with this is realising that *no one* has a guarantee that they won't get depressed. Depression has affected all kinds of people, from all kinds of walks of life, and from all kind of creeds, colours, and levels of intelligence.

Dozens of famous people have publicly reported or discussed their battles with depression during their lives. Celebrities are now 'coming out' about their suffering from depression or bipolar affective disorder (formerly known as manic depression). We hope that their actions can help to remove the stigma of mental health problems and enable more people to identify and seek help for depression.

Here are just a few famous types who've suffered from depression or bipolar affective disorder:

- Buzz Aldrin (astronaut)
- Ludwig van Beethoven (composer)
- William Blake (poet)
- Winston Churchill (British Prime Minister)
- John Cleese (comedian, actor and writer)
- Charles Dickens (writer)
- Germaine Greer (writer and journalist)
- Spike Milligan (comedian, actor, and writer)
- Isaac Newton (physicist)
- Mary Shelley (writer)
- Vincent Van Gogh (artist)
- Lewis Wolpert (embryologist and broad-caster)

Here is some advice on managing suicidal thoughts:

- ✔ Recognise your feelings of hopelessness about the future as a *symptom* of depression, not a fact.

- ✔ Remember that depression is a temporary state and there's lots of ways to treat it. Decide to tackle your depression for, say, six weeks, as an experiment to see whether things can improve.

- ✔ Tell a friend or family member how you're feeling.

- ✔ See a doctor and/or a therapist, or join a support group for further help and support if you're finding it difficult to overcome your depression alone.

- ✔ Try instigating the problem-solving process we outline in the previous section in this chapter, for any problem you currently see as hopeless.

Chapter 11

Overcoming Obsessions

In This Chapter

▶ Identifying obsessional problems

▶ Managing upsetting intrusive thoughts

▶ Facing fears and reducing rituals

▶ Decreasing preoccupations with health and appearance

*T*his chapter aims to introduce you to common obsessional problems and how to tackle them using CBT. Specifically, in this chapter we focus on obsessive-compulsive disorder (OCD), health anxiety, and body dysmorphic disorder (BDD). These problems can cause significant levels of distress and interference in daily living. However, if you have one or more of these disorders, you can use the CBT principles we outline in this chapter to reduce your obsessions and preoccupations. If you have a more severe form of these problems you should consider adding some professional help, but the core principles outlined here can still be of great help.

Many people have some degree of obsessional behaviour, such as checking or ordering, that don't particularly interfere with their lives. This level of problem is usually regarded as *subclinical*. However, problems like OCD are very disruptive and distressing when they reach more severe levels. A report from the World Health Organization (WHO) states that people with OCD can experience impact on their lives similar to those of people with AIDS.

Fortunately, obsessional problems are being diagnosed more accurately than ever before. Problems such as OCD are now among some of the most common psychiatric disorders. This increase is probably due to increased awareness and more accurate assessment measures. CBT is well-recognised as the psychological treatment of choice for obsessional problems, and has far superior relapse rates compared to medication.

Identifying and Understanding Obsessional Problems

Obsessional problems are among the most disabling of common emotional-behavioural problems. People with *obsessional problems* can spend many hours a day plagued by upsetting thoughts and feel driven to repeatedly carry out rituals or avoid situations. This section outlines three key obsessional problems, OCD, health anxiety, and BDD.

 Some degree of obsessionality is entirely normal – for example, around half of all people have a particular thing that they check more than they think is necessary, such as whether the gas cooker has been switched off or the door's been bolted. Obsessional problems have their roots in normal experiences, but the rituals and avoidance behaviours serve to make the frequency, severity, and duration of obsessions worse. The more you try to rid yourself of doubts, the more they tend to play on your mind.

We define the terms of obsessions in the list below:

- An *obsession* is a persistent, unwanted thought, image, doubt, or urge that intrudes into your mind, triggering distress. Obsessions are said to have reached a 'psychiatric problem' level when they cause significant levels of distress, interfere with your life, and are present for more than an hour a day.

- *Preoccupation* means being absorbed with something troubling that's on your mind. In this book we focus on preoccupations with appearance and health. Preoccupations are usually the result of you frequently focusing your attention on an idea (such as 'I'm seriously ill', or 'I'm repulsive to look at') or doubt that is distressing to you. Preoccupations are similar to obsessions in that they are regarded as problematic when they cause significant distress, interference in your life, and last for more than an hour per day.

- *Compulsions*, also called *rituals*, are the actions you may take in response to your obsessions or preoccupation, but do not particularly help you in your life. Compulsions can be observable behaviours (such as checking) or can be carried out in your mind (such as repeating a phrase in your head). Compulsions are usually attempts to either get rid of a thought, image, urge, or doubt; an attempt to reduce danger; or an attempt to reduce discomfort.

- *Avoidance behaviours* are things you do to avoid triggering your obsession or preoccupation. Your avoidance behaviour may be avoiding driving; avoiding visiting a hospital; or avoiding being seen in bright light.

Rituals and avoidance behaviours are the lifeblood of obsessional problems. Add to these catastrophic thinking (see Chapters 2 and 9), negative emotions (see Chapter 6), and attention bias (see Chapter 5), and you have the anatomy of obsessional problems.

Understanding obsessive-compulsive disorder (OCD)

According to the American Psychiatric Association, OCD is:

> *A problem in which the sufferer is plagued by either obsessions or compulsions, or usually both. Unwanted recurrent intrusive thoughts, impulses, or images that cause marked distress and are not simply excessive worries about real life problems. The sufferer makes attempts to ignore, suppress, neutralize the obsessions and recognises them as the products of their own mind.*

Common obsessions in OCD include the following:

- Fear of contamination

- Fear of accidentally causing harm to yourself or others

- Preoccupation with order or symmetry

- Religious obsessions, for example fear of offending God

- Sexual obsessions, for example fear of being a paedophile

- Fear of losing something important (such as a possession, paperwork, or ideas)

- Fear of becoming violent or aggressive

Compulsions frequently associated with OCD include the following:

- Checking (for example, if a light is switched off, or the front door is locked)

- Cleaning or washing (such as yourself, others, or home)

- Counting

- Repeating actions or special words, images, or numbers in one's mind

- Ordering and making things 'just so'

- Hoarding (excessive keeping of possessions such as newspapers that have no real, value, interest, or function)

✔ Making lists

✔ Replaying or repeating scenes, images, or actions in your mind

The prevalence of OCD is estimated to be around 2 per cent of the population, with some studies suggesting more. The severity and impact of OCD varies greatly, and in its most extreme form individuals can become totally housebound, even bedridden. Whilst the severity of symptoms can wax and wane, most people with OCD do function, do have relationships, and do hold down jobs or education, but will be under considerable extra strain. Clearly, very many people may recognise some degree of the excessive worries and rituals outlined above. The question is how much choice you feel you have to stop a ritual without distress, and how much interference OCD is causing in your life.

Recognising health anxiety

The American Psychiatric Association defines health anxiety as 'preoccupation with fears of having, or the idea that one has, a serious disease, based on misinterpretation of bodily sensations'. These preoccupations can:

✔ Persist despite medical evaluation and reassurance.

✔ Cause significant distress or impairment in social, occupational, or other areas of functioning

✔ Last at least six months

People with health anxiety misinterpret body sensations. Examples of common sensations and misinterpretations include the following:

✔ **Heart pounding:** 'I'm going to get heart disease.'

✔ **Lumps under the skin:** 'I have cancer.'

✔ **Tingling or numbness:** 'I have multiple sclerosis.'

✔ **Headache:** 'I must have a brain tumour.'

✔ **All of the above:** 'I'm dying.'

Compulsions commonly associated with health anxiety include the following:

✔ Seeking reassurance from medical professionals about the nature of physical sensations

✔ Seeking reassurance from others

✔ Checking body parts by poking, prodding, and touching

✔ Checking for symptoms in medical textbooks or on the Internet

✔ Examining oneself for signs of disease

✔ Monitoring physical sensations

Common avoidance behaviours associated with health anxiety include the following:

✔ Avoiding reading health-related stories in magazines or on TV

✔ Avoiding talking or thinking about death

✔ Avoiding touching body parts

✔ Avoiding having medical check-ups

Health anxiety is estimated to affect between 1–2 per cent of the population. It can result in people becoming tormented with fears that they have an illness that has not been properly diagnosed, or that they might become ill. Frequent trips to doctors are not uncommon when the person is gripped by anxiety and a fear that it would be irresponsible of them not to get themselves checked out. This can then result in even more worry that should they really be ill, they'll be dismissed as a hypochondriac. We've seen many people who've ended up badly bruised from repeatedly prodding an area of their body, or have spent hours doing research in desperate attempts to check and see what may be wrong with them.

Understanding body dysmorphic disorder (BDD)

BDD is defined by the American Psychiatric Association as follows:

> *A preoccupation with an imagined defect in appearance. If a slight physical anomaly exists, the person's concern is markedly excessive. The preoccupation causes clinically significant levels of distress and/or impairment in social, occupational or some other important area of functioning.*

Don't confuse BDD with an eating disorder, which is when a person restricts their weight, or binges and purges food. If you are very preoccupied with your overall size and shape and have difficulties with eating regular meals, consult with your doctor about whether you have an eating disorder. If this is the case, you may need help to tackle your eating behaviours as well as your preoccupation with how you look.

BDD preoccupations can focus on any area of the body and often affect multiple areas of the body. The face is the most common area of preoccupation, particularly the nose, facial skin, hair, eyes, teeth, lips, and chin. People with BDD believe that one or more of their features is too small or too big, or that their face doesn't 'fit together', is out of proportion, isn't symmetrical, or is just plain ugly.

Typical compulsions associated with BDD include the following:

- ✔ Gazing or checking appearance in mirrors or other reflective surfaces
- ✔ Avoiding mirrors or other reflective surfaces
- ✔ Seeking reassurance of attractiveness or how noticeable a 'defect' in appearance is, from other people
- ✔ Checking features by frequent touching or measuring
- ✔ Camouflaging features using clothing, padding, hairstyle, or make-up
- ✔ Attempting to distract others from the supposed defective feature with jewellery or by accentuating other body parts
- ✔ Frequently looking for and trying out new skincare, beauty, and haircare products
- ✔ Researching or seeking cosmetic surgery
- ✔ Excessive exercise
- ✔ Steroid abuse

Some common avoidance behaviours in people with BDD include the following:

- ✔ Avoiding social situations
- ✔ Avoiding 'attractive' people
- ✔ Choosing lighting carefully in social situations or near mirrors
- ✔ Carefully positioning yourself around (or avoiding) mirrors
- ✔ Changing posture or covering flaws with hands or other items

Frequently starting in adolescence, BDD affects around 1 per cent of the population, and has a relatively high suicide rate compared to many other emotional problems, proving that BDD is much more than mere vanity. BBD affects men and women roughly equally. Individuals can often spend many hours a day preoccupied with their appearance, perhaps having to get up hours early in order to work on their appearance just to feel less unacceptable.

Identifying Unhelpful Behaviours

As we note in Chapter 7, the things humans do to reduce their distress in the short term often maintain problems in the long run – so the solution is the problem! In the case of obsessional disorders, behaviours such as avoidance, checking, washing, seeking reassurance, comparing, readjusting, and repeating (to name but a few) are the maintaining mechanisms.

Most clients we work with on their obsessional problem agree *intellectually* that their behaviours perpetuate and aggravate their problems, but very often they say 'Now I really see what you mean!' after they experiment with them. Check out Chapter 4 for more information on designing and executing CBT experiments on your thinking.

The first step is to understand the concept of problem maintenance. The next step is to really experience how your behaviours affect your obsessions and preoccupation, by doing experiments.

In the broadest sense, you can try two kinds of experiment with your obsessional thinking:

- ✔ *Reduce* (or stop) a particular ritual and see how this affects the frequency, intensity, and duration of your upsetting thoughts.
- ✔ *Increase* a ritual or avoidance for a day and see what affect this has on the frequency, intensity, and duration of your upsetting thoughts.

Increasing a ritual or avoidance is often easier to do in the short term and often yields more results more rapidly.

Say you worry frequently about your house being burgled and you repeatedly check your doors and windows before leaving the house or going to bed. To find out whether your checking is part of the problem rather than the solution, record the frequency, duration, and intensity of your worry about burglary on a usual day of checking. Then spend another day trying as hard as you can to double your checking, and record the results. If you note a clear increase in your worry on the day of extra checking, the ritual behaviour's clearly part of your problem.

Acquiring Anti-obsessional Attitudes

Research and clinical observation shows that a number of thinking styles are related to the development of obsessional problems. Fortunately, you can also use thinking to combat obsessional problems. The following sections offer alternative ways of thinking that can help you in your fight against your obsessional problem.

Tolerating doubt and uncertainty

In our and many other therapists' experience, one of the main protestations that clients make about stopping rituals or avoidance behaviours is along the lines of 'How can you guarantee me that what I'm afraid of won't happen?'

The truth is, of course, that we can't. But no one without obsessional problems gets those kinds of guarantees either, so clearly the problem *isn't* a lack of certainty. We can offer a different kind of guarantee, however: As long as you continue to demand a guarantee or certainty that your fears won't come true, you're likely to have your obsessional problem.

Instead, practice *consistently* and *repeatedly* tolerating doubt and uncertainty without resorting to checking, washing, reassurance-seeking, or whatever you do compulsively. Your rituals only fuel your belief that you need certainty. Initially, staying with doubt may well feel uncomfortable, but if you stick with it your anxiety can reduce. Deliberately seek out triggers for your doubt and practice resisting the urge to carry out rituals, seek reassurance, or work things out in your mind.

Trusting your judgement

In an attempt to explain why individuals with obsessional problems check so much more than those without these problems, scientists explored the hypothesis that people with OCD have poorer memories. The rationale here was, perhaps, that people with OCD check or seek reassurance because they can't remember properly. The scientists do make an important discovery: People with obsessional problems have no memory deficiency. What they do have, however, is poor confidence in their memories.

Poor confidence in one's memory may be related to unrealistic demands for certainty (see the preceding section on how totolerate doubt and uncertainty), because no amount of checking removes that grain of doubt from your recall.

The best thing you can do to boost your confidence in your memory is to act as if you were more confident and cut back on rituals. Doing so consistently and repeatedly gradually helps you to build your confidence.

Treating your thoughts as nothing more than thoughts

One of the main thinking errors in obsessional problems is overestimating the importance of the intrusive doubts, thoughts, and images that occur naturally in your mind. Experts in OCD have shown that the following three key misinterpretations contribute to obsessional problems:

- ✔ **The probablity misinterpretation:** The idea that having a thought about an event in your mind affects the probability of that event occurring. For example, 'If I allow myself to picture myself hurting someone, then it's more likely that I'll do it.'

- ✔ **The moral misinterpretation:** The idea that an unpleasant thought entering your mind reveals something unpleasant about yourself. For example, 'Having thoughts of causing harm means I'm a bad and dangerous person.'

- ✔ **The responsibility misinterpretation:** The idea that having a thought about an event means that you have responsibility for it happening or for preventing it from happening. For example, 'Having an image of myself ill in a hospital bed means that I need to be more vigilant for signs of illness.'

Intrusive thoughts, images, doubts, and impulses are entirely normal. Your assumption that the thoughts that you're having aren't normal is the problem. The solution is to allow these thoughts to pass through your mind without engaging with them, trying to change them, trying to suppress them, or trying to hurry them along. As the song says, let it be! Refer to Chapter 5 for more suggestions on managing your mind without interfering with it.

Being flexible and not trying too hard

If you have an obsessional problem, you're almost certainly trying too hard at something. You may be trying too hard to get your appearance or desk looking just so. Or, you may be trying to ensure that you or someone you feel responsible for is safe from harm or disease. Or perhaps you're inclined to follow moral or religious instruction to the letter, rather than living within the spirit of these ideals.

Flexibility is one of the hallmarks of psychological health because it helps you adapt effectively to the real world. Consider carefully the real-life consequences of holding standards or ideals too rigidly. Do these ideals really help you live the kind of life you want? Are the costs on yourself and others worth the benefits? If not, try to define how you'd behave if you were free from your obsessional problem, or take a leaf from someone else's book and try acting accordingly. Refer to Chapter 8 for more on doing a cost–benefit analysis.

Using external and practical criteria

A crucial difference between people with and without obsessional problems is regarding the criteria they use to decide when to stop a particular behaviour. People without obsessions tend to use external observations, or practical criteria, to evaluate situations and make decisions.

By contrast, people with obsessional problems tend to use *internal criteria* – such as something feeling 'right', 'better', or 'comfortable' – to make decisions. Here are two examples of internal criteria with their external alternatives:

- ✔ A person with contamination OCD may wash her hands until she *feels* that her hands are clean enough. Someone without this problem may tend to stop washing when she can *see* her hands are clean or when she's been through a quick and convenient routine.

- ✔ A person with BDD may readjust her hair, trying to reduce her *feelings* of anxiety and to *feel satisfied inside* with how she looks. Someone without excessive concerns about her appearance may stop styling her hair when it *looks the same as usual* or isn't sticking up.

Strive to use 'external' criteria to decide when to stop an activity. Instead of stopping when you feel comfortable, force yourself to stop washing your hands or fixing your hair *before* you feel comfortable. Making this change can help reinforce the fact that your criteria for stopping rituals are the problem and proves to you that your discomfort and anxiety can diminish spontaneously. Importantly, this technique can also show you that you *can* tolerate the discomfort of resisting your rituals.

Allowing your mind and body to do their own things

Complete control of your thoughts and body is:

- ✔ **Impossible:** No one has it, not even highly trained doctors, athletes, monks, or psychologists!

- ✔ **Counterproductive:** Attempting to completely control your thoughts results in more of the thoughts and sensations you were trying to get rid of. You may seem even more out of control as a result.

- ✔ **Undesirable:** Being able to completely choose the thoughts that enter your mind effectively puts a stop to any originality and creative problem-solving. Being in control of your body would almost certainly result in your demise – after all, do you really know how to run a body?

Allowing your body and mind to go on autopilot is so much easier and more helpful than trying to control your thoughts and bodily sensations.

Normalising physical sensations and imperfections

Obsessional problems like OCD, BDD, and health anxiety can lead you to focus too much on your thoughts, physical sensations, and minor physical imperfections. These problems also lead you to attach undue importance and meaning to your sensations, physical imperfections, and upsetting thoughts.

- ✔ Health anxiety is underpinned by you attaching too much importance to normal physical sensations.

- ✔ OCD results from you attaching too much meaning to normal thoughts that intrude into your mind.

- ✔ BDD is caused by you attaching too much meaning to your appearance.

Your problem is not the content of your thought, the flaws in your complexion, or the variation in your heart rate. Your problem is *your belief* that these experiences are abnormal. To help yourself overcome your obsessional problems, take the view that your thoughts, flaws, and imperfections are *normal*. Conducting surveys (which we talk about in Chapter 4) is an excellent way of gathering evidence that many of the things you focus on and worry about are normal human experiences.

Facing Your Fears: Reducing (And Stopping) Rituals

In CBT, facing your fears and resisting the urge to carry out compulsions is called *exposure and response prevention*. This term has two important components:

- ✔ **Exposure:** Deliberately facing up to the places, people, situations, substances, objects, thoughts, doubts, impulses, and images that trigger off your feelings of anxiety and discomfort.

- ✔ **Response prevention:** Reducing and stopping the rituals and any other safety precautions that you adopt.

In order to reduce or potentially stop your reliance on rituals, you must tackle your obsessions head-on. To accomplish this, you need to get better at tolerating doubt, allow thoughts and images to come and go from your mind, and be realistic about responsibility. And yes, you need to practice these skills!

You can make faster progress if you *deliberately* trigger off your upsetting thoughts and anxiety in a regular and consistent way. Refer to Chapter 9 for more detail on designing an exposure programme to help combat your anxieties.

Facing your fears when overcoming an obsessional problem is different from many other kinds of anxiety problems, because the object of your fear may be more *internal* than *external*. For example, facing the *mental image* of pushing someone on to a train track is just as important as actually standing on the platform.

Resist! Resist! Resist!

To overcome an obsessional problem, you need to develop a list of your main fears as well as your typical rituals and safety behaviours.

Keeping a daily record of the frequency of the rituals you wish to reduce helps you to keep track of your progress and motivates you to keep reducing. You can record the frequency on paper or buy a 'tally counter' (a 'clicker' that counts each time you press it) from a stationery shop.

When you've written your list, you need to systematically expose yourself to your main fears, while simultaneously reducing and dropping your rituals and safety behaviours.

Stopping your rituals alone is not sufficient to overcome your obsessions. You need to incorporate deliberate exposure to your fears in order to get the practice you need.

Delaying and modifying rituals

Delaying and modifying a ritual can be also be a useful lead up to dropping a ritual entirely:

- ✔ **Delaying rituals.** If you find stopping your rituals difficult, start off by delaying them for a few minutes. Gradually build up the time delay until you can resist a ritual long enough for your anxiety to reduce of its own accord.

✔ **Modifying rituals.** If you can't gear yourself up to stop your ritual entirely just yet, modify your ritual. Instead of going for the full-blown version of a ritual, allow yourself to perform only a shortened version. For example, if you normally vacuum every corner of a room, try making yourself stick to the areas that you can see, without moving any furniture or other objects.

Overcoming your obsessional problems is supposed to be an uncomfortable experience. If you're working through the exercises in this chapter and not experiencing a temporary increase in your discomfort, then either you're not exposing yourself sufficiently or you're not resisting your rituals sufficiently.

If you plan to stop a particular ritual but end up doing it anyway, *re-expose* yourself rather than letting your obsessional problem win. For example, if you have a fear of contamination, touch the floor to re-expose yourself after washing your hands.

You may be very tempted to err on the safe side and allow yourself to carry out more rituals or safety measures than the average person. Retaining avoidance and rituals can leave you very prone to your obsessions returning. Keep working at your ritual reduction until your rituals are at least as low as those of the average person on the street. Think of rituals and avoidance as the roots of a weed you are trying to get rid of from your garden. If you don't get weeds up by the roots, they are sure to grow back.

Being Realistic about Responsibility

One of the hallmarks of obsessional problems is a tendency to take too much responsibility. Individuals with OCD, for example, often take excessive responsibility for causing or preventing harm to themselves or others. A person with health anxiety may have an overdeveloped sense of responsibility for spotting possible health problems. Someone with BDD may have an excessive sense of responsibility for not causing offence or being humiliated because of her appearance. In all cases, this sense of responsibility can drive the person to carry out rituals and leave them feeling guilty if they don't.

Dividing up your responsibility pie

A helpful technique for developing a more realistic perception of your personal responsibility is to create a *responsibility pie chart*, as follows:

1. **Identify an event you fear being responsible for** (such as, the house being burgled, causing harm, falling ill, being rejected).

2. Write down the level of responsibility you would feel for the event if it occurred as a percentage.

You can have between 0 and 100 per cent of the responsibility for an event occurring.

3. List all the possible contributing factors to your feared event occurring, including yourself.

4. Create a responsibility pie chart.

Use a large empty circle to represent 100 per cent, or all the responsibility for an event occurring. You can draw a circle yourself, or use the circle provided in Figure 11-1.

Proportionally divide the pie into wedges, based on how much responsibility you assign to each of the factors you list in step 3. Be sure to put yourself in last.

Figure 11-1:
The starting point for your respon- sibility pie chart.

5. Re-rate your estimation of your responsibility for your feared event.

Use the 0 to 100 per cent scale described in step 2.

For example, Figure 11-2 shows the responsibility pie chart for Terry, a mother with OCD who obsesses about harm coming to her children from poisonous substances. Initially, Terry believes that she would be totally to blame if any harm befell her children. However, after working through the responsibility pie chart activity, Terry is able to gain a more realistic perspective on her level of personal responsibility.

You can also use the responsibility pie chart with negative events that *have actually happened* and that you're blaming yourself for, for example losing a job, a failed relationship, someone treating you badly, or a loved one getting ill.

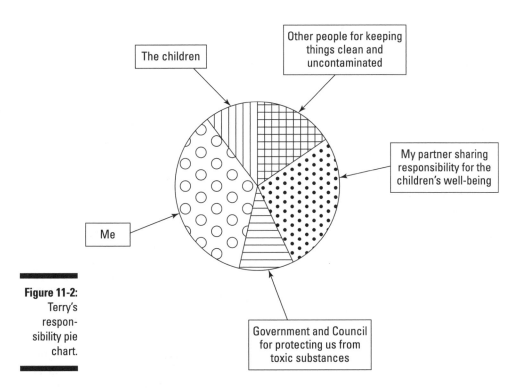

The children

Other people for keeping
things clean and
uncontaminated

My partner sharing
responsibility for the
children's well-being

Me

Government and Council
for protecting us from
toxic substances

Figure 11-2:
Terry's
respon-
sibility pie
chart.

The purpose of the responsibility pie is to help you see that you're not 100
per cent responsible for an event happening. Many obsessional people give
themselves more responsibility than is legitimate – or at least more than non-
obsessional people do.

Taking *less responsibility* is something that you steadily need to train your
mind to do. Actually, you're retraining your mind to break your habit of *taking
excessive-responsibility*.

Retraining your attention

If you think you're preoccupied with your appearance, health, or being
responsible for harm coming to yourself or others *because you focus on it too
much*, try to create a counterbalance by training your attention elsewhere.
Chapter 6 gives you some more guidance.

Seeking professional help

Use the following checklist to determine whether an obsession or compulsion is normal or a problem for which you should seek professional assistance.

✓ **Your obsessional problems are impacting on your physical health.** For example, you're not taking prescribed medication, attending medical appointments, or feeding and grooming yourself sufficiently.

✓ **Your obsessional problems are preventing you from leaving your home.** Sometimes, people with severe OCD or BDD become housebound.

✓ **Your obsessional problems are having a serious impact on your social and occupational life.** For example, you're unable to continue working, you've lost a job, you're avoiding contact with friends, or your partner has left you.

✓ **Your obsessional problems are preventing you from caring adequately for your children.** This is a particularly painful point for many people with OCD. People with OCD typically take too much responsibility for the welfare of their loved ones. However, if you contemplate the needs of your children and decide *impartially* that your problems are stopping you from meeting those needs, get in touch with a professional.

✓ **You've given self-help an earnest try but are unable to overcome your problem.**

Your family doctor may be familiar with obsessional disorders, but you may be better off seeking out a specialist. Make an appointment with a psychiatrist for assessment. If your problem is so severe that you're housebound, you may be able to get a home assessment via a community mental health outreach team. However, you may need to prepare yourself for going out of your safety zone and into a hospital or clinic.

Getting the best help for your obsessional problems is not always straightforward, but we do encourage you to not give up. If you meet the criteria on the checklist above, please do seek help. Appendix A lists relevant organisations you can consider contacting for more information.

Chapter 12

Overcoming Low Self-esteem by Accepting Yourself

· ·

In This Chapter

▶ Understanding low self-esteem

▶ Appreciating the principles of self-acceptance

▶ Strengthening your self-acceptance

▶ Dispelling myths about practising self-acceptance

· ·

Disturbing feelings, such as depression, anxiety, shame, guilt, anger, envy, and jealousy, are often rooted in low self-opinion. If you're prone to experiencing these feelings, then you may well have a problem with your self-esteem. You may assume that you're only as worthwhile as your achievements, love life, social status, attractiveness, or financial prowess. If you link your worth to these *temporary conditions* and for some reason they diminish, your self-esteem can plummet too. Alternatively, you may take a long-standing dim view of yourself: However favourable the conditions mentioned above, your self-esteem may be chronically low. Whatever the case, you can follow the philosophy of self-acceptance that we outline in this chapter, which can significantly improve the attitude you hold towards yourself.

Identifying Issues of Self-Esteem

Implicit in the concept of self-esteem is the notion of *estimating*, or rating and measuring, your worth. If you have high self-esteem, then your measure of your value or worth is high. Conversely, if you have low self-esteem, your estimate of your value is low.

Condemning yourself globally is a form of overgeneralising, known as *labelling* or *self-downing* (we talk about overgeneralisation in more detail in

Chapter 2). This thinking error creates low self-esteem. Labelling yourself makes you feel worse and can lead to counterproductive actions, such as avoidance, isolation, rituals, procrastination, and perfectionism (which we talk about in Chapter 7, 10, and 11), to name but a few.

Examples of labelling or self-downing include statements, such as the following:

I'm disgusting	I'm a failure	I'm stupid
I'm inferior	I'm useless	I'm less worthwhile
I'm inadequate	I'm not good enough	I'm bad
I'm unlovable	I'm worthless	I'm defective
I'm incompetent	I don't matter	I'm pathetic
I'm weak	I'm no good	I'm a loser

When you measure your worth on the basis of one or more external factors, you're likely to go up and down like a yo-yo in both mood and self-concept because life is changeable.

Developing Self-Acceptance

One approach to tackling your low self-esteem is to boost the estimate you have of your worth. The underlying problem, however, still remains; and like an investment, your self-esteem can go down, as well as up.

Self-acceptance is an alternative to boosting self-esteem and tackles the problem by removing self-rating. If you don't have a sturdy belief that your value is *intrinsic*, or built-in, you may have difficulty concluding that you have any worth at all when things go wrong for you.

Unconditional self-acceptance means untangling your self-worth from external 'measures' or 'ratings' of your value as a person. Eventually, you can become less likely to consider yourself defective or inadequate on the basis of failures or disapproval, because you view yourself as a *fallible human being*, whose worth remains more or less constant.

Self-acceptance involves making the following assertions:

- ✔ As a human being, you're a unique, multifaceted individual.
- ✔ You're ever-changing and developing.

✔ You may be able, to some degree, to measure specific aspects of yourself (such as how tall you are), but you'll never manage to rate the whole of yourself because you are too complex and continuously changing.

✔ Humans, by their very nature, are fallible and imperfect.

✔ By extension, because you're a complex, unique, ever-changing individual, you cannot legitimately be rated or measured as a whole person.

The following are the principles of self-acceptance. Read them, re-read them, think them over, and put them into practice in your daily life to significantly enhance your self-acceptance. The principles are good sense, but we're leaving it up to you to decide how 'common' this kind of sense is. The principles are derived from the rational (self-helping) thinking methods developed by Albert Ellis and Windy Dryden.

Understanding that you have worth because you're human

Albert Ellis, founder of rational emotive behaviour therapy – one of the very earliest approaches to CBT – states that *all human beings* have *extrinsic* value to others and *intrinsic* value to themselves. But we humans gamely confuse the two and classify ourselves as 'worthy' or 'good' on the basis of assumed value to others. We humans too easily allow our self-worth to be contingent upon the opinions and value judgements of others. Many cognitive behaviour therapists (and indeed other kinds of psychotherapists) hold the implicit value of a human being at the very heart of their perspective.

Imagine how much easier your life will be, and how much more stable your self-esteem will be, if you realise that you have worth as a person *independently* of how much other people value you. You can appreciate being liked, admired, or respected without it being a dire necessity to get it, or living in fear of losing it.

Appreciating that you're too complex to globally measure or rate

You may mistakenly define your whole worth – or even your entire self – on the basis of your individual parts. This is pointless, because humans are ever-changing, dynamic, fallible, and complex creatures.

Humans have the capacity to work on correcting less desirable behaviours and maximising more desirable behaviours. You have the distinctive ability to strive for self-improvement, to maximise your potential, and to learn from your and others' histories, mistakes, and accomplishments. In short, you have the ability to develop the ability to accept yourself as you are, while still endeavouring to improve yourself if you so choose.

Consider a bowl of fresh, hand-picked fruit, beautiful in almost every respect. Now imagine that one of the apples in the fruit bowl is bruised. Do you consider the whole bowl of fruit to be worthless? Of course not! It's a great bowl of fruit, with a single bruised apple. Avoid overgeneralising by seeing that your imperfections are simply *facets* of yourself and do not define the whole of you.

Letting go of labelling

Self-acceptance means deciding to resist labelling yourself at all and rather to entertain the idea that ratings are inappropriate to the human condition. For example:

- ✔ You lied to a friend once. Does that make you a liar forever and for all time?

- ✔ You used to smoke cigarettes but then you decided to give them up. Are you still a smoker because you once smoked?

- ✔ You failed at one or more tasks that were important to you. Can you legitimately conclude that you are an utter failure?

- ✔ By the same token, if you succeeded at one important task, are you now a thoroughgoing success?

As you can see by reviewing these examples, basing your self-esteem on one incident, one action, or one experience is a gross overgeneralisation.

Believing you're more than the sum of your parts

Take a look at Figure 12-1. The big *I* is comprised of dozens of little *is*. So, what's the point of the figure? When you evaluate yourself *totally* on the basis of one characteristic, thought, action, or intention, you're making the thinking error that a single part (the little i) equals to the whole (the big I).

Along similar lines, consider a finely woven tapestry comprised of countless variations of textures, colours, and patterns. Within this tapestry, you may find one or more flaws, where the colours fail to meet or the patterns are slightly out of sync. The flaws in the tiny details don't cancel out the beauty or value of the overall piece. And what about the *Venus de Milo*? Over the years, she's lost a limb or two, but the officials at the Louvre don't say, 'Um, sorry, she's flawed: Put her in the bin!' The fact that the statue is damaged does not diminish or *define* its overall worth. The statue is valued *as it is*, and the absence of arms does not negate the impact it has on our understanding of the evolution of art.

```
iiiiiiiiiiiiiiiiiiiiiiiiiiiiiiiiiiiiiiiiiiiiiiiiiiii
iiiiiiiiiiiiiiiiiiiiiiiiiiiiiiiiiiiiiiiiiiiiiiiiiiii
iiiiiiiiiiiiiiiiiiiiiiiiiiiiiiiiiiiiiiiiiiiiiiiiiiii
                iiiiiiiiiiiii
                iiiiiiiiiiiii
                iiiiiiiiiiiii
                iiiiiiiiiiiii
                iiiiiiiiiiiii
                iiiiiiiiiiiii
                iiiiiiiiiiiii
                iiiiiiiiiiiii
                iiiiiiiiiiiii
iiiiiiiiiiiiiiiiiiiiiiiiiiiiiiiiiiiiiiiiiiiiiiiiiiii
iiiiiiiiiiiiiiiiiiiiiiiiiiiiiiiiiiiiiiiiiiiiiiiiiiii
iiiiiiiiiiiiiiiiiiiiiiiiiiiiiiiiiiiiiiiiiiiiiiiiiiii
```

Figure 12-1:
Which do
you see
first: the big
I or all the
little *is*?

If your child, sibling, or nephew failed a spelling test, would you judge them a total loser? Would you encourage them to think of themselves as a global failure, based entirely on one action? If not, why are you doing this to yourself?

Start acting in accordance with the belief that your parts do not define your wholeness. If you truly believe this idea, what do you do when you fail at doing something, behave badly or wickedly, or notice that you have a physical imperfection or character flaw? How do you expect to feel when endorsing this belief?

Take a pack of self-adhesive notes and a large, flat surface. A wall or a door works well – or try a mate if he has a few spare minutes. Write down on one of the notes a characteristic that you, as a whole person, possess; then stick the note on the wall, door, or volunteer. Keep doing this, writing down all the aspects of yourself that you can think of until you run out of characteristics, or sticky notes. Now step back and admire your illustration of your complexity as a human being. Appreciate the fact that you cannot legitimately be rated globally.

Acknowledging your ever-changing nature

As a human being, your nature is to be an ever-changing person. Even if you measure all your personal characteristics today and come up with a global rating for yourself, it'll be wrong tomorrow. Why? Because each day, you change a little, age very slightly, and gather a few new experiences.

Consider yourself as work-in-progress and try holding a *flexible* attitude towards yourself. Every skill you acquire or interest you develop effectively produces a change within you. Every hardship you weather, every joyous event that visits you, and every mundane occurrence you endure causes you to develop, adapt, and grow.

Ellis theorises that your essential value or worth cannot be measured accurately because your *being* includes your *becoming*. Ellis suggests that each human is a *process* with an ever-changing present and future. Hence, you cannot conclusively evaluate yourself while you're still living and developing.

Forgiving flaws in yourself and others

Interestingly, you may overlook some imperfections in yourself while condemning the same shortcomings in others, or vice versa. To some degree, this relates to what you consider important, your flexibility, and your level of self-acceptance. Consider the following scenarios:

- Julian works in a computer shop. Whenever he's about to close a sale, he gets excited and trips over some of his words. He feels a bit foolish about this, although none of his customers has ever mentioned it.

- Margarita has a poor sense of direction. Sometimes she forgets which way is left and which is right. When she's driving, Margarita has difficulty following directions and frequently finds herself lost.

- Carlos is a good student, but has difficulty in exam situations. He studies earnestly, but come the day of the test, he forgets what he's read and performs poorly.

You can't always change things about yourself. Sometimes you can improve a bit, but sometimes you can't change at all. If you're a fully developed adult and five-foot tall, you're unlikely to be able to make yourself grow to six foot through sheer determination. The trick is to begin to recognise where you can make changes and where you can't. Living happily is about accepting your limitations without putting yourself down for them and capitalising on your strengths. So, taking the three examples above:

- Julian may be able to make himself less anxious about a potential sale; therefore, he

may speak more coherently. By accepting that he mangles his words sometimes, but not condemning himself for it, he may come some way towards overcoming this aspect of his behaviour.

- Margarita may simply be someone who's not particularly good at navigation. She may improve with practice, but she may also do well to accept that she's the person who turns up late for parties two streets away from her home.

- Carlos can look at his studying habits and see whether he can study more effectively. However, he may simply be someone who does better on practical assignments rather than tests.

Overall, Julian, Carlos, and Margarita can choose to accept themselves as fallible human beings and work to improve in the areas described, while also accepting their personal limitations. They can choose to embrace their inherent fallibility as part of the experience of being a human, and understand that their 'less good' traits are part of their individual composition as much as their 'good' traits.

Alternatively, they can choose to evaluate themselves on the basis of their 'less good' traits and judge themselves as worthless, or less than worthy. But where, oh where, do you go from there?

Accepting your fallible nature

Sorry if we're the ones to break it to you, but human beings are flawed and imperfect. You may be the pretty impressive product of evolution, but essentially you're just the smartest animal on the planet. Even if you believe you're the creation of a divine entity, do you really think the design brief was perfection? Maybe being complex, different, and with an in-built tendency to make mistakes are all part of the plan. When people say 'You're only human,' they have a point: Never, ever, can you be flawless or stop making mistakes. And neither can anyone else. It's just how we're built.

During the process of accepting yourself, you may experience sadness, disappointment, or remorse for your blunders. These healthy negative emotions may be uncomfortable, but usually they can lead to self-helping, corrective, and 'adaptive' behaviours. Self-condemnation or self-depreciation, on the other hand, are likely to lead to far more intense, unhealthy negative emotions, such as depression, hurt, guilt, and shame. So, you're more likely to adopt self-defeating, 'maladaptive' behaviours, such as avoidance or giving up.

Valuing your uniqueness

Who else do you know who's exactly – and yes, we do mean *exactly* – like you? The correct answer is no one, because the human cloning thing hasn't really taken off yet. So, you are, in fact, quite unique – just like everyone else!

You alone are possessor of your own little idiosyncrasies. So learn to laugh it up, because the mistakes and foot-in-mouth moments will just keep on coming, whether you like it or not.

Taking yourself overly seriously is not a successful path to obtaining good mental health (which we talk about in Chapter 22). Your individual human fallibility can be both amusing and illuminating. Think about comedy programmes and films. Much of what makes these shows funny is the way the characters *behave*, the mistakes they make, their social blunders, their physicality, their personal peculiarities, and so on. When you laugh at these characters, you aren't being malicious – you just recognise echoes of yourself and of the entire human experience in them. Furthermore, you're unlikely to put down these characters on the basis of their errors. Give yourself a similar benefit of the doubt. Accepting the existence of personal shortcomings can help you to understand your own limitations and identify areas that you may wish to target for change.

Why self-acceptance beliefs work

At first glance, self-acceptance and self-acceptance beliefs may seem like a tall order or 'not what people think'. However, incorporating self-accepting beliefs into your life can really make a difference in your life, and we recommend it for the following reasons:

✔ **Self-acceptance beliefs are helpful.** You're inspired to correct your poor behaviour or address your shortcomings on the basis that you give yourself permission to be flawed. You allow yourself a margin for error. When problems occur or you behave poorly, you can experience appropriate and proportionate negative emotions and then move on. People are generally more effective problem-solvers when they're not severely emotionally distressed.

✔ **Self-acceptance beliefs are consistent with reality.** Do you know anyone who's entirely

flawless? If you have only conditional self-acceptance, you're subscribing to a belief that you cease to be acceptable, or worthwhile, when you fall short of those conditions or ideals. Basically, you're telling yourself that you must succeed at any given task. Because you can (and do) both fail and succeed, the evidence suggests that your demand to always succeed is erroneous.

✔ **Self-acceptance beliefs are logical.** Just because you *prefer* to behave in a certain way, doesn't mean that you *must* behave in a certain way. Nor, does your failing to act in that manner logically render you a failure in all respects. Rather, this 'failure' supports the premise that you're a fallible human capable of behaving in differing ways at various times. To broaden the point, this 'failure' highlights your humanness and your inherent capacity to do both 'well' and 'less well'.

For example, we have a couple of our own quirks that we try to accept, and even celebrate, as unique. Rob does this weird little twitch every now again when he's tired. The twitch is a bit disconcerting when he's driving, but most of the time it's just something that Rob does. Rhena tends to fiddle with her jewellery when she's thinking or just idle – irritating to some, endearing to others.

You're unique because no one is a facsimile of you. At the same time, you're also not special or unique in any way, because *everyone* is an individual and, hence, unreplicable. Your uniqueness means that you're *different* from all others and paradoxically that you're the *same* as all others.

Using self-acceptance to aid self-improvement

As we touch upon in the nearby sidebar, which covers accepting flaws in others and yourself, self-acceptance can lead to healthy and *appropriate* negative emotional responses to adverse experiences. This type of emotional response tends to lead to functional or *adaptive* behaviours. Self-denigration, on the other hand, leads to unhealthy, *inappropriate* emotional responses, which in turn tend to produce unhelpful or *destructive* behaviours. Look at the following situation:

Wendy's been a full-time mum for the past ten years. Before she had her children, she worked as a legal secretary. Now that her children are older, she wants to return to work. Wendy attends a job interview. During the interview, she becomes very nervous and is unable to answer some of the questions adequately. She notices that she's becoming flustered and hot. It also becomes clear to her that secretarial work has evolved in the past ten years and that she lacks the computer skills necessary for the post. Unfortunately, she doesn't get the job.

Now consider two very different responses to the interview:

> **Response A:** Wendy leaves the interview, ruminating on her poor performance all the way back home. 'I looked such an idiot,' she tells herself. 'They must have thought me a real amateur, blushing and stuttering like that. I'm such a failure. Who'd want to hire someone as lacking in skills as me? I don't know what made me think I'd be able to get into work again anyway. I'm clearly not up to standard at all.' Wendy feels depressed and hopeless. She mopes around the house and continues to think about what a failure she is. She feels so ashamed about failing the interview that she avoids talking about it to her friends, thus denying herself the opportunity to receive feedback, which may be useful or help her feel more balanced. Wendy stops looking in the employment pages.

> **Response B:** Wendy leaves the interview and thinks: 'I really didn't present very well in there. I wish I hadn't been so obviously nervous. Clearly, I need to get some computer skills before I'm likely to get a job offer.' Wendy feels very disappointed about not getting the job, but she doesn't conclude that failing one important task makes her a failure. She feels regretful, but not ashamed, about her performance and talks to a few friends about it. Her friends give her some encouragement. Wendy then enrols on an IT course at her local college. She continues to look through the job ads in the paper.

In response B, Wendy is understandably disappointed with how the interview turned out. She's able to recognise her skills' deficit. Because she accepts herself with this *specific deficit*, she takes concrete steps towards increasing her skills base.

In response A, Wendy is not thinking about how to do better at the next interview. She's thinking about how she'd like to crawl under the carpet and spend the rest of her days there. A bit of an extreme reaction considering the circumstances, but Wendy isn't considering the circumstances. She has decided that messing up an interview equals total failure, and she's feeling far too depressed and ashamed to start problem-solving.

Generally, your failures and errors are not as important or calamitous as you think they are. Most of the time, your failures mean a lot more to you than they do to other people.

Understanding that acceptance doesn't mean giving up

In the example of Wendy, we don't suggest that she must resign herself to a life of unemployment simply because she lacks computer skills. Why should she? Clearly, she can do things to ensure that she stands a good chance of getting back into the job market.

In Wendy's case, self-acceptance means that she can view herself as worthwhile, while getting on with self-improvement in specific areas of her life. By contrast, if Wendy refuses to accept herself and puts herself down, she's far more likely to resign – perhaps even condemn – herself to her current state of unemployment.

Resignation requires little or no effort, but self-acceptance can involve a lot of personal effort.

- **High frustration tolerance** (HFT) is the ability to tolerate discomfort and hard work in the *short term*, en route to achieving an identified *long-term* goal. In response B in the job-interview example, Wendy accepts herself and holds an HFT attitude. She is prepared to do the work necessary to reach her goal of getting a job.

- **Low frustration tolerance** (LFT) is unwillingness to tolerate *short-term* pain for *long-term* gain. An LFT attitude is present in statements, such as 'It's too difficult to change – this is just the way I am', and 'I may as well just give up'. Resignation and LFT go hand in hand. In Wendy's response A, she refuses to accept herself in view of her recent experience and resigns herself to unemployment.

Resignation may seem like an easier option than self-acceptance because it means that you have to *do* less. However, people tend to feel pretty miserable when they resign and condemn themselves, refusing to put effort into improving their situation.

Being Inspired to Change

You may think that self-acceptance is all fine and well when talking about human error, social gaffes, and minor character flaws, but the dice are more loaded in instances where you've transgressed your personal moral code.

If you've behaved in an antisocial, illegal, or immoral manner, you may have more difficulty accepting yourself. But you can! Accepting *yourself* does not mean accepting the negative behaviour and continuing to do it. On the contrary, accepting yourself involves recognising that you – an acceptable human being – have engaged in a poor, or unacceptable, behaviour. Accepting yourself makes you more likely to learn from your mistakes and act more constructively – which is in both your interest and in the interest of those around you.

Consider the following two scenarios:

- ✔ Malcolm has an anger problem. He puts unreasonable demands on his wife and children to never get on his nerves. He has a bad day at work and comes home to find no dinner on the table and his two young children playing noisily in the sitting room. Malcolm shouts at his wife and slaps her. He calls his children names and hits them. His family is afraid and upset. This happens on a regular basis.

- ✔ Fiona works in a shoe shop. She's been stealing money from the till to buy alcohol and codeine-based painkillers. Usually, she takes the tablets throughout the day and drinks heavily in the evenings, until she passes out. Lately, she has called in sick to work more often because she has terrible hangovers and feels very depressed. Fiona often calls herself a 'useless drunk' and 'a low-life thief', and then drinks more to stop herself thinking. She works hard to hide her drinking and stealing, and feels ashamed of herself most of the time.

Are Malcolm and Fiona bad people, or are they just currently exhibiting bad behaviours? If you condemn Malcolm or Fiona – or, indeed, yourself – as a 'bad person' on the basis of bad behaviour, you're missing the point that a person is more complex than a single act.

In order to overcome destructive or socially unacceptable behaviours, you need to do the following:

- ✔ **Take personal responsibility for your bad behaviour.** Rather than deciding you're just a bad person who has no control or responsibility for your actions, accept that you're doing bad things.

    In the example above, Malcolm's doing very bad things when he takes out his anger on his family. But, if he decides that he's a bad person overall, he relinquishes his responsibility to change. Basically, he's saying: 'I beat my family because I'm a bad person through and through and therefore I can't change.' He's also more likely to attribute his violence to external factors rather than to his own unreasonable demands: 'They know what I'm like and they should bloody-well stay out of my way when I come in from work.'

> ✔ **Identify clearly what you're doing that's wrong or unacceptable.** You must be specific when pinpointing bad behaviours.
>
> For example, Fiona has two definite serious problems or 'bad' behaviours. First, she has an addiction; second, she's stealing to support that addiction. Fiona's shame and self-condemnation are very likely going to get in the way of her overcoming her problems. She cannot put in the hard work needed to recover from her addiction (which includes seeking professional help) if she can't accept herself as worth the effort.

To move on in life in a way that contributes to the kind of world you'd like to live in, assume personal responsibility and keep working on your self-acceptance.

Actioning Self-Acceptance

Just like virtually all skills worth acquiring, you're going to have to work hard and practice in order to achieve successful self-acceptance skills. This section focuses on ways to start integrating self-acceptance into your daily life.

Self-talking your way to self-acceptance

What's in a name? Rather a lot, actually. As we discuss in Chapters 3 and 9, most people largely *feel* the way they *think*. In other words, the meanings you assign to events have a great deal to do with how you ultimately feel about those events.

Similarly, meaning is attached to the names your call yourself. If you use abusive, harshly critical, or profane terminology to give utterance to your behaviours or traits, then you're heading towards emotional disturbance.

The notion that you may start to believe something if you tell yourself it enough times, is partly true. Fortunately, you can *choose* what messages you give yourself and, therefore, choose how you think and feel about yourself.

How you talk to yourself impacts immediately, or obliquely, on your self-concept. Try the following self-talk strategies to make the best impact on yourself:

> ✔ **Desist with global labels.** Humans often call themselves losers, idiots, failures, stupid, or unlovable because of certain events or actions they've been involved in or done. You may use even worse language on yourself in the privacy of your own head. Why? Because, you're caving in to the temptation to rate your entire selfhood on the evidence of one, or more, isolated incidents.

✔ **Be specific with your self-assessments.** Before you classify yourself as a failure, ask yourself the following questions: 'In what specific way have I failed?' 'In what specific way have I acted stupidly?' It's far less easy to fall into global self-rating when you force yourself to be specific.

✔ **Say what you mean and mean what you say.** You may be saying to yourself right now: 'Oh, but I don't *mean* it when I call myself those bad names.' No? Then don't say them! Get into the practice of using language that describes accurately your behaviour and is in keeping with self-acceptance beliefs. Instead of muttering 'I'm such an idiot for missing that deadline,' try saying: 'Missing that deadline was a really bad move. I'm really disappointed about it.'

Resisting self-abusive language cuts two ways. This chapter focuses on self-acceptance, but much of the advice applies to acceptance of others, too. Generally, people are nicer and more forgiving to their mates than they are to themselves. But, people are still capable of damning others and calling them ugly names. Start exercising a different type of consistency: Stop name-calling, full stop. When you do put a halt on name-calling, it can lead you to feel less intense anger and hurt when others behave poorly, which helps to reinforce your self-acceptance beliefs. If you're practicing not globally rating others, then you're also minimising the tendency to globally rate yourself.

Following the best-friend argument

Out of habit, most humans employ double standards: You judge your friends by an entirely different, often more accepting, standard than you use on yourself.

Try to take the same attitude of acceptance towards yourself that you take towards your friends and family. Consider the following:

✔ **Act like your best friend by judging your behaviour but not judging yourself.** Eustace has been having difficulties in his marriage. He has been staying out late, drinking with his mates, before going home and being verbally abusive to his wife. His best mate, Lucian, has highlighted Eustace's poor behaviour in their conversations but he has maintained an understanding attitude towards his friend's unhappiness. Lucian is not about to define Eustace as a complete bastard on the strength of his recent, excessive drinking and arguments with his wife.

✔ **Accept your failings as you would those of a dear friend.** Laura just failed her driving test for the fourth time. She feels very down about it. Her best friend Maggie tells her to try again and to be less hard on herself. Maggie wants Laura to do the driving test again. She doesn't view Laura as a total failure based simply on her difficulty in passing a test. Even if Laura never drives, Maggie will likely remain her friend because of other things she likes and appreciates about Laura.

✔ **View your behaviour within the context of your circumstances, and above all, be compassionate.** Rivka had a pregnancy terminated following a short affair. She feels very guilty and can't imagine putting the event behind her. Rivka's close friend, Carla, reminds her of the unfortunate circumstances she found herself in at the time, and tells her that she's still someone that she likes and respects very much. Carla can see that Rivka has made a difficult decision. She compassionately considers that Rivka has acted out of a degree of desperation. Rivka may have been unlucky, or a bit careless, with respect to birth control, but Carla does not judge her on the basis of the abortion.

Ask yourself whether the punishment fits the crime. Are you being fair on yourself? What punishment would you dole out to your best friend for the same behaviour? Be aware that you may be making yourself feel extremely guilty, or ashamed, inappropriately. If you wouldn't like to see anyone else feeling such extreme emotions in response to the same transgression you've committed, then you're applying a double standard that's loaded against you.

Are you created so differently that you must subscribe to an exceptional code of conduct? (Consider this an inverted inferiority complex.) Having some exceptional code of conduct implies that you, and you alone, are somehow designed exclusively to transcend the ubiquitous human essence of fallibility. However, you are human. You don't fail any more extravagantly than any of your peers – nor do you succeed more dramatically than they do. If you're going to exercise compassion towards your friends' failures and wobbles, you need to consistently apply the same rules of compassion and understanding towards yourself.

Dealing with doubts and reservations

Many people feel that by accepting themselves, they're simply letting themselves off the hook. But, self-acceptance is about taking personal responsibility for your less good traits, actions, and habits. Self-acceptance is about targeting areas that you both *can* and *wish to* change and then taking the appropriate steps towards change. Self-acceptance is not saying: 'Hey, I'm human and fallible! Therefore, I just am the way I am and I don't need to think about changing anything.'

You are, at baseline, worthy and acceptable, but some of your behaviours and attitudes may be simultaneously unacceptable.

Another common fear is that by accepting yourself, you're actually condoning undesirable aspects of yourself: 'Hey, I'm an acceptable human being and, therefore, all I think and do is acceptable.' Not so.

Work on accepting your overall self on the basis of your intrinsic human fallibility, and be prepared to judge *specific aspects* of yourself. You can both
condone your personhood and also condemn, or reject, certain things that
you do.

Selecting the Self-help Journey to Self-Acceptance

A common reason for people persistently putting themselves down, is that
they hope to become better by calling attention to their mistakes, flaws, and
failings. Unfortunately, this process frequently includes feeling depressed or
anxious, which may well already be underpinned by low self-esteem.

Trying to solve an emotional problem at the same time as calling yourself
useless, worthless, and pathetic is much like trying to learn a foreign language while hitting yourself over the head with a textbook – your actions are
likely to make both jobs much harder.

Accepting yourself has two interesting implications for overcoming emotional
problems and personal development. First, you're equal in worth to other
human beings just as you are, which helps to reduce emotional pain. Second,
because you're not distracted by beating yourself up, you can focus better on
coping with adversity, reducing disturbance, and self-improvement.

Imperfect self-acceptance

As you're a fallible human, you won't be perfect at
self-acceptance either. You'll very probably slip
into putting yourself down from time to time, as
everyone does – us included. The aim is to accept
yourself more often and to accept yourself again
more quickly, if you notice that you're putting
yourself down. Such acceptance definitely gets
easier and more consistent with practice.

Broadly speaking, you may be using one of two
common strategies to manage low self-esteem:

Avoiding doing things, or doing things excessively. For example, a person who believes
they're worthless unless they're liked by everybody may try extra hard to avoid rejection or to
win people's approval, while a person who
regards themselves as a 'failure' may try to avoid
situations in which they might fail. Have a look at
Chapter 21 for more avoiding potential failure.

Chapter 13

Cooling Down Your Anger

In This Chapter
▶ Knowing when your anger's problematic
▶ Developing healthy anger
▶ Communicating effectively to combat unhealthy anger

Anger's a pretty common emotion. However, anger is also increasingly recognised as an important emotional problem. Anger can be bad for your relationships, your health, and your self-esteem.

In the bad old days of psychological treatment for anger, people were encouraged simply to 'get it out', often by beating pillows to vent their fury. The result? Just like anything you practise, these people got better at being angry. The notion that expressing your rage can 'get it out of your system' is something of a myth. More often you wind yourself up further, generating even more anger. A better solution is to get to grips with managing your angry feelings responsibly, and to master skills that can help you to feel less angry, less often.

CBT offers clear and effective management of anger, by tackling the thinking that underpins your anger and helping you express that anger in a healthy manner. This chapter focuses on CBT techniques that can help you deal directly with your feelings of anger.

Discerning the Difference between Healthy and Unhealthy Anger

Essentially, two different types of anger exist – healthy and unhealthy:

✔ **Healthy anger is helpful annoyance and irritation.** This is the kind of anger that spurs you on to assert your rights when it is important that you do so.

✔ **Unhealthy anger is unhelpful rage, and hate.** This type of anger leads you to behave aggressively or violently even in response to mild or unimportant provocation.

All emotions have *themes* – that is, sets of circumstances or triggers from which they arise (we explain this a bit more in Chapter 6). Themes for anger include someone breaking one of your personal rules, or threatening your self-esteem through word or deed. Another anger theme is frustration, when someone or something gets in the way of you reaching a goal.

The triggers for healthy and unhealthy anger are the same, but the behavioural responses they typically produce are very different. Both anger types are also associated with different ways of thinking and attention focus.

Key characteristics of unhealthy anger

Unhealthy anger is far more likely than healthy anger to cause fractures in your personal relationships, create trouble in your workplace, or land you in prison. You're also likely to feel more physically and emotionally uncomfortable when you're unhealthily angry.

Several ways of thinking typically underpin unhealthy anger:

✔ Holding rigid demands and rules about the way other people must or must not behave

✔ Insisting that other people must not insult or ridicule you

✔ Demanding that life conditions and other people don't get in the way of you getting what you want

✔ Overestimating the degree to which people deliberately act in undesirable ways towards you

✔ Assuming automatically that you're right and the other person's wrong

✔ Refusing to consider another person's point of view

Common behavioural characteristics associated with unhealthy anger include the following:

✔ Attacking or wanting to attack another person physically or verbally

✔ Attacking another person in an indirect – also known as *passive-aggressive* – way, for example trying to make someone else's job difficult

✔ Taking out your anger on innocent parties, such as another person, an animal, or an object

✔ Plotting revenge

✔ Attempting to turn others against the person you believe has behaved undesirably

✔ Sulking

✔ Looking for evidence that someone has acted with malicious intent

✔ Searching for signs of an offence being repeated

✔ Being overvigilant for people breaking your personal rules or acting disrespectfully towards you

Common physical signs of unhealthy anger include the following:

✔ Clenched fists

✔ Muscular tension, especially in the neck and shoulder muscles

✔ Clenched jaw

✔ Trembling or shaking

✔ Raised heart rate

✔ Feeling hot

For many people, anger can come on hot and fast. Familiarising yourself with your own early warning signs of anger can help you to intervene earlier.

Hallmarks of healthy anger

In general, people experience healthy anger as intense but not overwhelming experience. You can feel intensely angry in a healthy way without experiencing a loss of control. Healthy anger does not lead you to behave in antisocial, violent, or intimidating ways.

In addition, healthy anger is typically underpinned by the following ways of thinking:

✔ Holding strong preferences rather than rigid demands about how people should act

✔ Having flexibility in the rules you expect people to abide by

✔ Strongly preferring that others don't insult or ridicule you

✔ Desiring that other people and life conditions don't get in the way of you getting what you want

✔ Thinking realistically about whether other people have deliberately acted undesirably towards you

✔ Considering that both you *and* the other person may be right *and* wrong to a degree

✔ Trying to see the other person's point of view

Behavioural characteristics typical of healthy anger include:

✔ Asserting yourself with the other person

✔ Staying in the situation with the intent of resolving any disagreement

✔ Requesting the other person to modify her behaviour – and respecting her right to disagree with you

✔ Looking for evidence that the other person may not have behaved with malicious intent

Assembling Attitudes That Underpin Healthy Anger

If you're serious about overcoming your unhealthy anger, you have to take a long hard look at some of the attitudes you hold. This involves honestly looking at the way you believe that other people and the world at large *must* treat you. You may hold some common toxic beliefs that frequently lead to unhealthy anger in people. Some of these toxic thoughts include:

✔ No one must ever treat me poorly or disrespectfully.

✔ The world must not be unjust or unfair and *especially* not to me!

✔ I must get what I want when I want it and nothing should get in my way.

✔ I must never be led into feeling guilty, inadequate, embarrassed, or ashamed by other people or life events.

✔ No one and nothing must ever expose my weaknesses or errors.

Having looked long and hard at your attitudes, you need to make your toxic attitudes more helpful and realistic (see Chapter 3 for more on tackling toxic thoughts in general). Yes! Once again, positive emotional change comes from changing the way you think about yourself, about other people, and the world in general. If you want to be emotionally healthy and high-functioning, you need to start developing flexible, tolerant, and accepting attitudes.

High-functioning individuals experience fewer disturbing emotional responses, they are able to enjoy life, and they bounce back fairly readily from everyday hassles and annoyances. It's all in the way you look at life and the kind of attitude you take toward life's ups and downs (particularly with regard to anger).

We can explain the types of attitude that are likely to help you overcome unhealthy anger. However, *you* must decide to agree with these attitudes and ultimately *act in accordance with them* if you want to see a change in the amount of anger you experience.

The following sections describe the healthy attitudes that you need to take in order to overcome your unhealthy anger.

Putting up with other people

Other people exist in the same universe as you. Sometimes, this can be a rather pleasant state of affairs, but on occasions you may find that these other people are a damnable inconvenience. Whether you like it or not, other people can exist, do exist, and will continue to exist in your universe for the foreseeable future. Accepting that these other people have as much right as you to inhabit the planet just makes sense. And while cohabitating, you may as well accept the reality that sometimes other people may get on your nerves. As you're not in charge of the universe, you'd better accept that other people are *allowed* to act according to their rules and values – not yours.

You've probably noticed that humans come in a variety of shapes, sizes, and colours. No doubt you've seen that not all people share the same religion, culture, political opinions, moral codes, or rules of social conduct. Now, without going into a long-winded speech about the value of diversity, accepting individual difference is terribly important. Acknowledging that other people have a right to their own ideas about how to live their lives – even when you flatly disagree with their ideas – can save you a lot of emotional upset. People will continue to exercise these rights, whatever your opinion.

Accepting others can save you a world of unhealthy anger. Consider this: Every morning Jill and Tim travel to work together by bus. Every time she boards the bus, Jill says a pleasant 'Good morning!' to the driver, who always ignores her completely. One day, Tim asks Jill why she persists in greeting the driver, even though he never acknowledges her. Jill says: 'Because I choose to behave in line with my standard of politeness rather than to respond to his standard of rudeness.'

Jill's high tolerance to rudeness from the bus driver means that she can avoid making herself unhealthily angry. She does this by:

- Accepting that the driver has the right to be rude. No law exists against responding (or not) to another person's greeting.

- Not taking the driver's rudeness over-personally. The driver doesn't know Jill, so it is highly unlikely that he is actually 'out to get her' specifically. He's probably foul-tempered to many people in addition to Jill.

- Exercising her right to behave according to her own standard of politeness, even in the face of another person's rudeness. Although the bus driver is rude to Jill, she chooses not to respond in the same way. She can carry on being a generally polite person even in the face of another person's rudeness if she so chooses.

Forming flexible preferences

Wanting others to treat you well and with respect makes sense. Similarly, you probably want other people to do their jobs well and to help you to get what you want. You're likely to want life to roll your way and for world events to gel with your personal plans.

However, expecting and demanding these conditions to be met all the time doesn't make sense!

Keeping your attitudes flexible and based on *preferences*, rather than demands or expectations, can keep your anger in the healthy camp. Rigid and demanding attitudes can land you in unhealthy destructive anger, time and time again.

Consider the relationship of Ade and Franco: Ade holds rigid beliefs about other people showing him respect and courtesy. Franco holds the same principal attitudes, but flexibly. Ade and Franco go for lunch together and sit near a table of young men, who drink a bit too much and end up talking very loudly and rudely. Franco and Ade can't hear each other and their lunch is being ruined by the behaviour of these young men. Franco suggests that he and Ade move to another table, where they won't be disturbed by the men's antisocial behaviour. Ade, however, gets up and shouts at the men, ending up in a brawl outside the cafe. He's lucky not to be hurt more seriously than he is.

Ade's rigid attitudes about the situation are:

'How dare these idiots treat me this way?'

'I won't tolerate being disrespected like this.'

'I've got to show these idiots who's the boss.'

Franco's more flexible attitudes about the situation are:

'These guys are behaving like idiots.'

'These guys are really annoying me with their disrespectful behaviour.'

'I don't want to put up with this, so I think I'll get away from these guys.'

Flexible preferences for things like respect allow for the possibility of you being treated disrespectfully. Rigid demands don't allow for the possibility of life and other people treating you in ways that you think they shouldn't. Inevitably, you can end up feeling outraged if you always demand that others behave in a specific way. People behave according to how *they* want to behave – not how *you* want them to behave.

Accepting other people as fallible human beings

When you angrily condemn another person as 'useless', 'no good', or 'idiotic', you make a gross overgeneralisation. The other person isn't a thoroughgoing idiot just because she's acting idiotically – she surely acts in different ways in other situations, just like you do.

The critical point here is also a practical point: Putting down other people makes respecting others difficult. You need to sustain a level of respect for others in order to be able to consider behaviours objectively and act appropriately assertive.

The alternative to putting down others is to accept them as FHBs – fallible human beings – who may act in objectionable ways (to you). When you consider others as FHBs, you can appropriately condemn the behaviour but not the person. This acceptance is critical in helping you to keep a level head and master your angry feelings.

Accepting other people is the other side of the coin to accepting yourself. You can eventually accept yourself because you're essentially applying the same philosophy to everyone.

Accepting yourself

Sometimes, people default to unhealthy anger because they have a fragile sense of their own worth. If someone treats you poorly, insults you, or seems to hold a negative opinion of you, you may be reminded of how low an opinion you have of yourself. In order to protect your self-worth, you may attack the other person. Think of the rationale as 'If I can put you down, then I can avoid putting myself down.'

By believing that you're an unrateable, complex, ever-changing, fallible human, you may see that you can never be less worthwhile, even when people treat you poorly. In Chapter 12, we offer more guidance on self-acceptance.

Developing high frustration tolerance

Frustration occurs most often when something or someone gets in the way of you achieving your specific goals and aims. The more important your goal is to you, the more angry or annoyed you're likely to feel when something blocks your attempts to reach that goal.

People who frequently experience unhealthy anger tend to have a low tolerance for frustration. Their low threshold for tolerating hassle, mishaps, or obstruction from others is echoed in statements like these:

'I can't stand it!'

'It's intolerable!'

'I just can't take it anymore!'

Increasing your tolerance for frustration helps you to experience appropriate levels of healthy annoyance in response to goal obstruction. Having a *high frustration tolerance* (HFT) makes you more effective at solving problems. So, your anger doesn't get in the way of you seeing possible solutions to everyday hassles and setbacks. High frustration tolerance is present in statements such as:

'This is an uncomfortable situation but I can stand the discomfort!'

'This event is hard to bear but I can bear it – some difficult things are worth tolerating.'

'Even if I *feel* like I can't take it anymore, chances are that I can.'

To increase your tolerance for frustration, ask yourself these kinds of questions when life pulls a fast one on you:

'Is this situation really terrible or is it just highly inconvenient?'

'Is it true that I can't stand this situation or it is it more true that I don't like this situation?'

'Is this situation truly unbearable or is it really just very difficult to bear?

Being less extreme in your judgement of negative events can help you to have less extreme emotional responses, such as unhealthy anger.

Doing your ABCs

Practise writing down your unhealthy angry thoughts on paper and replacing them with healthier thoughts. Refer to Chapter 3 to see how to use an ABC form to tackle toxic thoughts and replace them with realistic renderings, pertinent preferences, additional acceptances, self-acceptance, and high frustration tolerance.

Most of what you think is intolerable isn't as bad as it seems. Many things are difficult to tolerate but are tolerable, hard to bear but bearable, unpleasant and inconvenient – but you *can* stand them!

To underscore the point, imagine getting stuck in traffic on your way to the airport and then missing your flight. Deeply annoying! However, by you getting angry and screaming at the traffic, isn't going to make the cars move any faster. Of course, becoming healthily annoyed about the traffic doesn't change the situation either. But your healthy anger is less likely to cause you such extreme discomfort and is more likely to help you create a contingency plan. Rather than using up your energy swearing and bashing your mobile against the dashboard, you can focus your efforts on phoning the airline and trying to get yourself bumped on to the next available flight.

Pondering the pros and cons of your temper

Believe that you're *right* to be angry and steadfastly stick to this perception, is one of the more common obstacles to conquering unhealthy anger.

You certainly have the *right* to feel angry. You may even *be right* to be angry, in the sense of objecting to something you don't like. However, you may feel better and behave more constructively if you have *healthy* anger rather than *unhealthy* anger.

To commit more fully to changing your anger, review the costs and benefits of your current anger, and of a healthier alternative. Refer to Chapter 8 for some pointers on completing a cost–benefit analysis, which can help you to facilitate this change.

Imparting Your Indignation in a Healthy Way

Expressing your feelings readily when they occur can be a good antidote to bouts of unhealthy anger. On the other hand, bottling up your feelings can mean that you fester on your emotions until they bubble up to the surface and you explode.

People who talk openly and appropriately about their emotional responses to events are less prone to unhealthy feelings like anger and depression. The following sections offer tips and techniques to improve your communication skills and to deal with dissatisfaction in a healthy manner.

Asserting yourself effectively

Assertion involves standing up for yourself, voicing your opinions and feelings, and firmly ensuring that your basic rights are considered. Assertion differs from aggression, in that it does not involve violence, intimidation, or disregard for the rights of others.

Using assertion rather than aggression is more effective in getting you what you want. When you're being assertive, you're still in control of your behaviour, but when you're unhealthily enraged much of your behaviour is impulsive.

People are likely to respond to your wishes when you're being assertive simply because you're making yourself clear – not because they're afraid of your anger.

Often, your aggression is about winning an argument and getting the other person to back down and agree that you're right. Assertion is not about winning per se. Rather, assertion is about getting your point across but not insisting that the other person agrees with you or backs down.

If you have a tendency to become angry, and get verbally or physically aggressive quickly, give yourself time out and go and count to ten (or as high as you need to feel calmer). You can then consider your next thinking and behavioural steps.

Assertion is a skill that you can practice. Many people with anger problems benefit from breaking down assertion into the following steps:

1. **Get the other person's attention.** For example, if you want to make a complaint in a shop, wait until you have the shop assistant's attention rather than shouting at them when they are busy with another task. If you want to talk to your partner about a specific issue, ask for some of her time.

2. **Be in the right place.** The best time to assert yourself may depend on where you are when you get irked. If your boss makes a comment that undermines you during a board meeting, you're probably best to bring it up with her a bit later in less public surroundings.

3. **Be clear in your head about what you want to say.** If you're new to assertion, but more familiar with the shouting and screaming thing, give yourself time to really think about what you want to get across.

4. **Stick to your point and be respectful.** Don't resort to name-calling or hurling insults.

5. **Take responsibility for your feelings of annoyance.** Don't blame the other person for *making* you feel angry. Use statements like 'I feel angry when you turn up an hour late for our appointments', or 'I felt let down and angry that you didn't invite me to your wedding reception'.

Assertion doesn't always work. Simply because you make the superlative effort to stop yelling your lungs out and to stop battering other people about the head and ears, doesn't mean that you're always going to get what you want. Oh, no, siree Bob! In fact, some people may even meet your assertion with their own aggression. So, strive to maintain your healthy anger and to behave assertively, even when other people don't. Remind yourself that other people have the right to choose to behave badly and that you have the right to remove yourself from them rather than responding in kind.

Before you assert yourself, decide whether the situation's really worth your time and energy. Ask yourself whether the problem merits you being assertive. Is the issue more trouble than it's worth? If you're a former unhealthy anger junkie, you're probably not used to just letting things go. You can practise deciding when asserting yourself is in your best interests and when you're wiser to simply not respond at all.

Coping with criticism

Criticism isn't always intended to anger or undermine the receiver. Well-delivered specific criticism can provide useful information and need not cause offence. Most people like to hear positive feedback – it's the negative stuff that really gets under your skin.

People who demand perfection from themselves, or expect approval from significant others, can often take criticism badly. They tend to take criticism overly seriously and personally. They often assume that any form of negative comment means that they're less than worthy. If you're this sort of person, a comment from your boss such as 'I'm not entirely happy with this report you've written' gets translated in your head something like this:

> *My boss thinks my report is rubbish = All my reports are rubbish = I'm rubbish at my job = I'm rubbish*

You may even become unhealthily angry in an attempt to defend your self-worth, and launch a counteroffensive on the person you feel has attacked you.

You can take the sting out of criticism by keeping these points in mind:

✔ Criticism can help you to improve your work performance and your relationships.

✔ You can assess criticism, decide how much of it you agree with, and reject the rest.

✔ Criticism is something pretty much everyone experiences from time to time. You cannot reasonably expect to always avoid being criticised.

If someone criticises you in a global way – for example, your sister calls you an incompetent loser – try asking her to be more specific: 'In what specific ways am I an incompetent loser?' Asking questions can make the criticism more useful to you. Or, if the person cannot be more specific, your question can disarm her. The following section discusses disarming in greater detail.

Using the disarming technique

Okay, not all the criticism that you get is well-intended. Sometimes, another person may bombard you with a load of negative remarks or insults. What are your options? You *can* get unhealthily angry and shout at or otherwise attack your antagonist. Or, you can keep your annoyance in the healthy camp and try non-defensively disarming your critic. The disarming technique works on the following principles:

✔ Look for a grain of truth in what the other person is saying and agreeing with her on that specific point.

✔ Show your critic some empathy

✔ Ask your critic for more information about her point of criticism

✔ Express your own point of view as 'I feel' statements

For example, Hilda's friend criticises her for being late to meet her for coffee. Hilda's friend says angrily: 'You're always late. You're just so disorganised!' Hilda would usually be defensive and hostile about criticism, resulting in many past arguments. Instead, this time Hilda uses the disarming technique and replies, 'You're right! I'm not the most organised person in the world' (partial agreement). 'Are you feeling really annoyed?' (empathy/asking for more information). This takes the heat from her friend's anger, who then goes on to say how frustrated she's feeling in general.

Using the disarming technique, you come out on top by keeping your cool. You also gain the satisfaction of having managed a critical comment well. Who knows – you may even *improve* your relationship with your critic.

Dealing with Difficulties in Overcoming Anger

Even if you know that your anger responses are causing you problems in your life, you may still be reluctant to let go of your anger. Sometimes, people are reluctant to break free from unhealthy anger and related behaviours because they can't see an alternative, and think that they may end up being passive or getting walked over instead.

However, if you develop your assertion skills, you may well be more inclined to let go of your anger. Nevertheless, here are some common obstacles to getting rid of unhealthy anger and some suggestions to help you take on healthy anger instead:

- ✓ **You lack empathy and understanding of the impact your unhealthy anger responses have on those near to you.** When you're not angry, ask your loved ones how they feel about your anger. Try to remember times when you've been on the receiving end of aggressive or intimidating behaviour and how it affected you. Use feedback about your anger, and your own experiences of aggression from others, to help you change how you express feelings of annoyance in the future.

- ✓ **Letting go of your anger means that you're weak.** You may consider yourself an angry person, and you may like it that way. You may think that if you don't continue to be angry, other people may discover that you're weak, a pushover, someone they can mess with. Work to realise that people who're assertive – firm but fair – tend to earn respect. You don't need to be angry to be strong.

✔ **You think that your unhealthy anger helps you to control other people and encourages them to respect you.** If you're very aggressive, people who are important in your life, such as your children or your partner, may go out of their way to avoid incurring your wrath. Don't mistake fear and dislike for respect. You may control the people in your life by your anger, but their compliance is likely born of fear and loathing, not from genuine regard for you. When you behave respectfully and assertively, people are likely to respond out of a genuine regard for your feelings rather than out of fear.

✔ **Your unhealthy anger makes you feel powerful.** Although some people find the intensity of their unhealthy anger pretty uncomfortable and even scary, others feel invigorated by the rush of their fury. Unhealthy anger is based on putting down another person. Unhealthy anger often means that you are stepping on another person's rights, or abusing, or intimidating somebody else. If you enjoy these aspects of your anger, you probably hold a low opinion of yourself generally. Look for other ways to experience your personal power without undermining those around you.

✔ **Your anger is self-righteous.** You may be clinging stubbornly to your anger because you think it's justified. You may be refusing to admit that you could be wrong or that the other person could be right. Rarely are confrontations as cut and dry as one party being utterly in the right and the other utterly in the wrong. Remind yourself that it is okay to be wrong. It is not a sign of weakness or inferiority. Allow yourself to admit that you may be wrong and that the other person may have a good point.

Feeling a bit sceptical? Test out your predictions about adopting healthy anger and behaving in an assertive rather than an aggressive manner. You can use the blank behavioural experiment sheet in Chapter 4. (Refer to Chapter 4 for more help on conducting behavioural experiments.)

Body benefits for bridling your anger

Being angry, especially feeling frequently hostile towards other people and the world, is bad for you. Scientific research shows an association between hostility and raised blood pressure, which can lead to heart problems. Take the pressure off your mind, your interactions with other people, and your heart by controlling – rather than being controlled by – your anger.

Part IV
Looking Backwards and Moving Forwards

The 5th Wave   By Rich Tennant

"My hunch, Mr. Pesko, is that you're still making mountains out of mole hills."

In this part . . .

Putting your present problems into context based on your past experiences is central to CBT, and this part helps you to do just that. You'll also find information on how to consolidate new ways of thinking, as well as tips about making productive behavioural changes stick. We'll help you to overcome common obstacles to positive change and show you how to get and best use professional help.

Chapter 14

Taking a Fresh Look at Your Past

In This Chapter

▶ Putting your current problems into context

▶ Identifying your core beliefs

▶ Dealing with early experiences

▶ Developing alternative beliefs

*Y*our past experiences have an effect on how you think and function now. Sometimes, you may endure bad experiences and be able to make some good things happen from them. At other times, you may be wounded by unpleasant events and carry that injury with you into your present and future.

This chapter encourages you to examine openly whether your past experiences have led you to develop *core beliefs* that may be causing your current emotional difficulties.

People are sometimes surprised to find out that CBT considers the past an important aspect of understanding one's problems. However, rather than focusing intensively on childhood relationships and experiences, CBT specifically investigates past experiences in order to see how these early events may still be affecting people in their *present* lives.

Exploring How Your Past Can Influence Your Present

We don't know what your childhood and early adulthood were like, but many people share relatively common past experiences. The following examples highlight various aspects of past experience that may resonate with your life history. Rather than focusing on the differences between these examples and your own experiences, use the examples to identify similar things that have happened to you in your own life.

> ✓ Sybil grew up with parents who fought a lot. She learnt to be very quiet and to keep out of the way so that her parents' anger would not be directed at her. She always tried to be a very good girl and no trouble to anyone.

✔ Rashid had critical parents. The demands Rashid's parents made on him to be a 'high achiever' made it clear to him that he would get their love and approval only when he did well in sports and at school.

✔ Beth had a violent father who would frequently beat her and other family members when he was in a bad mood. At other times, her father was very loving and funny. Beth could never predict accurately what mood her father would be in when he came through the front door.

✔ Milo's relationships have never lasted for very long. Most of the women he's dated have been unfaithful to him. Milo's partners often complain that he is too insecure and suspicious of their friendships with members of the opposite sex.

✔ Mahesh lost the family business and his oldest son in a fire five years ago. His wife has been depressed since the fire, and their marriage seems to be falling apart. Recently, his teenage daughter has been in trouble with the police. No one seems to offer Mahesh support. He feels dogged by bad luck.

Many other different kinds of difficult experiences can contribute to the development of negative core beliefs:

✔ Death of loved ones

✔ Growing up with neglectful, critical, or abusive parents or siblings

✔ Divorce

✔ Being bullied at school

✔ Being abandoned by a parent or significant other

✔ Undergoing a trauma, such as rape, life-threatening illness, accidents, or witnessing violent attacks on other people

These are just some examples of the types of events that can have a profound effect on mental health generally. Negative events that contribute to the way you think about yourself, other people, and the world often occur in childhood or early adult life. However, events occurring at any stage of your life can have a significant impact on the way you think about the world.

Identifying Your Core Beliefs

Your *core beliefs* are enduring ideas or philosophies that you hold very strongly and very deeply. These ideas are usually developed in childhood or early in adult life. Core beliefs are not always negative. Good experiences of life and of other people, generally lead to the development of healthy ideas about yourself, other people, and the world. In this chapter we deal with neg-ative core beliefs because these are the types of beliefs that cause people's emotional problems.

Sometimes, the negative core beliefs that are formed during childhood can be reinforced by later experiences, which seem to confirm their validity.

For example, one of Beth's core beliefs is 'I'm bad'. She develops this belief to make sense of her father beating her without any real or obvious reason. Later, Beth has a few experiences of being punished unreasonably by teach-ers at school, which reinforces her belief in her 'badness'.

Core beliefs are characteristically global and are absolute, like Beth's 'I'm bad'. People hold core beliefs to be 100 per cent true under all conditions. You often form your core beliefs when you're a child to help you make sense of your childhood experiences, and so you may never evaluate whether your core beliefs are the best way to make sense of your adult experiences. As an adult, you may continue to act, think, and feel as though the core beliefs of your childhood are still 100 per cent true.

Your core beliefs are called 'core' because they're your deeply held ideas and they're at the very centre of your belief system. Core beliefs give rise to rules, demands, or assumptions, which in turn produce *automatic thoughts* (thoughts that just pop into your head when you are confronted with a situation). You can think of these three layers of beliefs as a dartboard with core beliefs as the bull's-eye. Figure 14-1 shows the interrelationship between the three layers, and shows the assumptions and automatic thoughts that surround Beth's core belief that she's bad.

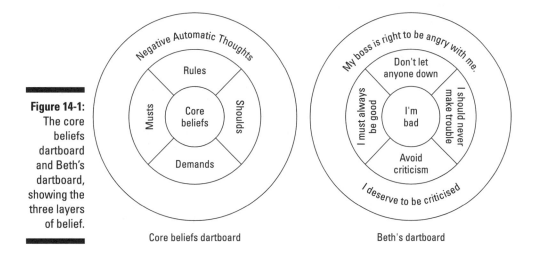

Figure 14-1:
The core beliefs dartboard and Beth's dartboard, showing the three layers of belief.

Core beliefs dartboard   Beth's dartboard

Another way of describing a core belief is as a lens or filter, through which you interpret all the information you receive from other people and the world around you.

The three camps of core beliefs

Core beliefs fall into three main camps: beliefs about yourself, beliefs about other people, and beliefs about the world.

Beliefs about yourself

Unhelpful negative core beliefs about yourself often have their roots in damaging early experiences. Being bullied or ostracised at school, or experiencing neglect, abuse, or harsh criticism from caregivers, teachers, or siblings can inform the way in which you understand yourself.

For example, Beth's experiences of physical abuse led her to form the core belief 'I'm bad'.

Beliefs about other people

Negative core beliefs about others often develop as a result of traumatic incidents involving other people. A traumatic incident can mean personal harm inflicted on you by another person or witnessing harm being done to others. Negative core beliefs can also develop from repeated negative experiences with other people, such as teachers and parents.

For example, because Beth's father was violent and abusive towards her but also could be funny when he wanted to be, she developed a core belief that 'people are dangerous and unpredictable'.

Beliefs about the world

People who have experienced trauma, lived with severe deprivation, or survived in harmful, insecure, unpredictable environments are prone to forming negative core beliefs about life and the world.

Beth holds a core belief that 'the world is full of bad things', which she developed from her early home situation and events at school later on.

Sometimes, core beliefs from all three camps are taught to you explicitly as a child. Your parents or caregivers may have given you *their* core beliefs. For example, you may have been taught that 'life's cruel and unfair' before you have any experiences that lead you to form such a belief yourself.

Seeing how your core beliefs interact

Identifying core beliefs about yourself can help you to understand why you keep having the same problems. However, if you can also get to know your fundamental beliefs about other people and the world, you can build a fuller picture of why some situations distress you. For example, Beth may find being yelled at by her boss depressing because it activates her core belief 'I'm bad', but the experience also seems to confirm her belief that people are unpredictable and aggressive.

Like many people, you may hold core beliefs that you're unlovable, unworthy, or inadequate – these beliefs are about your basic worth, goodness, or value. Or perhaps you hold beliefs about your capability to look after yourself or to cope with adversity – these beliefs are about how helpless or powerful you are in relation to other people and the world.

Mahesh, for example, may believe 'I'm helpless' because he has experienced tragedy and a lot of bad luck. He may also hold beliefs that 'the world is against me' and 'other people are uncaring'. Looking at these three beliefs together, you can see why Mahesh is feeling depressed.

Detecting Your Core Beliefs

Because core beliefs are held deeply, you may not think of them or 'hear' them as clear statements in your head. You're probably much more aware of your negative automatic thoughts or your rules than you are of your core beliefs (refer to Figure 14-1).

The following sections show you some methods you can use to really get to the root of your belief system.

Following a downward arrow

One technique to help you pinpoint your problematic core beliefs is the *downward arrow* method, which involves you identifying a situation that causes you to have an unhealthy negative emotion, such as depression or guilt. (For more on healthy and unhealthy negative emotions, check out Chapter 6.)

After you've identified a situation that brings up negative emotions, ask yourself what the situation means or says about you (or others, or the world). Your first answer is probably your *negative automatic thought* (NAT). Keep asking yourself what your previous answer means or says about you until you reach a global, absolute statement, such as 'other people are dangerous' or 'I am bad' in Beth's case.

For example, when Rashid uses the downward arrow method to examine his feelings about failing a university entrance exam, he has the negative automatic thought:

NAT: 'I'll never get into a good university.'

What does this NAT mean about me?

'I've disappointed my parents again.'

What does disappointing my parents mean about me?

'Every time I try to do well at something, I fail.'

What does failing mean about me?

'I'm a failure.' (Rashid's core belief.)

You can use the same downward arrow technique to get to your core beliefs about other people and the world. Just keep asking yourself what your NAT *means about others or the world.* Ultimately, you can end up with a conclusive statement that is your core belief. The following is an example of how to do this, using the situation of getting a parking ticket:

NAT: 'These kinds of things are always happening to me.'

What does this mean about the world?

'Bad things are always just around the corner.'

What does this mean about the world?

'The world is full of tragedy and hardship.'

What does this mean about the world?

'Life is against me.' (Core belief.)

Picking up clues from your dreaming and screaming

Imagine your worst nightmare. Think of dream scenarios that wake you up screaming. Somewhere in these terrifying scenarios may be one or more of your core beliefs. Some examples of core beliefs that can show themselves in dreams and nightmares include:

- ✔ Drying up while speaking publicly

- ✔ Being rejected by your partner for another person

- ✔ Being criticised in front of work colleagues

- ✔ Getting lost in a foreign country

- ✔ Hurting someone's feelings

- ✔ Doing something thoughtless and being confronted about it

- ✔ Letting down someone important in your life

- ✔ Being controlled by another person

- ✔ Being at someone else's mercy

Look for the similarities between your nightmare scenarios and situations that upset you in real life. Ask yourself what a dreaded dream situation may mean about yourself, about other people, or about the world. Keep considering what each of your answers means about yourself, others, or the world until you reach a core belief.

Tracking themes

Another way of journeying to the core of your core beliefs is to look for themes in your automatic thoughts. A good way of doing this is by reviewing your completed ABC forms (which we describe in Chapter 3).

For example, if you find that you often have thoughts related to failure, getting things wrong, or being less capable than other people, you may have a core belief of 'I'm inadequate' or 'I'm incompetent'.

Filling in the blanks

Another method of eliciting your core beliefs is simply to fill in the blanks. Take a piece of paper, write the following, and fill in the blanks:

I am _____

Other people are _____

The world is _____

This method sort of requires you to take a wild guess about what your core beliefs are. Ultimately, you're in a better position than anyone else to take a guess, so the exercise is worth a shot.

You can review written work that you have done, which is a good technique for discovering your core beliefs. Going over what you've written again enables you to refine, tweak, or alter your beliefs. Be sure to use language that represents how you truly speak to yourself. Core beliefs are very idiosyncratic. However you choose to articulate them is entirely up to you. The same is true of the healthy alternative beliefs you develop (see the section that covers how to acquire alternatives to your core beliefs, later in this chapter). Make sure that you put alternative beliefs into language that reflects the way that you speak to yourself.

Understanding the Impact of Core Beliefs

Core beliefs are your fundamental and enduring ways of perceiving and making sense of yourself, the world, and other people. Your core beliefs have been around since early in your life. These core beliefs are so typically engrained and unconscious that you're probably not aware of their impact on your emotions and behaviours.

Spotting when you are acting according to old rules and beliefs

People tend to behave according to the beliefs they hold about themselves, others, and the world. To evaluate whether your core beliefs are unhealthy, you need to pay attention to your corresponding behaviours. Unhealthy core beliefs typically lead to problematic behaviours.

For example, Milo believes that he's unlovable and that other people cannot be trusted. Therefore, he tends to be passive with his girlfriends, to seek reassurance that they're not about to leave him, and to become suspicious and jealous of their interactions with other men. Often, Milo's girlfriends get fed up with his jealousy and insecurity and end the relationship.

Because Milo operates according to his core belief about being unlovable, he behaves in ways that actually tend to drive his partners away from him. Milo doesn't yet see that his core belief, and corresponding insecurity, is what causes problems in his relationships. Instead, Milo thinks that each time a partner leaves him for someone else, it is further evidence that his core belief of 'I'm unlovable' is true.

Sybil believes that she mustn't draw attention to herself because one of her core beliefs is 'other people are likely to turn on me'. Therefore, she's quiet in social situations and is reluctant to assert herself. Her avoidant, self-effacing behaviour means that she doesn't often get what she wants, which feeds her core belief 'I'm unimportant'.

Sybil acts in accordance with her core belief that other people are likely to turn on her and, subsequently deprives herself of the opportunity to see that this is not always going to happen. If Sybil and Milo identify their negative core beliefs, they can begin to develop healthier new beliefs and behaviours that can yield better results. We look more closely at how to develop new, more positive core beliefs later in this chapter.

Understanding that unhealthy core beliefs make you prejudiced

When you begin to examine your core beliefs, it may seem to you that every-thing in your life is conspiring to make your unhealthy core belief ring true. More than likely, your core belief is leading you to take a prejudiced view of all your experiences. Unhealthy beliefs, such as 'I'm unlovable' and 'other people are dangerous', distort the way in which you process information. Negative information that supports your unhealthy belief is let in. Positive information that contradicts the negative stuff is either rejected, or twisted to mean something negative in keeping with your unhealthy belief.

The prejudice model in Figure 14-2 shows you how your unhealthy core beliefs can reject positive events that may *contradict* them. At the same time, your core beliefs can collect negative events that may *support* their validity. Your unhealthy core beliefs can also lead you to distort positive events into negative events so that they continue to make your beliefs seem true.

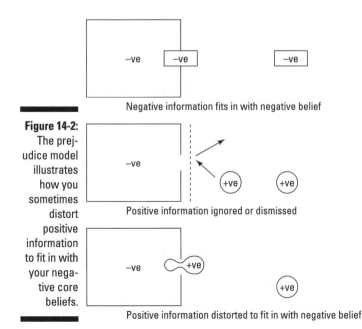

Negative information fits in with negative belief

Figure 14-2: The prej-udice model illustrates how you sometimes distort positive information to fit in with your nega-tive core beliefs.

Positive information ignored or dismissed

Positive information distorted to fit in with negative belief

For example, here's how Beth's core belief 'I'm bad' causes her to prejudice her experiences:

- **Negative experience:** Beth's boss is angry about a missed deadline, affirming her belief that 'I'm bad'.
- **Positive experience:** Beth's boss is happy about the quality of her report, which Beth distorts as 'he's happy about this report only because all my other work is such rubbish', further affirming her belief that 'I'm bad'.

Beth also ignores smaller *positive* events that don't support her belief that she's bad, such as:

- People seem to like her at work.
- Co-workers tell her that she's conscientious at work.
- Her friends telephone her and invite her out.

However, Beth is quick to take notice of smaller *negative* events that do seem to match up with her belief that she's bad, for example:

- Someone pushes her rudely on a busy train.
- Her boyfriend shouts at her during an argument.
- A work colleague doesn't smile at her when she enters the office.

Beth's core belief of 'I'm bad' acts as a filter through which all her experiences are interpreted. It basically stops her from re-evaluating herself as anything other than bad; it makes her prejudiced against herself. This is why identifying negative core beliefs and targeting them for change is so important!

Making a Formulation of Your Beliefs

When you have identified your core beliefs using the techniques outlined in the previous sections, you can use the form below (Figure 14-3) to make a formulation of your beliefs and rules. Filling out this form gives you an 'at a glance' reference of what your negative core beliefs are and how they lead you to act in unhelpful ways. The form is a handy reminder of the beliefs you need to target for change and why.

Follow these steps to fill out the form:

1. **Relevant Early/Past Experiences. In this box, write down any significant past events that you think may have contributed to the development of your specific negative core beliefs.**

FORMULATION OF MY BELIEFS AND RULES

RELEVANT EARLY/PAST EXPERIENCES

CORE UNHELPFUL BELIEFS
I am...., The world is...., Other people....

RULES/ ASSUMPTIONS
If....then...., Demands about self, the world, others.

AVOIDANCE AND COMPENSATORY BEHAVIOURS
Situations you tend to avoid or things you do excessively
as a consequence of your beliefs/rules

WHAT I'VE GOT GOING FOR ME
List your personal strengths and assets

Figure 14-3:
Make a
formulation
of your
beliefs with
the help of
this form.

For example, Beth records:

- Father was physically abusive and had unpredictable mood swings

- Father told me that I was bad

- I received severe and unreasonable punishment from teachers

2. **Core Unhelpful Beliefs. Write your identified core beliefs about yourself, other people, and the world in this box.**

Beth records her beliefs like this:

- I am bad

- Other people are unpredictable and dangerous

- The world is full of bad things

3. **Rules/Assumptions. In this box write down the rules or demands you place on yourself, other people, and the world *because of* your core negative beliefs.**

Beth writes:

- I must be 'good' at all times (demand on self).

- *If* I am criticised *then* it means that I am a bad person (conditional rule).

- Other people must not find fault with me or think badly of me (demand on others).

- The world must not conspire to remind me of how bad I am by throwing negative experiences my way (demand on the world).

4. **Avoidance and Compensatory Behaviours. Use this box to record how you try to avoid triggering your negative core beliefs, or unhelpful things you do to try and cope with your negative core beliefs when they are triggered.**

Beth records:

- Being a perfectionist at work in order to avoid any criticism

- Avoiding confrontation and thereby not asserting myself at work or with friends

- Overapologising when I do get criticised or make a small mistake

- Always assuming that other people's opinions are 'right' and that my own opinions are 'wrong'

- Being timid in social situations to avoid being noticed

- Not trusting others and assuming that they are ultimately going to hurt me somehow

5. **What I've got going for me. Write down positive things about yourself that fly in the face of your negative core beliefs.**

Beth writes:

- My work colleagues seem to like me.

- I am very conscientious at work and this has been commented on by my boss and by colleagues.

- I have some good friends who are trustworthy.

- There have been some good things that have happened to me like finishing college and getting a good job.

- I am generally hardworking and honest.

- I care about other people's feelings and opinions.

Information you write down in this box is important because it can be used to help you develop more balanced and helpful alternative core beliefs. (We explain more about how to construct healthy core beliefs in the following sections.)

Limiting the Damage: Being Aware of Core Beliefs

To reduce the negative impact of your unhelpful core beliefs, try to get better at spotting the beliefs being activated. Step back and consider a more unbiased explanation for events rather than getting swept along by the beliefs.

One way of improving your awareness of your core beliefs is to develop a *core belief flashcard*. This written-down statement includes the following:

- ✔ What your core belief is.

- ✔ How your core belief affects the way you interpret events.

- ✔ How you tend to act when the core belief is triggered.

- ✔ What a more unbiased interpretation of events is likely to be.

- ✔ What alternative behaviour may be more productive.

For example, Sybil wrote the following core belief flashcard:

> *When my core belief of 'I'm unimportant' is triggered, I'm probably taking something personally and wanting to withdraw. Instead, I can remember that most people don't hold this view of me, and then I can stay engaged in the social situation.*

Carry your flashcard around with you and it review it often, even several times a day. Use your flashcard, especially when you notice that your core belief has *been* triggered, or just before you enter a situation where you know that your old core belief is *likely* to be triggered.

Developing Alternatives to Your Core Beliefs

When you've put your finger on your core beliefs and identified those that are negative and unhealthy, you're in a position to develop healthier alternative beliefs.

Your new core belief doesn't need to be the extreme opposite of your old belief. Changing an extreme belief, such as 'I'm unlovable' to 'I'm lovable',may be too difficult when you're just starting out. Instead, cut yourself some slack and realise that simply by beginning to understand that an unhealthy core belief is not 100 per cent true all the time is enough. Here are some examples:

- Beth's alternative to her unhealthy belief 'I'm bad' is 'there are good things about me'.

- Rashid replaces his unhealthy belief 'I'm a failure' with 'I succeed at some things'.

- Mahesh chooses the alternative 'good things do happen in the world' to replace his old belief 'the world's against me'.

- Sybil replaces her belief 'other people will turn against me' with the healthier belief 'many people can be kind'.

- Milo substitutes his old core belief 'I'm unlovable' with the more accurate belief 'some people do like me, and some people will love me'.

Generating alternatives for your unhealthy and absolute core beliefs is not about positive thinking or platitudes, but is about generating less absolute, more accurate, more realistic opinions about yourself, other people, and the world around you.

Shaping your world

When you start to adopt healthy core beliefs, it can feel as if you're going against the grain because in fact that is what you are trying to do. Your old, negative core beliefs are familiar, deeply entrenched, and 'feel' like they must be true. New, healthy beliefs can 'feel' false and unnatural at first. Remind yourself that just because you've believed something for a long time doesn't make it true. People believed the earth was flat for a long time but that old belief doesn't change the fact that the world is round!

Some things are true, regardless of whether you believe them. Other things will never be true, no matter how fervently you believe them.

Revisiting history

Many people can look back over their lives and get a fairly clear picture of where their core beliefs have come from. Sometimes though, the source of core beliefs is not so clear.

Although most core beliefs arise from your early experiences, you can still form deep entrenched ideas about yourself, life, and other people when you're older. For example, Mahesh develops his core beliefs about the world being against him following a string of bad luck and tragic events during his adult years.

Revisit your history with a view to come up with some reasons behind the ways that you think and behave in the present. Be compassionate with yourself, but recognise that you're the only one who can retrain your brain into updated and healthier ways of understanding your experiences.

Replacing old meanings with new meanings

Experiences that you had earlier on in life were given a meaning by you at the time. As an adult, you're in the fortunate position of being able to reassess the meanings you originally gave certain events and to assign more sophisticated meanings where appropriate.

For example, Beth forms the belief 'I'm bad' based on the information she had when her father was abusing her. She was young and worked on various assumptions, including:

- Daddy tells me that I've been bad, and this must be true.
- You get punished when you're bad.
- I must've done something bad to deserve this treatment.

Now that she's no longer a child and recognises that she has this core belief, Beth can choose to look at her father's abuse and assign different meanings to his treatment of her:

- ✔ My father had an anger problem that had nothing to do with me.

- ✔ No child should be punished so severely, no matter how disobedient they've been.

- ✔ My father was wrong to beat me, and I didn't deserve to be beaten.

- ✔ My father did a bad thing by beating me and his bad behaviour doesn't mean that I am bad.

Use the three-column old meaning/new meaning worksheet in Appendix B, to review past events that contributed to the development of your core beliefs and reinterpret them now as an older, wiser person.

The sheet has the three headings. Fill them in as follows:

1. **In the first column, 'Event', record what actually happened.**

2. **Under 'Old Meaning' in the second column, record what you believe the event means about you.**

   This is your unhealthy core belief.

3. **In the 'New Meaning' third column, record a healthier and more accurate meaning for the event.**

   This is the new belief that you want to strengthen.

Table 14-1 shows an example of Beth's worksheet.

Table 14-1	Beth's Old Meaning–New Meaning Worksheet	
Event	*Old Meaning*	*New Meaning*
My Dad yelling, telling me I was bad when I was little.	I must be bad for him to say this so often.	I was much too young and afraid to be 'bad'. It was my father's anger that was the problem.

Incorporating new beliefs into your life

Constructing newer, healthier, more accurate core beliefs is one thing, but beginning to live by them is another. Before your new beliefs are really stuck in your head and heart, you need to act *as if* they're already there. For Beth, this may mean her forcing herself to face up to criticism from her boss and making appropriate adjustments to her work without berating herself. In short, she needs to act *as if* she truly believes that there are good things about herself, even in the face of negative feedback. She needs to operate under the assumption that her boss's anger is a reasonable (or possibly an unreasonable) response to an aspect of her work, rather than proof of her intrinsic badness.

In Chapter 15, we suggest several techniques for strengthening new alternative beliefs.

Starting from scratch

We won't tell you that changing your core beliefs is easy, because that simply isn't true. In fact, erasing your old belief systems is so difficult that we think the best way of dealing with them is to make alternative healthy beliefs stronger so that they can do battle with your unhealthy beliefs.

Think of your old beliefs as well-trodden paths through an overgrown field. You can walk quickly and easily down these paths, as they've been worn down from years of use. Developing new alternative beliefs is like making new paths through the field. At first, the new paths are awkward and uncomfortable to walk on, because you need to break down the undergrowth.

You may be tempted to walk along the old paths because they're easier and more well-known, but with practice, your new paths can become familiar and natural to walk along. Similarly, with regular practice, thinking and acting along the lines of your alternative beliefs can become stronger and more automatic, even when the going gets tough!

Thinking about what you'd teach a child

When you're challenging your negative core beliefs, try to think about what you'd tell a child. Act as your own parent by reinstructing yourself to endorse healthy ways of viewing others, yourself, and the world.

Ask yourself what types of belief you'd teach a child. Would you encourage him to grab hold of the negative core beliefs that you may hold about yourself, or would you want him to think of himself in a more positive and accepting way? Would you wish for him to think of other people as evil, mistrustful, danger-ous, and more powerful than himself? Or, would you rather he had a more balanced view of people, such as variable but basically okay, generally trust-worthy, and reliable? Would you want him to believe that he can stand up for himself?

Considering what you'd want a friend to believe

When challenging your core beliefs, think about having a friend like Mahesh, Beth, Rashid, Milo, or Sybil. What advice would you give them? Would you say 'Yes, Rashid, you're a failure'? 'I agree, Mahesh – life's against you'? 'Beth, you're bad'? 'Sybil, no one ever thought you were important anyway'?

Or, would you be quietly horrified to spout these unhealthy and damaging beliefs? We assume the latter.

If you wouldn't want your dear friends to believe such things, why believe them yourself? Talk to yourself like you would to your best friend when your negative core beliefs are activated.

Chapter 15

Moving New Beliefs from Your Head to Your Heart

In This Chapter

▶ Strengthening your new, helpful attitudes and beliefs

▶ Dealing with doubts about a new way of thinking

▶ Testing out your new ways of thinking in difficult situations

▶ Preparing for setbacks

After you've identified your unhelpful patterns of thinking and developed more helpful attitudes (refer to Chapters 2, 3, 12, and 14), you need to reinforce your new thoughts and beliefs. The process of reinforcing new beliefs is like trying to give up a bad habit and develop a good habit in its place. You need to work at making your new, healthy ways of thinking second nature, at the same time as eroding your old ways of thinking. This chapter describes some simple exercises to help you develop and nurture your new beliefs.

In many ways, *integrating* your new method of thinking with your mind, emotions, and actions is *the* critical process in CBT. A parrot can repeat rational philosophies, but the parrot doesn't understand or *believe* what it's saying. The real work in CBT is turning intellectual understanding into something you that know in your gut to be true.

Defining the Beliefs You Want to Strengthen

Many people who work at changing their attitudes and beliefs complain: 'I know what I *should* think, but I don't believe it!' When you begin to adopt a new way of thinking, you may *know* that something makes sense but you may not *feel* that the new belief is true.

When you're in a state of *cognitive dissonance* you know that your old way of thinking isn't 100 per cent right, but you aren't yet convinced of the alternative. Being in a state of cognitive dissonance can be uncomfortable because things don't feel quite right. However, this feeling is a good sign that things are changing.

In CBT, we often call this disconnection between thinking and truly believing the *head-to-heart problem*. Basically, you know that an argument is true in your head, but you don't feel it in your heart. For example, if you've spent many years believing that you're less worthy than others or that you need the approval of other people in order to approve of yourself, you may have great difficulty *internalising* (believing in your gut) an alternative belief. You may find that the idea that you have as much basic human worth as the next person, or that approval from others is a bonus but not a necessity, difficult to buy.

Your alternative beliefs are likely to be about three key areas:

✔ Yourself

✔ Other people

✔ The world

Alternative beliefs may take the following formats:

✔ A *flexible preference*, instead of a rigid demand or rule, such as 'I'd very much prefer to be loved by my parents, but there's no reason they absolutely *have* to love me.'

✔ An *alternative assumption*, which is basically an if/then statement, such as '*If* I don't get an A in my test, *then* that won't be the end of the world. I can still move on in my academic career.'

✔ A *global belief,* which expresses a positive healthy general truth, such as 'I'm basically okay' rather than 'I'm worthless', or 'The world's a place with some safe and some dangerous parts' instead of 'The world's a dangerous place'.

When you do experience the head-to-heart problem, we recommend acting *as if* you really do hold the new belief to be true – we explain how to do this in the following section.

One of your main aims in CBT, after you've developed a more helpful alternative belief, is to increase how strongly you endorse your new belief or raise your *strength of conviction* (SOC). You can rate how much you believe in an alternative healthy philosophy on a 0–100 percentage scale, 0 represents a total lack of conviction and 100 represents an absolute conviction.

Acting As If You Already Believe

You don't need to believe your new philosophy entirely in order to start changing your behaviour. Starting out, it's enough to *know* in your head that your new belief makes sense and then *act* according to your new belief or philosophy. If you consistently do the 'acting as if' technique, which we explain here, your conviction in your new way of thinking is likely to grow over time.

You can use the 'acting as if' technique to consolidate any new way of thinking, in pretty much any situation. Ask yourself the following questions:

- How would I behave if I truly considered my new belief to be true?

- How would I overcome situational challenges to my new belief if I truly considered it to be true and helpful?

- What sort of behaviour would I expect to see in other people who truly endorse this new belief?

You can make a list of your answers to the above questions and refer to it before, after, and even during an experience of using the 'acting as if' technique. For example, if you're dealing with social anxiety and trying to get to grips with self-acceptance beliefs, use the 'acting as if' techniques that follow, and ask yourself similar kinds of questions, such as:

- **Act consistently with the new belief:** If I truly believed that I was as worthy as anyone else, how would I behave in a social situation?

    Be specific about how you'd enter a room, the conversation you may initiate, and what your body language would be like.

- **Troubleshoot for challenges to your new belief:** If I truly believed that I was as worthy as anyone else, how would I react to any social hiccups?

    Again, be specific about how you may handle lulls in conversation and moments of social awkwardness.

- **Observe other people.** Does anyone else in the social situation seem to be acting as if they truly endorse the belief that I am trying to adopt?

    If so, note how the person acts and how they handle awkward silences and normal breaks in conversation. Imitate their behaviour.

When you act in accordance with a new way of thinking or a specific belief, you reinforce the truth of that belief. The more you experience a belief *in action*, the more you can appreciate its beneficial effects on your emotions. In essence, you are rewiring your brain to think in a more helpful and realistic way. Give this technique a try, even if you think that it's wishful thinking or seems silly. Actions do speak louder than words. So if a new belief makes sense to you, follow it up with action.

Building a Portfolio of Arguments

When an old belief rears its ugly head, try to have on hand some strong arguments to support your new belief. Your old beliefs or thinking habits have probably been with you a long time, and they can be tough to shift. You can expect to argue with yourself about the truth and benefit of your new thinking several times, before the new stuff well and truly replaces the old.

Your portfolio of arguments can consist of a collection of several arguments against your old way of thinking and several arguments in support of your new way of thinking. You can refer to your portfolio anytime that you feel conviction in your new belief is beginning to wane. The following sections help to guide you towards developing sound rationales in support of helpful beliefs and in contradiction of unhelpful beliefs.

Generating arguments against an unhelpful belief

To successfully combat unhealthy beliefs, try the following exercise. At the top of a sheet of paper, write down an old, unhelpful belief you want to weaken. For example, you may write: 'I have to get approval from significant others, such as my boss. Without approval, I'm worthless.' Then, consider the following questions to highlight the unhelpful nature of your belief:

✔ **Is the belief untrue or inconsistent with reality?** Try to find evidence that your belief isn't factually accurate (or at least not 100 per cent accurate for 100 per cent of all of the time). For example, you don't *have* to get approval from your boss: The universe permits otherwise, and you can survive without such approval. Furthermore, you cannot be defined as worthless on the strength of this experience, because you're much too complex to be defined.

Considering why a certain belief is *understandable* can help you to explain why you hold a particular belief to be true. For example, 'It's understandable that I think I'm stupid because my father often told me I was when I was young, but that was really due to his impatience and his own difficult childhood. So, it follows that I believe myself to be stupid because of my childhood experiences, and not because there is any real truth in the idea that I am stupid. Therefore, the belief that I am stupid is consistent with my upbringing but inconsistent with reality.'

✔ **Is the belief rigid?** Consider whether your belief is flexible enough to allow you to adapt to reality. For example, the idea that you *must* get approval or that you *need* approval in order to think well of yourself, is overly rigid. It is entirely possible that you will fail to get approval from significant others at some stage in your life. Unless you have a flexible belief about getting approval, you are destined to think badly of yourself whenever approval is not forthcoming. Replace the word *must* with *prefer* in this instance, and turn your demand for approval into a flexible preference for approval.

✔ **Is the belief extreme?** Consider whether your unhelpful belief is extreme. For example, equating being disliked by one person with worthlessness is an extreme conclusion. It is rather like concluding that being late for one appointment means that you will always be late for every appointment you have for the rest of your life. The conclusion that you draw from one or more experiences is far too extreme to accurately reflect reality.

✔ **Is the belief illogical?** Consider whether your belief actually makes sense. You may want approval from your boss, but logically she doesn't *have* to approve of you. Not getting approval from someone significant doesn't logically lead to you being less worthy. Rather, not getting approval shows that you've failed to get approval on this occasion, from this specific person.

✔ **Is the belief unhelpful?** Consider how your belief may or may not be helping you. For example, if you worry about whether your boss is approving of you, you'll probably be anxious at work much of the time. You may feel depressed if your boss treats you with indifference or visibly disapproves of your work. You're less likely to say no to unreasonable requests or to put your opinions forward. You may actually be less effective at work because you're so focused on making a good impression. You may even assume that your boss is disapproving of you when actually this isn't the case. So, is worrying about your boss's approval helpful? Clearly not!

Running through the preceding list of questions is definitely an exercise that involves putting pen to paper or fingertips to keyboard. Try to pick out your unhelpful beliefs and to formulate helpful alternatives, then generate as many watertight arguments against your old belief and in support of your new belief as you can. Try to fill up one side of A4 paper for each belief you target.

You can include in your portfolio evidence gathered from other CBT techniques you use to tackle your problems, such as ABC forms (Chapter 3) and behavioural experiments (Chapter 4). You can use any positive results observed from living according to new healthy beliefs as arguments to support the truth and benefits of these new beliefs.

Generating arguments to support your helpful alternative belief

The guidelines for generating sound arguments to support alternative, more helpful ways of thinking about yourself, other people, and the world, are similar to those suggested in the preceding section, 'Generating arguments against an unhelpful belief'.

On a sheet of paper, write down a helpful alternative belief that you want to use to replace a negative, unhealthy view you hold. For example, a helpful alternative belief regarding approval at work may be: 'I want approval from significant others, such as my boss, but I don't *need* it. If I don't get approval, I still have worth as a person.'

Next, develop arguments to support your alternative belief. Ask yourself the following questions to ensure that your helpful alternative belief is strong and effective:

- ✓ **Is the belief true and consistent with reality?** For example, you really can want approval and fail to get it sometimes. Just because you want something very much doesn't mean to say you'll get it. Lots of people don't get approval from their bosses, but it doesn't mean they're lesser people.

- ✓ **Is the belief flexible?** Consider whether your belief allows you to adapt to reality. For example, the idea that you *prefer* to get approval but that it isn't a dire necessity for either survival or self-esteem, allows for the possibility of not getting approval from time to time. You don't have to form any extreme conclusions about your overall worth in the face of occasions of disapproval.

- ✓ **Is the belief balanced?** Consider whether your helpful belief is balanced and non-extreme. For example, 'Not being liked by my boss is unfortunate but it's not proof of whether I'm worthwhile as a person.' This balanced and flexible belief recognises that disapproval from your boss is undesirable and may mean that you need to reassess your work performance. However, this recognition does not hurl you into depression based on the unbalanced belief that you're unworthy for failing to please your boss on this occasion.

- ✓ **Is the belief logical and sensible?** Show how your alternative belief follows logically from the facts, or from your preferences. It follows logically that your boss's disapproval about one aspect of your work is undesirable and may mean that you need to work harder or differently. It does not follow logically that because of his disapproval you are an overall bad or worthless person.

✓ **Is the belief helpful?** When you accept that you want approval from your boss but that you don't *have* to get it, you can be less anxious about the possibility of incurring your boss's disapproval or failing to make a particular impression. You also stand a better chance of making a good impression at work when you prefer, but are not desperate for, approval. You can be more focused on the job that you're doing and less preoccupied by what your boss may be thinking about you.

Imagine you're about to go into court to present to the jury arguments in defence of your new belief. Develop as many good arguments that support your new belief as you can. Most people find that listing lots of ways in which the new belief is helpful makes the most impact. Try to generate enough arguments to fill one side of A4 paper for each individual belief.

Review your rational portfolio regularly, not just when your unhealthy belief is triggered. Doing so helps you reaffirm your commitment to thinking in healthy ways.

Understanding That Practice Makes Imperfect

Despite your best efforts, you may continue to think in rigid and extreme ways and experience unhealthy emotions from time to time. Why? Well, – oh yes, we say it again – you're only human.

Practicing your new, healthy ways of thinking and putting them to regular use minimises your chances of relapse. However, you're never going to become a perfectly healthy thinker – human beings seem to have a tendency to develop thinking errors and you need a high degree of diligence to resist unhelpful and unhealthy thinking (refer to Chapter 2).

Be wary of having a perfectionist attitude about your thinking. You're setting yourself up to fail if you expect that you can always be healthy in thought, emotion, and behaviour. Give yourself permission to make mistakes with your new thinking, and use any setbacks as opportunities to discover more about your beliefs.

Dealing with your doubts and reservations

You must give full range to your scepticism when you're changing your beliefs. If you try to sweep your doubts under the carpet, those doubts can re-emerge when you least expect it – usually when you're in a stressful situation. Consider Sylvester's experience:

> Sylvester, or Sly for short, believes that other people must like him and goes out of his way to put people at ease in social situations. Sly takes great care to never hurt anyone's feelings and puts pressure on himself to be a good host. Not surprisingly, Sly's often worn out by his efforts. Because Sly's work involves managing other staff, he also feels anxious much of the time. Sly also worries about confrontation and what his staff members think of him when he disciplines them.
>
> After having some CBT, Sly concludes that his beliefs need to change if he's ever going to overcome his anxiety and feelings of panic at work. Sly formulates a healthy alternative belief: 'I want to be liked by others, but I don't always *have* to be liked. Being disliked is tolerable and doesn't mean I'm an unlikeable person.'
>
> Sly can see how this new belief makes good sense and can help him feel less anxious about confronting staff members or being not-so-super-entertaining in social situations. But deep inside, Sly feels stirrings of doubt. Still, Sly denies his reservations about the new belief and ignores niggling uncertainty. One day, when Sly's confronting a staff member about persistent lateness, his underlying doubts rear up. Sly resorts to his old belief because he hasn't dealt with his doubts effectively. Sly ends up letting his worker off the hook and feeling angry with himself for not dealing with the matter properly.

Had Sly faced up to his misgivings about allowing himself to be disliked, he may have given himself a chance to resolve his feeling. Sly may then have been more prepared to deal with the stressful situation without resorting to his old belief and avoidant behaviour.

Zigging and zagging through the zigzag technique

Use the zigzag technique to strengthen your belief in a new healthy alternative belief or attitude. The zigzag technique involves playing devil's advocate with yourself. The more you argue the case in favour of a healthy belief and challenge your own attacks on it, the more deeply you can come to believe in it. Figure 15-1 shows a completed zigzag form based on Sly's example.

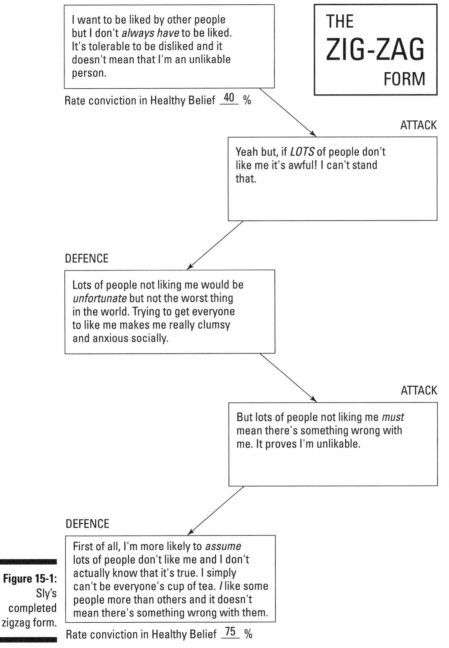

HEALTHY BELIEF

I want to be liked by other people but I don't *always have* to be liked. It's tolerable to be disliked and it doesn't mean that I'm an unlikable person.

Rate conviction in Healthy Belief __40__ %

THE
ZIG-ZAG
FORM

ATTACK

Yeah but, if *LOTS* of people don't like me it's awful! I can't stand that.

DEFENCE

Lots of people not liking me would be *unfortunate* but not the worst thing in the world. Trying to get everyone to like me makes me really clumsy and anxious socially.

ATTACK

But lots of people not liking me *must* mean there's something wrong with me. It proves I'm unlikable.

DEFENCE

First of all, I'm more likely to *assume* lots of people don't like me and I don't actually know that it's true. I simply can't be everyone's cup of tea. *I* like some people more than others and it doesn't mean there's something wrong with them.

Rate conviction in Healthy Belief __75__ %

Figure 15-1:
Sly's completed zigzag form.

You can find a blank zigzag form in Appendix B. To go through the zigzag technique, do the following steps:

1. **Write down in the top left-hand box of the zigzag form a belief that you want to strengthen.**

   On the form, rate how strongly you endorse this belief, from 0 to 100 per cent conviction.

   Be sure that the belief's consistent with reality or true, logical, and helpful to you. Refer to the section that covers generating arguments to support your helpful alternative beliefs, for more on testing your healthy belief.

2. **In the next box down, write your doubts, reservations, or challenges about the healthy belief.**

   Really let yourself attack the belief, using all the unhealthy arguments that come to mind.

3. **In the next box, dispute your attack and redefend the healthy belief.**

   Focus on defending the healthy belief. Don't become sidetracked by any points raised in your attack from Step 2.

4. **Repeat Steps 2 and 3 until you exhaust all your attacks on the healthy belief.**

   Be sure to use up all your doubts and reservations about choosing to really go for the new, healthy alternative way of thinking. Use as many forms as you need and be sure to stop on a defence of the belief you want to establish rather than on an attack.

5. **Re-rate, from 0 to 100 per cent, how strongly you endorse the healthy belief after going through all your doubts.**

If your conviction in the healthy belief hasn't increased or has increased only slightly, revisit the previous instructions on how to use the zigzag form. Or, if you have a CBT therapist, discuss the form with her and see whether she can spot where you zigged when you should have zagged.

Putting your new beliefs to the test

Doing pen-and-paper exercises is great – they really can help you to move your new beliefs from your head to your heart.

However, the best way to make your new ways of thinking more automatic is to put them to the test. Putting them to the test means going into familiar situations where your old attitudes are typically triggered, and acting according to your new way of thinking.

So, our friend Sly from earlier in the chapter may choose to do the following to test his new beliefs:

- ✔ Sly confronts his member of staff about her lateness in a forthright manner. Sly bears the discomfort of upsetting her and remembers that being disliked by one worker doesn't prove that he's an unlikeable person.

- ✔ Sly throws a party and resists the urge to make himself busy entertaining everyone and playing the host.

- ✔ Sly works less hard in work and social situations at putting everyone at ease and trying to be super-likeable mister nice guy.

If you're really, really serious about making your new beliefs stick, you can *seek out* situations in which to test them. On top of using your new beliefs and their knock-on new behaviours in everyday situations, try setting difficult tests for yourself. Sit down and think about it: If you were still operating under your old beliefs, what situations would really freak you out? Go there. Doing this will 'up the ante' with regard to endorsing your new beliefs.

Coping with everyday situations, such as Sly's previous example, is very useful, and they're often enough to move your new belief from your head to your heart. But if you really want to put your new beliefs under strain, with a view to making them even stronger, put yourself into out-of-the-ordinary situations. For example, try deliberately doing something ridiculous in public or being purposefully rude and aloof. See if you can remain resolute in your new belief such as 'disapproval does not mean unworthiness' in the face of your most feared outcomes. We think you can! This is a tried and tested CBT tool for overcoming all sorts of problems, such as social anxiety. (Refer to Chapter 12 for more guidance on developing *self-acceptance* and Chapter 22 for more on devising *shame attacking* exercises.)

Here are some tests that Sly (or we could now call him 'Braveheart') may set up for himself:

- ✔ Go into shops and deliberately be impolite by not saying 'thank you' and not smiling at the shop assistant. This test requires Sly to bear the discomfort of possibly leaving the shop assistant unhappy after making a poor impression.

- ✔ Say good morning to staff without smiling and allow them to form the impression that he was 'in a bad mood'.

- ✔ Mooch about, deliberately trying to look moody and aloof in a social setting.

- Make a complaint about faulty goods he's purchased from a local shop where the staff know him.

- Bump into someone on public transport and do not apologise.

You may think that Sly's setting himself up to be utterly friendless as a result of this wretched belief change lark. *Au contraire, nos chere!* Sly has friends. Sly still has a reputation of being a generally kind and affable bloke. What Sly doesn't have now is a debilitating belief that he has to please all the people all the time. Rather, Sly can come to truly believe that he can tolerate the discomfort of upsetting people occasionally and that being disliked by one or more people is part of being human. That's life. That's the way it goes sometimes. Sly can believe in his heart that he's a fallible human being, just like everyone else, that he's capable of being liked and disliked but basically he's okay.

Nurturing Your New Beliefs

As you continue to live with your alternative helpful beliefs, gather evidence that supports your new beliefs. Becoming more aware of evidence from yourself, other people, and the world around you that supports your new, more helpful way of thinking, is one of the keys to strengthening your beliefs and keeping them strong.

A *positive data log* helps you overcome the biased, prejudiced way in which you keep unhelpful beliefs well-fed, by soaking up evidence that fits with them and discounting or distorting evidence that doesn't fit. Using a positive data log boosts the available data that fit your new belief and helps you to retrain yourself to take in the positive.

Your positive data log is simply a record of positive results arising from acting in accordance with a healthy new belief and evidence that contradicts your old unhealthy belief. You can use any type of notebook to record your evidence. Follow these steps:

1. **Write your new belief at the top of a page.**

2. **Record any experiences that support your new belief.**

   Be specific and include even the smallest details that encourage you to doubt your old way of thinking. For example, even a newspaper vendor making small talk when you buy your paper can be used as evidence to support a belief that you are likeable.

3. **Record positive reactions that you get from others when you act in accordance with new beliefs.**

4. **Record evidence that your new belief is helpful to you; include changes in your emotions and behaviour.**

   Fill up the whole notebook if you can.

If you still have trouble believing that an old, unhelpful belief is true, start by collecting evidence on a daily basis that your old belief isn't 100 per cent true, 100 per cent all of the time. Collecting this sort of evidence can help you steadily erode how true the belief seems.

In your positive data log, you can list the benefits of operating under your new belief, including all the ways in which your fears about doing so have been disproved.

For example, Sly might record the following observations:

- His staff members still seem to generally like being managed by him, despite the fact that he disciplines them when needed.

- Being less gregarious at parties doesn't stop others from having a good time or from engaging with him.

- His anxiety and panic about the possibility of being disliked have reduced in response to his belief change.

Your positive data log can not only remind you of the good results you have reaped from changing your unhealthy beliefs to healthy ones, but also help you be *compassionate* with yourself when you relapse to your unhealthy beliefs and corresponding behaviours. Use your positive data log to chart your progress, so when you *do* fall back you can assure yourself that your setback need be only temporary. After all, practice makes imperfect.

Many people add to their positive data log for months or even years. Keeping the log provides them with a useful antidote to the natural tendency to be overly self-critical.

Be sure to refer to your positive data log often, even daily, or several times each day when you are bedding down new beliefs. Keep it in your desk or handbag or wherever you are most likely to be able to access it during the day. As a general rule, you can't look at your positive data log too often!

Chapter 16

Heading for a Healthier and Happier Life

. . . .

In This Chapter

▶ Discovering and choosing healthy activities

▶ Taking care of yourself, your life, and your relationships

▶ Communicating effectively

. . . .

*T*he way that you think influences the way that you feel and behave. How you behave also influences the way you end up feeling and thinking . . . and round and round the cycle goes.

So, how you *live* from day to day has an effect on your overall mood. In this chapter, we look at what makes a lifestyle *healthy*. Developing a healthy lifestyle can contribute enormously to keeping you in tiptop physical and psychological condition.

We use the term 'healthy' to mean looking after your physical self, which includes exercise, sleep, sex, your eating habits, and keeping your living envi-ronment a pleasant place to be. Psychological health overlaps with this and is about doing things that give you a sense of enjoyment and achievement, holding helpful and balanced attitudes toward life, and building satisfying relationships.

Make looking after yourself a priority rather than an afterthought. An ounce of prevention really is worth a pound of cure.

Planning to Prevent Relapse

Once you start to recover from your problems, your next step is to devise a plan to prevent a resurgence of symptoms – to ensure that you don't suffer a *relapse*. A relapse basically means that you return to your original state of mind. An important part of your relapse prevention plan is nurturing yourself and guarding against falling back into old, unhelpful lifestyle habits, such as working too late, eating unhealthily, drinking too much caffeine and alcohol, or isolating yourself. Chapter 18 deals with relapse prevention in depth. The following sections in this chapter provide some pointers on how you can make your life fuller and how to take care of yourself.

Filling In the Gaps

When you start to recover from some types of emotional problems, such as depression, anxiety, or obsessions, you may find that you have a considerable amount of spare time available to you, which previously your symptoms took up. Indeed, you may be astounded to find out just how much energy, attention, and time, common psychological difficulties can actually consume.

Finding constructive and enjoyable things to do to fill in the gaps where your symptoms once were is important. Keeping yourself occupied with pursuits that are meaningful to you gives you a sense of well-being and leaves less opportunity for your symptoms to re-emerge.

Choosing absorbing activities

Activities that you used to enjoy may take a back seat while you wrestle with your problems. However, maybe you can think of some new activities that interest you and that you may like to try. The following are a few pointers to help you generate ideas about what activities and hobbies you can begin building into your life:

- Make a list of things you used to do and would like to start doing again.

- Make a separate list of new activities that you'd like to try.

- Try to create a balance between activities that do and don't involve physical exercise.

- Include everyday activities like cooking, reading, DIY, and keeping up social contacts. These activities are often neglected when you're over-whelmed by symptoms.

- Choose to focus on around five activities to revive or pursue, depending on how full your life is with work and family commitments.

In case you're still at a loss as to what you want to do, here's some ideas – but remember that this list is by no means exhaustive: Antiques, art appreciation, astronomy, baking, chess, dance, drama, dressmaking, enamelling, fishing, football, gardening, golf, interior decorating, kick boxing, languages, motoring, painting, pets (get a kitty – Rhena's cat Jack has transformed her life!), quizzes, tennis, voluntary work, wine-tasting, writing . . .

Don't just think about it! Decide *when* you're going to begin doing your chosen activities. If you don't give yourself a concrete start date, forgetting about things or putting them off can be all too easy.

Matchmaking your pursuits

You know yourself better than anyone else, so you're the best person to judge which hobbies can bring you the most satisfaction. Try to match your recreational pursuits to your character. If you know that you love paying attention to detail, you may enjoy needlework or making jewellery. Extreme sports may appeal to you if you've always been good at physical activities and like adrenalin rushes. Conversely, if you've never been very musical, taking up an instrument may not be the best choice for you.

We recommend that you stretch yourself by trying things that you haven't done before. Who knows – you may end up really liking the new activities. However, if you choose pursuits that are too far removed from your fundamental personality or natural abilities, you might lose heart and abandon them.

Putting personal pampering into practice

Oh, the joys of a good massage, a hot foamy bath, or a trip to the opera (okay, we understand that not everyone feels the same about opera). You can't overcome your problems without a significant degree of personal effort. Congratulate yourself for your hard work, and treat yourself to a few nice things.

Take care of yourself on a day-to-day basis, and look out for times when you deserve a few extra special treats. Friday nights are a good time to regularly treat yourself after a long week at work.

Your treats don't have to be expensive. You can do many small things – such as putting some cut flowers in a vase, making your living space smell nice, playing pleasant music, watching a favourite film or television programme – which are free or inexpensive.

Consider pampering yourself as part of your *relapse-prevention plan* (see Chapter 18 for more on relapse prevention). Even doing little things like using nice bath oils or eating a special meal once a week can remind you to value yourself and to treat yourself with loving care.

Overhauling Your Lifestyle

We suggest that you take a close look at the way you currently live and decide on the things that are good, and the things that are not so good for you. Be sure to consider the following key areas:

- ✔ **Regular and healthy eating.** The principle is relatively simple: Have three meals and a couple of healthy snacks a day, with plenty of fruit, vegetables, and wholegrain foods. Minimise your consumption of sugar and simple carbohydrates, like white bread, and don't overdo the saturated fat. Have what you fancy in moderation. If you think you need extra help with healthy eating, talk to your doctor, who can refer you to a dietitian.

Try keeping a record of everything you eat, for a week. Identify where you can make positive changes towards eating more regularly and more healthily. If you find that your actions don't match with your good intentions, use the Tic-Toc technique (which we discuss in Chapter 17) to tackle the thoughts and attitudes that can get in the way of healthy eating.

- ✔ **Regular exercise.** Ample evidence suggests that exercise is very beneficial for both your mental health and your physical health. Aim for at least three sessions of physical exercise, lasting 20-30 minutes each, per week. Consult your doctor if you haven't exercised regularly for some time.

- ✔ **Leisure pursuits.** Include activities that bring you pleasure or satisfaction and aren't attached to your job or home life. Remind yourself of what you used to do and of what you've been meaning to do, when choosing activities and hobbies.

- ✔ **Social contact.** Get to know new people or reinvigorate your existing relationships. Sometimes relationships suffer as a result of psychological illness; read more about getting intimate further on in this chapter, which address issues of intimacy and communication.

- ✔ **Vitally-absorbing interests.** Get involved with causes you feel are important, such as recycling or animal rights campaigns.

- ✔ **Resource management.** This catch-all may involve you doing a budget, getting an accountant, developing a system to deal with your household bills efficiently, renegotiating your working hours, or hiring a cleaner.

Ideally, you can create a nice balance between the different aspects of your life so that none is neglected.

Look at the things you do on a daily or weekly basis, and decide what you're doing *too much of,* such as drinking in the pub, working late, or eating fast food. Try to replace some of these activities with others that you're doing too little of, such as getting exercise, spending time with your family, or studying.

Walking the walk

The best-laid plans of mice and men are apt to go astray. And how.

You're really serious about making positive changes to your lifestyle; however, just thinking about it and setting out plans aren't enough – although they *are* a great first step. The next step is to *do it*! Actions speak louder than words, so act on your intentions sooner, rather than later.

Keep your body moving

We cannot emphasise enough about the multiple benefits of you taking regular exercise. It's so darn good for you, in so darn many ways. If you don't believe us, try it out! Exercise a few times each week and see if you don't end up feeling better – we defy you to contradict us.

You can exercise in ways that don't involve going to the gym. Gardening, walking, cycling, dancing, and housework, all give your body a workout. Find out which activities suit you, your interests, your schedule, and your current level of fitness – *and do them!*

Be careful that you're exercising for the right reasons, such as to enjoy yourself, and to keep yourself physically and mentally healthy. Check that you're not exercising obsessively. The following are unhealthy motivations for taking exercise:

- ✔ **To keep your weight lower than is medically recommended.** People who suffer from eating disorders may often exercise fanatically.

- ✔ **To improve your looks if you are anxious about your appearance.** People with body dysmorphic disorder (BDD), sometimes use exercise to compensate for imagined defects in their physical appearance (Chapter 11 has more about this psychological problem).

- ✔ **To punish yourself.** People with feelings of shame and low self-worth may exercise to excess as a means of self-harming.

Ask your physician to work out your *body mass index* or 'BMI', which gives you a weight range that is normal for your age and height.

Using your head

Perhaps your emotional problems get in the way of your work or study. Maybe your difficulties interfer with you making progress in your career or changing jobs – after all, many people with psychological problems also experience work and education difficulties.

Start to set goals for how you'd like your work or academic life to develop. Build a realistic plan of action for reaching your professional or educational goals by following these steps:

1. **Start your plan by considering where you'd like to be and what you need to do in terms of study and training to get there.**

2. **Break your ultimate goal down into smaller bite-sized chunks.** You may need to gather references, build a portfolio, write a CV, or apply for a loan or grant to fund your studies.

3. **Investigate facilities for learning.** Use the Internet to look for specific courses, contact universities and colleges for a prospectus, see a careers advisor, or visit an employment agency.

4. **Build your study or training plan into your life with a view to keeping a balance between study, work, social, and leisure activities.**

5. **Set a realistic time frame to achieve your goal.** Pushing yourself to get there too fast is likely to cause you stress, impair your enjoyment of the journey to your goal, or even lead you to abandon your goal all together.

Go out and study just for the sake of it. Developing a new skill or exploring a new subject area can be highly rewarding for you, whether or not the studying is applicable directly to your work. Adult education classes and intensive workshops can be a great way for you to explore new topics – and for you to meet new people, which can be beneficial if your social life has suffered during your illness.

Getting involved

Think about the kind of world you want to live in and how you can contribute towards creating it. You can get involved with anti-litter campaigns, local building-restoration projects, charities, or whatever you feel is important. You can usually choose how much time to devote to these pursuits.

Becoming spiritual

Sometimes, people with specific disorders such as obsessive-compulsive disorder (OCD) or extreme guilt, can find that their religion or spiritual beliefs get mixed up with their problems. Re-establishing a healthy understanding of your faith can be an important aspect of your recovery. Resuming your usual manner of worship – be it mediation, attending mass or going to a synagogue – can help you to reintegrate with your religious beliefs or your community. You might also find that discussing your recent problems with a religious leader or a member of your congregation is helpful.

Talking the talk

Emotional problems can have a detrimental effect on your personal relationships. Sometimes, your symptoms can be so all-consuming that you have little space to show interest in what others around you are feeling and doing. Therefore, you may need to do some work to rebuild your existing relationships when you feel better.

When your symptoms subside, you may want to give more of your attention to the other people in your life. This may involve playing with your kids, talking to your partner about how your problems have affected your relationship (without blaming yourself, of course), or renewing contact with friends and extended family.

People in your life are likely to be aware of how troubled you've been and they may notice recent positive changes in you. Let them talk about the changes they've noticed within you. Listening to other people's experiences of your problems can help to reinforce the idea that the other people in your life care about you. Improving your relationships and simply spending time in the company of other people can help you keep your symptoms at bay. You can also involve others in your relapse-prevention plan, if appropriate.

A supportive relationship with a significant other can help you to stay healthy. This relationship doesn't need to be a romantic relationship – platonic relationships are important as well. Research has shown that having a network of social contacts, as well as having someone you're able to confide in, helps to reduce your emotional problems in general.

It's never too late for you to make friends. Even if your problems have led you to isolate yourself, now's the time to go out and meet people. Be patient and give yourself the time and opportunity to start forming good relationships. Go to where the people are! Join some clubs or classes.

Getting intimate

Your specific problems may lead you to avoid intimate relationships with other people. You may have been too preoccupied by your problems to be able to form or maintain intimate relationships. If you want to be close to others, you've got to get your head round the concept of letting others into your life. Allowing yourself to trust others enough to share at least some of your personal history can make you feel closer to your listeners. Intimacy is a give-and-take affair – ideally, the balance is roughly equal.

Six steps for talking and listening

Good relationships are sustained by thoughtfulness, effort, and time. Many of the changes in your relationships may occur naturally because as you become less preoccupied with your problems you are more able to focus on the world around you.

Effective communication is the cornerstone of good relationships. Bear in mind that you can communicate not only with what you say, but also with how you *listen*. Your body language can also convey a message to others. Things like eye contact and physical contact are also means of getting the message across. A simple hug can really mean a lot.

Try the following six steps to improve your communication skills:

1. When you have something important to discuss with someone, find a mutually good time to do so. Make sure that you both have ample time to talk and listen to each other.

2. Use 'I feel' statements, such as '*I feel* disappointed that you came home late', rather than blaming language, such as '*You* made me so angry'.

3. If you want to give negative feedback to someone about his behaviour, keep it clear, brief, and specific. Remember to also give positive feedback about the behaviour you want to reinforce, for example thank your partner for calling to say he'll be late.

4. After you've given positive or negative feedback, ask the person how he feels and what he thinks about what you've said.

5. Don't fall into the trap of thinking that a right or true way of doing things exists. Accept that different people value different things. Seek compromises when appropriate. Listen to the other person's point of view.

6. Be prepared to accept negative feedback and criticism from others. Look for points that you agree with in what the other person is saying. Give the other person a chance to air his views before you get defensive or counteractive. Give yourself time to assess the feedback you receive.

If you think you're incapable of getting truly close to someone else, you're probably wrong. Give other people – and yourself – a chance to be honest with one another. Reciprocally enhancing relationships usually evolve naturally, but you need to be open to the possibilities of intimate relationships for this evolution to happen.

Sex and other animals

Your interest in sex, regardless of your age or gender, may diminish as a result of your emotional disturbance. Many people dealing with emotional problems can lose interest in sex. When you begin to feel better, getting your sex life back on track may take some time.

Sex drive is a bit like appetite: You don't always realise you're hungry until you start eating.

Sometimes, couples stop having sex regularly but don't ever discuss the change. Often, both partners get into a routine of not being sexually intimate and try to ignore the problem. Some people are too shy to talk about sex or feel guilty for having lost their interest in sex. Additionally, many people are afraid of discussing their loss of sex drive with their doctors, or friends, for fear of embarrassment.

Taking the plunge and talking about changes in your sex drive with your therapist or doctor can be very worthwhile. Your therapist or doctor may offer you useful suggestions and may even tell you that certain medications you've been taking may contribute to your decreased interest in sex.

Loss of interest in sexual activities is a normal side effect of certain experiences. Many psychological disorders, such as depression, post-traumatic stress disorder, obsessional problems, health anxiety, postnatal depression, and low self-esteem, can impact on your ability to feel aroused. Bereavement, physical illness, and stress can also put your sexual desires on the backburner. Fortunately, decreased libido is often temporary.

Talking about sex

'Birds do it, bees do it, even educated fleas do it', but sometimes the issue of sex is like an elephant in a tutu doing the dance of the seven veils in the middle of your bedroom. Both you and your partner can end up studiously ignoring its presence, even though it's right there, begging for your attention.

If you can't bring yourself to broach the topic of sex with your partner as you begin to recover, you can do a few things to help rekindle the flames of desire. Try some of the following:

- **Resume non-sexual physical contact.** Hold hands, stroke your partner's arm or back as you chat, sit closer to each other on the sofa, and reintroduce cuddling. Non-sexual contact can help you to get comfortable with touching one another again, and set the scene for a revival of more intimate contact.

- **Kiss.** If you've got into the habit of a quick kiss on the cheek as you leave the house, aim for the mouth instead. Kissing is a powerful form of communication. It also can be highly sensual and enjoyable.

- **Create opportunities.** Getting into bed at the same time before you're both bone tired, and then snuggling up, can create a non-threatening reintroduction to sexual relations.

- ✔ **Take the pressure off.** If you tell yourself that you've *got* to get aroused or you've *got* to have sex tonight, you can work yourself into such a state that all spontaneity is quashed. Try to take the attitude that if it happens, it happens.

- ✔ **Give yourself a chance to get in the mood.** You don't have to feel very aroused to start getting intimate. Sometimes you may need to have a lot of low-level sexual contact like stroking, petting, and kissing before you're ready to go further. Be patient with yourself and try to talk to your partner about how you're feeling. Sometimes, just talking about sex is enough to relax you to let nature take its course.

- ✔ **Take the onus off orgasm.** Any sexual or close physical contact can be fulfilling. You may not be able to achieve orgasm for some time, so instead enjoy foreplay like you may have done in the early stages of your relationship. You can really get your sex life back on track, and you may even be able to make it better than it was before, if you give a lot of attention to the preliminaries.

Whatever turns you on is worth exploring further. Talk to your partner: You may be able to find things that can help you both get more in the mood for lovemaking. Try to be open-minded about your sex life. Just be careful to set your own personal boundaries about what turns you on and what has the opposite effect.

Chapter 17

Overcoming Obstacles to Progress

· ·

In This Chapter

▶ Getting to know the feelings that bind you

▶ Taking a progressive attitude

▶ Avoiding getting stuck on the road to recovery

· ·

*H*uman beings have a keen way of blocking their progress and sabotaging their goals. Maybe you get in the way of your progress without even being aware that you're doing it. Or perhaps you're conscious that you're sabotaging yourself with faulty thinking. Whatever the case, this chapter explores common obstacles that get in the way of positive change, and suggests some tips for overcoming blocks to progress.

Tackling Emotions That Get in the Way of Change

As if having an emotional problem isn't enough, you may be giving yourself an extra helping of discomfort and distress by some of the meanings you attach to your original problems. Some of the feelings that you may experience about your primary emotional problems, such as shame, guilt, or even pride, can result in *progress paralysis*.

Shifting shame

When people feel ashamed of their problems, they usually believe that their symptoms are a sign that they're weak, flawed, or defective. If you feel ashamed, you're less likely to seek help, because you worry that other people may judge you harshly for having a psychological problem, such as depression, or perhaps they may think that you're silly for having other types of problems, such as anxiety or social phobia. You may worry that anyone you tell about your problem will be horrified by some of your thoughts or actions, and reject you. If you suffer with obsessive-compulsive disorder

(OCD), a disorder typified by unpleasant and unwelcome thoughts or ideas, you may worry that other people won't understand you. People with OCD frequently assume that no one else in the world experiences the kind of upsetting thoughts that they do. In fact, everyone has intrusive and upsetting thoughts from time to time. In Chapter 11, we talk about some of the intrusive thoughts that are common in OCD.

You may be too ashamed to even admit to yourself that you have a problem. Blaming the problem on external events or other people is often a result of shame. Shame is really corrosive to change because it can have the following effects:

- ✔ Shame can make you isolate yourself, which can lower your mood even further.

- ✔ Shame can lead you to deny the problem. And you can't work on problem-solving if you're unwilling to acknowledge that the problem exists in the first place.

- ✔ Shame can result in you blaming other people and events for your problems, robbing you of your personal power for change.

- ✔ Shame can make you overestimate your symptoms as 'abnormal', 'weird', or 'unacceptable'.

- ✔ Shame can lead you to overestimate the harsh degree by which others judge you for having the problem.

- ✔ Shame can stop you from seeking out more information that can help to make you realise that your problem isn't so unusual.

- ✔ Shame can prevent you from getting appropriate psychological help, or the right medication.

Fight back against shame by refusing to hide your problems from yourself. Seek out information to make some of your experiences seem more normal. Practise self-acceptance beliefs like the ones we outline in Chapter 12. Take responsibility for overcoming your emotional problems – but resist blaming yourself for your symptoms.

Getting rid of guilt

Guilt is an unhealthy negative emotion that's particularly notorious for blocking positive change. You may be telling yourself guilt-provoking things like the following:

- ✔ 'I'm causing my family a lot of bother through my problems.'

- ✔ 'Other people in the world are so much worse off than me. I've no right to feel depressed.'

- ✔ 'I should be more productive. Instead, I'm just a waste of space.'

Guilt sabotages your chances of taking positive action. Guilty thoughts, such as the preceding examples, can lead you to put yourself down further, thereby making yourself more depressed. Your depression leads you to see the future as hopeless and saps your motivation. (Have a peek at Chapter 6 for more information about unhealthy negative emotions and how they work against you.)

Even if the thoughts that are making you feel guilty about your depression, anxiety, or other emotional problem hold some truth, try to accept yourself as someone who's *unwell*. For example, your diminished ability to be productive is a side effect of depression, not an indication that you're a bad or selfish person.

Shame and guilt grow in the dark. Hiding your problems, and your feelings *about* your problems, from other people tends to make things worse over time. Talking about your obsessions, depression, addiction, or other problems gives you the chance to share your fears and discomfort with someone else, who may be far more understanding than you imagine.

Putting aside pride

Having too much pride can get in the way of your progress. Sometimes, pride is a sort of compensatory strategy for feelings of shame. Your pride may protect you from the shame that you think you'd experience if you were to accept that the methods you've used thus far to overcome your problems have been less than ideal. The following are common pride-based attitudes that may be stopping you from making positive changes:

- ✔ **'It's absurd to say that I can help myself – if I could make myself better, I'd have done it ages ago!'** Actually, people very rarely know how best to help themselves out of emotional problems. Often, you need to read some self-help books or have techniques explained to you before you really understand how to implement specific techniques, and why these methods work.

- ✔ **'I'm an intelligent person and I should be able work out this stuff on my own!'** Maybe you *can* work out how to help yourself overcome emotional problems without any help whatsoever. But remember: Even the most intelligent people need to see specialists for advice from time to time. For example, you may be very bright but you still need to take your car to a mechanic to be fixed.

- ✔ **'I like to think of myself as strong. Admitting to having these problems shows me up as weak.'** Getting a bout of 'flu doesn't make you a weak person – and neither does a bout of depression or anxiety. For example, refusing to seek medical treatment for an infected wound is foolish, not an example of strength.

Book now to avoid disappointment

Many people with emotional problems wait months or even years before sharing their problems with anyone else. For example, people with OCD put up with their symptoms for an average of ten years before they seek professional help – they may even keep their problems secret from their friends and family. People with depression and other anxiety problems can also wait for months or years before talking about their problems with another person.

The most common reason for keeping problems under wraps is shame. Thinking that you need to keep problems a secret is quite tragic, because you end up suffering in silence needlessly. You can refer to the list of professional resources we supply in Appendix A. Exploring your options *now* can assure you that your symptoms are common and that you have nothing to be ashamed of. Get yourself on the road to recovery now to avoid feeling disappointed that you didn't get help sooner, and you can start to begin reclaiming enjoyment from life.

Swallow your pride and be ready to seek advice and help. Recognising and accepting that you have a problem and that you need to get guidance on how to deal with it, takes strength, not weakness.

Seeking support

After you begin to get over your shame, guilt, and pride, you can start to look for help in earnest. The help you seek may take the form of reading a self-help book like this one, approaching a therapist, talking things over with a friend (who could even support you using this book), or looking through some online resources. Some people find that self-help techniques are enough. But if you think you need more support, be sure to get help sooner rather than later. Putting off seeking professional help when you need it only prolongs your discomfort. Don't wait until your problem has advanced to the stage where your relationships, employment situation, or daily functioning are suffering, before you take positive action. (In Chapter 19, we explain how to seek professional help.)

Trying a little tenderness

Shame and guilt involve kicking yourself – and really putting the boot in – when you're already feeling down. Kicking someone in an attempt to get them back on their feet just doesn't make sense.

You haven't *chosen* your problems, although you may accept that you're stuck in a pattern that's making your problems worse. Take other contributing factors into account when you think about how your problems may have started.

You can take responsibility for overcoming your emotional disturbances and you can be compassionate with yourself in the process. Being kind to yourself when you're working hard to get better makes sense, particularly if you consider that a lot of the work involves making yourself uncomfortable in the short term. Surely you deserve to give yourself a little encouragement during exposures and behavioural experiments, rather than piling on the self-criticism.

Try being your own best friend instead of your own worst critic for a while, and see whether this helps you to make some positive strides. (Have a look at Chapter 12 for more tips on how to treat yourself with compassion.)

Adopting Positive Principles That Promote Progress

Some of the attitudes you hold probably aren't going to do you any favours as you try to overcome your emotional problems. Fortunately, you can swap your unhelpful attitudes for alternative beliefs that can give you a leg-up on the ladder to better emotional health.

Understanding that simple doesn't mean easy

Most of the steps to overcoming psychological problems with CBT are relatively simple. CBT isn't rocket science – in fact, many of the principles and recommendations may seem like common sense. However, CBT may be sense, but it ain't that common – if it was, fewer people would be suffering with emotional problems.

Even if CBT is as simple as ABC, the actual application of CBT principles is far from easy. Using CBT to help yourself requires a lot of personal *effort*, *diligence*, *repetition* and *determination*.

Because CBT seems so simple, some people get frustrated when they discover that they're not getting well fast or easily enough for their liking. If you want to make CBT work for *you*, take the attitude that getting better doesn't have to be easy. Your health is worth working for.

Being optimistic about getting better

One of the biggest blocks that prevent you from getting better is when you refuse to believe that change is possible. Be on the lookout for negative predictions that you may be making about your ability to get better. Challenge any thoughts you have, like the following:

- ✔ 'Other people get better, but they're not as messed up as me.'
- ✔ 'I'll never change – I've been like this for too long.'
- ✔ 'This CBT stuff will never work for someone as useless as me.'

If these thoughts sound familiar, check out the section that covers how to try to be a little kinder to yourself earlier in this chapter. Would you encourage a friend to believe such thoughts, or would you urge your friend to challenge their thinking? Try to give yourself the kind of good advice that you'd give another person with your type of problem.

Look for evidence that you *can* make changes. Remind yourself of other things you've done in the past that were difficult and required lots of your effort to overcome. If you don't give a new treatment method a fair shot, then how can you possibly *know* it can't work?

Staying focused on your goals

If you want to continue making healthy progress, occasionally you need to renew your commitment to your goals. You may find that you stop dead in your tracks because you've forgotten what the point is. Or perhaps you find yourself feeling ambivalent about getting over your problems. After all, staying anxious, depressed, or angry may seem easier than changing.

Remind yourself regularly of your goals and the benefits of striving to achieve these goals. You can sse the cost–benefit analysis (CBA) form to reaffirm the benefits of making goal-directed changes. In Chapter 8, we describe the CBA form and give you some more information about setting goals. Turn to Appendix B for a blank version of the CBA form.

Always try to set goals that are within your grasp, and you can establish shorter-term goals along the way. For example, if your goal is to move from being largely housebound to being able to travel freely, set a goal of being able to go to a particular shop to buy something specific. You can then concentrate on the steps needed to reach that particular smaller goal, before moving on to tackle larger goals.

Persevering and repeating

We often hear people say that they tried a technique or experiment once but that it didn't make them feel better. The reason for this lack of success is that once is very rarely enough. When you work at changing ingrained patterns of thinking and behaving, you're likely to have to try out new alternatives many times before you appreciate any beneficial change. You need to give yourself plenty of opportunity to get used to the new thought or behaviour. Also, you can expect new ways of thinking and behaving to feel very unnatural at first.

Think of your core beliefs and old ways of behaving as automatic responses, just like using your right hand to shave. If you break your right arm, and are unable to use it for a while, you have to use your left hand to shave. Imagine that your new healthy beliefs and behaviours are represented by your left hand. Each time you go to use your new beliefs, they feel awkward and don't seem to work very well. Every morning when you reach for the razor with your broken right arm, you have to remind yourself to struggle with using your left arm instead. You nick yourself shaving and miss a few places. However, over time you get better and better at using your left hand to shave, until one day your automatic response is to reach for the razor with your left hand.

People can retrain themselves into using new patterns of behaviour all the time. Think about people who are giving up smoking or changing their diets. Even moving house and altering your route to work are examples of behavioural retraining. You can retrain your thinking as well as your behaviour – perseverance and repetition apply to both.

Tackling Task-Interfering Thoughts

The 'Tic-Toc' technique is a simple yet effective way of unblocking obstacles to change. The technique gives you a helping hand toward achieving your goals.

TICs are *task interfering cognitions*, the thoughts, attitudes, and beliefs that get in the way of your progress. You need to respond with *TOCs – task orienting cognitions*, which are constructive alternatives to TICs. The list of unhelpful attitudes (sand traps) in the nearby sidebar is helpful for getting some ideas about task interfering cognitions.

Fill out the Tic-Toc sheet by following these steps:

1. **Identify the goal or task you want to focus on.**

2. **In the left column (TICs), list your thoughts, attitudes, and beliefs that get in the way of you achieving your aim.**

3. **In the right column (TOCs) put responses to each of your TICs that will help you achieve your goal or task.**

You can find a blank Tic-Toc form in Appendix B. Use it whenever you notice that you are not pursuing a goal or carrying out a self-helping task. Table 17-1 is an example of a Tic-Toc sheet.

Table 17-1	Example of a Tic-Toc Sheet

Goal or task: Setting time aside and filling out my university application forms.

Task Interfering Cognitions (TICs)	*Task Orienting Cognitions (TOCs)*
1. If I start I'll get too stressed.	1. Doing this is a hassle, but if I take it a step at a time I'll cope.
2. It's too complicated; I'm bound to get it wrong.	2. If I read the guide carefully I'll probably do a good enough job.
3. I'm bound to be rejected.	3. I've got a good chance and I'll really regret it if I miss the deadline.
4. There's no point in trying, I always end up putting it off.	4. I have put it off but it's not inevitable that I'll keep doing it, especially if I start now!

Sidestepping sand traps

Along the path to better mental health, you're sure to encounter obstacles. The following are popular reasons for abandoning your goals or not getting started with pursuing goals in the first place.

✔ **Fearing change.** Despite feeling really miserable, you may be afraid of what'll happen if you take steps to change. You may have been depressed or anxious for so long that you can't really imagine doing anything else. Perhaps some of the people in your life are helping you to live with your problems, and you fear that by getting better you may lose those people. However, getting yourself well gives you a chance to build more fulfilling relationships and to develop your independence.

✔ **Having low-frustration tolerance.** When the going gets tough, the tough go home to bed, right? No! You may be tempted to go to bed, but you just wake up every morning with the same old problems. The only way to increase your tolerance to frustration in all its forms is to grit your teeth and stick with it. However uncomfortable you may be while working on changing yourself, the effort is almost certainly a lot less painful than staying unwell for the rest of your life.

✔ **Being passive.** Maybe if you wait long enough, someone else will get better for you! Perhaps a miracle will happen to change your life, or a magic button will appear for you to push! Hey presto! – and you're fixed. Maybe, but don't hold your breath waiting. Take responsibility for doing the work needed to get you feeling better.

✔ **Having a fear of being bossed around.** Some people have a very strong sense of autonomy and they can be sensitive to other people trying to influence or coerce them. If you're one of these people, you may think that your therapist, or somebody close to you, is trying to take over when they suggest you try new strategies. Try to be open-minded to what professionals and people who care about you suggest. Deciding to give someone else's ideas a try is up to you. No one else can really control you or your decisions.

✔ **Being fatalistic.** Perhaps your motto is 'This is the way I am and how I'm destined to be for all time.' Being convinced that your moods are governed by forces beyond your control, such as chemicals, hormones, biology, the past, fate, or God, means that you're prone to surrender yourself to your symptoms. Why not put your theories to the test by making a real effort to rewrite your supposed destiny? You never know: Your original assumptions may be wrong!

✔ **Love is the drug that I'm thinking of . . .** You may be convinced that love is the only true path to happiness. You may be unable to imagine that you can have a satisfying life by learning to cope with your problems on your own. You may think that you will remain unhappy and emotionally disturbed until your special someone rides in on a steed to rescue you from this crazy mixed up world. Love is a real bonus to human existence, make no mistake. However, the healthiest relationships are those where both parties are self-sufficient and enjoy the companionship of one another without being overly dependant.

✔ **Waiting to feel motivated.** A lot of people make the mistake of waiting to feel like doing something before they get started. The problem with waiting for inspiration, or motivation, is that you may hang about for far too long. Often, action precedes motivation. When overcoming emotional disturbance, you often need to do an experiment (check out Chapter 4) or you can stick to an activity schedule (in Chapter 10), even when doing so is the last thing that you feel like doing. Positive action is the best remedy for overcoming the feelings of being lethargic and hopeless.

Chapter 18

Psychological Gardening: Maintaining Your CBT Gains

In This Chapter

▶ Taking care of the fruits of your hard work

▶ Avoiding potential relapse and overcoming actual relapse

▶ Sowing the seeds of love (and compassion)

*L*ooking after the positive changes you've made is a major part of helping you stay emotionally healthy. You can nurture your belief and behaviour changes everyday. The process is a bit like watering a plant to keep it thriving. The more care you take of yourself both generally and specifically – for example, by practising your new ways of thinking and acting – the more you reduce the chances of returning to your old problematic ways.

This chapter provides tips and advice that can help you avoid relapses and manage setbacks if they do occur.

Knowing Your Weeds from Your Flowers

Think of your life as a garden. Unhealthy, rigid ways of thinking and corresponding behaviours like avoidance, rituals, safety strategies, perfectionism, and trying too hard to please (to name but a few) are the weeds in your garden. The flowers consist of your healthy flexible thinking, such as acceptance of self and others, acceptance of uncertainty, and allowing yourself to be fallible, and your healthy behaviours, such as assertion, communication, problem-solving, and exposure (refer to Chapters 4 and 11 for more about exposure and response prevention).

No garden's ever weed-free. Planting desirable plants isn't enough. You need to continuously water and feed the flowers, and uproot the weeds to keep your garden healthy. If you tend your garden regularly, the weeds don't get a chance to take hold because there you are with your trowel, digging 'em out at the first sign of sprouting. Depending on the virulence of your weeds, you may need to use some weedkiller from time to time in the form of appropriately prescribed medication. So, *know thy garden*.

After you've identified your unhealthy behaviours and thinking tendencies, and bedded down some healthy alternatives, you can keep a better look out for emerging weeds and keep an eye on the health of your flowers.

Ask yourself the following questions, which can help you to know your weeds from your flowers:

- **What areas do I most need to keep working at in order to maintain my CBT gains?** The areas you identify are those where weeds are most likely to first take root.

- **What CBT strategies aid me most in overcoming my emotional problems?** Think about the new attitudes you've adopted towards yourself, the world, and other people. These areas are your tender, new flowers – their delicate shoots need your attention.

- **What are the most useful techniques that I've applied to overcoming my emotional problems?** Think about the new ways of behaving that you've adopted (daffodils) and the old ways of behaving that you've dropped (thistles). Stick to your new healthy behaviours and be aware of slipping back into your former unhealthy patterns of behaviour. Use an activity schedule to help you carry out beneficial routines and behaviours (jump to Chapter 10 for more about activity scheduling).

Write down the answers to the preceding questions so that you can look at them often to remind yourself of where to put in the hoe.

Working on Weeds

This section deals with weed-related topics and offers you some suggestions on how to stop weeds from taking over your garden, anticipating where weeds are likely to grow, and how to manage the weeds that keep coming back.

Nipping weeds in the bud

Out of the corner of your eye, you see a weed sticking up its insidious little head. You may be tempted to ignore the weed. Maybe it'll go away or whither and die on its own. Unfortunately, weeds seldom eliminate themselves. Assume that any weed you identify needs killing.

A common reason for ignoring resurging problems is shame (which we talk about in Chapter 17). If you feel ashamed that your problems are recurring, you may try to deny the problems, and you may avoid seeking help from professionals or support from friends, or family. You may be less likely to make a personal effort to whack down the problems in the way you did the first time.

Setbacks are a normal part of development. Human beings have emotional and psychological problems just as readily as physical problems. You don't have to be ashamed of your psychological problems, any more than you should be ashamed of an allergy or a heart condition.

Another common reason for people ignoring the reappearance of psychological problems is *catastrophising* or assuming the worst (head to Chapter 2 for more info on thinking errors). Many people jump to the conclusion that a setback equals a return to square one – but this certainly doesn't have to be the case. You can take the view that a problem you conquered once is at a fundamental disadvantage when it tries to take hold again. This is because you know your enemy. Use what you already know about recognising and arresting your old thinking and behaviour to help you pluck that weed before it gets too far above the ground.

Some emotional and psychological problems are more tenacious than others, for example bipolar disorder, obsessive-compulsive disorder (OCD), and eating disorders. Just because a problem's tenacious, it doesn't mean that it has to take over your life, or even cause you too much interference in your life. However, you can expect to meet tenacious problems again. Keep up with treatment strategies even when your original problems are no longer in evidence; doing so will help prevent a relapse.

For example, if you have a history of depression, you may notice that weeds are popping up when you do some of the following:

- ✔ Begin to think in a pessimistic way about your future and your ability to cope with daily hassles.
- ✔ Ruminate on past failures and on how poor your mood is.
- ✔ Lose interest in seeing your family and friends.
- ✔ Have difficulty getting out of bed in the morning, and you want to sleep more during the day instead of doing chores or taking exercise.

If you spot these stinging nettles making their way into your otherwise floral existence, try some of these techniques:

- ✔ Challenge your pessimistic thinking bias, and remind yourself that your thoughts are not accurate descriptions of reality but symptoms of your depression. (See Chapter 2 for more on thinking errors.)

✔ Interrupt the rumination process by using task-concentration and mind-fulness techniques. (We explain these in Chapter 5.)

✔ Continue to meet with family and friends, despite your decreased interest, on the basis that doing so makes you feel better rather than worse.

✔ Force yourself out of bed in the morning and keep an activity schedule. (Have a read of Chapter 10 for more on activity schedules.)

Whatever your specific problems, follow the preceding example: Write down your descriptions of anticipated weeds and some specific weed-killing solutions to have at hand.

Don't ignore signs that your problems are trying to get their roots down. Be vigilant. But also be confident in your ability to use the strategies that worked before and in your ability to use them time and again, whenever you need to.

Spotting where weeds may grow

To prevent relapse, become aware of where your weeds are most likely to take root.

Most people, regardless of their specific psychological problems, find themselves most vulnerable to setbacks when they're run down or under stress. If you're overtired and under a lot of environmental stress, such as with work deadlines, financial worries, bereavement, or family/relationship difficulties, you can tend to be more prone to physical maladies, such as colds, 'flu, and episodes of eczema. Psychological problems are no different from physical ones in this regard: They get you when you're depleted and at alow ebb.

You may notice that some problems, like OCD, anxiety, and depression, are more evident when you're recovering from a physical illness. Recognising this common human experience can help you to combat any shame that you may feel, and to de-catastrophise a return of your symptoms.

Compile a list of situations and environmental factors that are likely to give your weeds scope to take on triffid-like power. For example, you may be able to pinpoint *environment triggers* for your depression, such as the following:

✔ Seasonal change, especially during autumn, when the days get shorter and the weather becomes colder.

✔ Sleep deprivation, due to work commitments, young children, illness or any other reason.

✔ Lack of exercise and physical activity.

> ✔ Day-to-day hassles piling up at once, such as the boiler breaking down in the same week that the washing machine explodes and a few extra bills arrive.
>
> ✔ Reduced opportunity for positive social interaction with friends and family.

You can also identify *interpersonal* triggers for your depression, such as the following:

> ✔ Tired and tetchy partner.
>
> ✔ Disagreements with your partner, children, parents, or extended family.
>
> ✔ Critical or demanding boss.
>
> ✔ Disagreeable work colleagues.

Compile a list of high-risk situations for yourself, including situations that are most likely to fire up your unhealthy core beliefs (we explain core beliefs in Chapter 13), and situations that put you under strain. Creating such a list helps you to keep a clear idea of when you're most vulnerable to relapse and identify which psychological soil is the most fertile for weed growth.

Dealing with recurrent weeds

Some weeds just seem to keep coming back. You may think you're rid of them, only to open your garden door to a scene from *Little Shop of Horrors* ('Feed me, Seymour!').

Some unhealthy beliefs are harder to erode than others. *Core beliefs* (refer to Chapter 13) are those that typically you've held to be true for a very long time – most of your life even. These beliefs will keep trying to take root and may be particularly resistant to your attempts to kill them off.

The best way to deal with these recurrent weeds is to not become complacent. Keep reinforcing your alternative beliefs. Keep up with activities that fill the gaps left by your addictions or preoccupation with food. Keep doing exposure and response-prevention activities (refer to Chapter 11) to combat your OCD. Trust that over time and with persistence, your new ways of thinking and acting will get stronger.

Are you unwittingly feeding your weeds? Avoidance is a major weed fertiliser. You may have developed a healthy belief, such as 'I want to be liked by people, but I don't have to be. Not being liked by some people doesn't mean that I'm unlikeable.' And yet, if you still avoid social situations, self-expression, and confrontation, you're giving your old belief that 'I must be liked by everyone or it means that I am an unlikeable person!', the opportunity to germinate.

Check out your reasons for avoiding certain situations and experiences. Are you not going to a party because you don't want to, or because you want to avoid the possibility of others judging you negatively in some way? Are you not visiting a farm because it doesn't interest you, or because you want to avoid contamination from pesticides?

When you spot a recurrent, mulish weed in your garden, dig it out from the root. You can kill off weeds entirely by getting the roots, *and* the shoots, out of the soil. Try not to make half-hearted efforts at challenging your faulty thinking. Dispute your thinking errors (Chapter 2) and push yourself back into challenging situations using your healthy coping strategies (we cover thinking errors in Chapter 2, and we talk about coping strategies in Chapters 4, 11, and 13.)

Tending Your Flowers

Knowing when you're most prone to the symptoms of your original problems re-sprouting, is one thing. But knowing how to troubleshoot problems and prevent weeds from growing back, is another thing altogether.

The techniques, behavioural exercises, and experiments that helped you to overcome your problems in the first place will probably work again. So, go back to basics. Keep challenging your negative thinking and thinking errors. Keep exposing yourself to your feared situations. If your life is in turmoil due to inevitable things like moving house, work difficulties, or ill health, try to keep to your normal routine as much as possible.

Above all, even when things are going well, water your pansies! *Psychological watering* involves keeping up with your new ways of thinking and behaving, by giving yourself plenty of opportunity to consistently practice and test your new ways of living. As we mention in Chapter 13, Healthy, alternative beliefs take time to become habitual (refer to Chapter 13). Be patient with yourself and keep doing healthy things, even when you're symptom-free.

Developing a plan for times of crisis is another good idea. Here are some examples of what you may wish to include in your plan in the event of a potential relapse:

✔ Consider seeing your GP or psychiatrist to determine whether you need to go on medication for a while.

✔ Talk about your feelings to someone you trust. Pick a person who you can rely on to be supportive. Seek the help of a professional if talking to a friend or family member is not enough.

✔ Review your efforts from previous CBT work and re-use the exercises that were most effective.

✔ Keep your lifestyle healthy and active.

Planting new varieties

Digging out a weed (unhealthy belief and behaviour) is important, but you also need to plant a flower (healthy belief and behaviour) in its place. For example, if you notice that an old belief like 'I have to get my boss's approval, otherwise it proves that I'm unworthy' resurging, dispute the belief with arguments about the logic, helpfulness, and truth of the belief. (Chapter 13 has more about disputing unhealthy beliefs.)

You also need to plant a healthy belief, such as 'I want my boss's approval, but I don't have to get approval in order to be a worthwhile person'. You can strengthen the new belief by gathering arguments for the logic, helpfulness, and truth of the alternative healthy belief.

To strengthen new beliefs and behaviours further, you can devise situations that you know are likely to trigger your old unhealthy beliefs, and work at endorsing and acting according to your new beliefs instead. For example, deliberately seek your boss's feedback on a piece of work that you know is not your best. Resist your old behaviours that arise from the unhealthy belief that 'I must get my boss's approval', such as over-apologising or making excuses. Instead accept yourself for producing a less than good piece of work and take note of constructive criticism (refer to Chapter 12 for more about self-acceptance, and head to Chapter 15 for more techniques to strengthen new beliefs).

You can dig out unhealthy behavioural weeds and plant behavioural flowers in their place. For example, you may note that you drink more alcohol in the evenings as your mood lowers with the shortening days. You know that the onset of winter gets you down because you spend more time in the house. You can make the choice to stop drinking more than one glass of wine in the evening and start going to a local dance class or some other activity instead. You can also make a list of activities to do indoors, which will keep you occupied during the winter evenings.

A happy gardener's checklist

Here are some points to help you prevent and overcome relapse. Use this checklist to stop your marigolds getting choked by bindweed.

✔ **Stay calm.** Remember that setbacks are normal. Everyone has ups and downs.

✔ **Make use of setbacks.** Your setbacks can show you the things that make you feel worse as well as what you can do to improve your situation. Look for preventive measures that you may have used to get better, but that you may have let slide when your symptoms reduced.

✔ **Identify triggers.** A setback can give you extra information about your vulnerable areas. Use this information to plan how to deal with predictable setbacks in the future.

✔ **Use what you have learned from CBT.** Sometimes you think that a setback means that you're never going to get fully well, or that CBT hasn't worked for you. But if the stuff you did worked once, then chances are, the same stuff can work again. Stick with it; you've nothing to lose by trying.

✔ **Put things into perspective.** Unfortunately, the more you've improved your emotional health, the worse black patches will seem in contrast. Review your improvement and try to see this contrast in a positive way – as evidence of how far you've come.

✔ **Be compassionate with yourself.** People often get down on themselves about setbacks. No one is to blame. You can help yourself get back on track by seeing a setback as a problem to overcome, rather than a stick with which to beat yourself.

✔ **Remember your gains.** Nothing can take your gains away from you. Even if your gains seem to have vanished, they can come back. You can take action to make this happen more quickly.

✔ **Face your fears.** Don't let yourself avoid whatever triggered your setback. You can devise further exposure exercises (refer to Chapters 11 and 15) to help you deal with the trigger more effectively next time it happens.

✔ **Set realistic goals.** Occasionally, you may experience a setback because you bite off more than you can chew. Keep your exercises challenging but not overwhelming. Break bigger goals into smaller, mini-goals.

✔ **Hang on!** Even if you aren't able to get over a setback immediately, don't give up hope. With time and effort, you can come out of the setback. Don't hesitate to get appropriate support from friends and professionals if you think you need to. Remind yourself of times in the past when you felt as despairing and hopeless as you do now. Remind yourself of how you got out of the slump – and use the same strategies now.

Happy gardening!

Plant flowers in place of weeds, and tend those flowers to keep them hardy. Your weeds will have greater difficulty growing again where healthy flowers are thriving.

How does your garden grow?

Research shows that CBT has a better relapse-prevention rate than medication on its own or other types of therapy. This difference may be because CBT encourages you to become your own therapist. Doing behavioural and written exercises does seem to help people to stay well, and for longer. Try to continue to be an active gardener throughout your life. Left to their own devises, most gardens become overrun with weeds. Think of maintaining the health of your psychological garden as an ongoing project.

Being a compassionate gardener

What do you do if one of your precious plants isn't doing so well? If you notice that you've got blight on your prize rose, do you deprive it of food and water, or do you try to treat the disease? It's better not to abuse or neglect the plants in your garden for failing to thrive because – if you do, they may only wilt further. You probably don't blame the plant for ill-health, so why should you blame yourself when you relapse?

Yes, take responsibility for anything that you may be doing that's self-defeating. And yes, accept responsibility for taking charge of your thinking, and ultimately, for engineering your own recovery. But, also take a compassionate view of yourself and your problems. Some of your unhealthy tendencies may have taken root partly due to childhood and early adulthood experiences. Others may have some biological underpinnings. Some of your problems may have arisen from a trauma. You're not alone in having emotional problems. You're part of the human race, and there is no reason to expect more of yourself than you do of others with regard to staying emotionally healthy.

If you take a responsible, compassionate view of setbacks, you will be more able to help yourself get well again.

 You know that 'they' say you should talk to your plants to make them grow? Well, it may sound a bit daft, but maybe there's something in it. Try imagining yourself as a little pot plant on your kitchen windowsill. Talk to yourself encouragingly and lovingly when you notice your leaves drooping. Give yourself the types of messages that nurture rather than deplete you.

Chapter 19

Working with the Professionals

In This Chapter

▶ Deciding to work with a professional CBT therapist

▶ Getting the most from your CBT therapist

▶ Identifying the characteristics of a good CBT therapist

CBT has gained popularity in recent years, due in part to research showing that CBT is an effective treatment for many common psychological problems. These days, you can access CBT treatment by books, by the Internet, in groups, and in one-to-one sessions (Appendix A lists Web sites and organisations that you may want to contact). This chapter helps you determine how to seek further help, how to select a CBT therapist, and how to get the most out of your treatment.

Procuring Professional Help

The information in this book may be all you need to overcome your emotional problems. Or, you may consider checking out some of the other self-help books we recommend in Chapter 23, which can give more guidance on specific problems.

As well as self-help, you may decide that you want or need additional help from a qualified therapist. If you have problems that are severe or difficult to overcome, your doctor may also prescribe medication, or refer you to a psychiatrist for a more specialised assessment of your difficulties. Psychiatrists can usually refer you to a psychotherapist who is qualified to treat your specific problems. Your GP may also be able to suggest a therapist, whether or not you have also been referred to a psychiatrist.

Self-help approaches, such as books like this one, have the advantage of costing little, being easily available – even in the middle of the night and during holidays – and providing enduring advice for years to come. Perhaps most importantly, when you use a self-help book, you know that the person who's making the changes in your life is *you*. A good self-help book can be invaluable, even if you're also seeking professional help. In fact, most CBT therapists recommend a book or two during treatment. Your therapist may collaborate with you, using a book of your choice – such as this one – as a resource. Alternatively, ask your therapist whether she has any suggestions for material you can read to help you get the most from your treatment.

Ask yourself the following questions to determine whether *now* is the right time for you to look for professional help:

- ✔ **How severe are your current problems?** For example, if you have severe depression or if you feel like you can't go on any more, seeking expert help is strongly recommended, as you may be too ill to benefit fully from self-help techniques. By 'severe' we mean that your problem is interfering significantly with your relationships, ability to work or carry on with normal daily activities. If you have experienced uninterrupted symptoms for more than two months, or if you notice that your symptoms are coming back more often, you must seek out professional help.

- ✔ **Have you tried self-help approaches in a consistent and systematic manner for at least two (and ideally six) weeks?** If you feel you're making some progress on your problems, you may not need to work with a professional at this time. However, if you are not satisfied with your rate of progress and still feel bad much of the time, then structured therapy sessions may help you.

Check out how long you need to wait for NHS (National Health Service) treatment in the UK. Putting your name on a waiting list sooner, rather than later, is a good plan if resources are overstretched in your area.

- ✔ **Do your problems interfere with your ability to concentrate and utilise self-help material?** If so, a therapist may well be able to help you digest information and techniques at a pace you can manage.

- ✔ **Do you see the sense in self-help principles but struggle to apply them to your own life?** Most therapists are much more experienced than you in applying psychological principles to specific types of problems. They can suggest more ways to help you move forward and guide you on how best to use the therapeutic techniques described in self-help books.

- ✔ **Have you reached a plateau or obstacle in your self-help programme that you can't overcome on your own?** By working with a trained and experienced therapist, you may develop the ability to overcome barriers and jump-start your treatment. A therapist can often have suggestions that you may not have tried, which can serve as a motivator to get your treatment moving again.

- ✔ **Are you ready to share your problems with someone and team up with her on achieving shared goals for therapy?** Therapy is a team effort. Therapists don't 'fix' you. Your treatment still needs lots of input from you.

Thinking about the right therapy for you

Doctors and psychologists often recommend CBT because research evidence supports its effectiveness (refer to Chapter 1). Specifically:

- ✔ CBT is an active problem-solving approach that helps you develop skills and enables you ultimately to become your own therapist.

- ✔ CBT focuses on the present, whereas many other therapies focus on personal history. In CBT, you use your childhood experiences to help you and your therapist understand how you may have developed specific beliefs and ways of behaving. However, the focus is on your *current* problems and the ways in which your thinking and acting perpetuate your problems.

- ✔ CBT emphasises a collaborative relationship in therapy. CBT therapists can help you build skills and they are likely to expect you to carry out assignments in between sessions.

In addition to CBT, you may come across dozens more therapeutic approaches when you investigate your treatment options. Some of the more common psychotherapies practiced today include the following:

- ✔ **Transactional analysis:** Focuses on the internal relationship between the parent, adult, and childlike aspects of human personalities.

- ✔ **Person-centred therapy:** Emphasises the therapist displaying warmth, empathy, and genuineness towards the client, but without directing the client.

- ✔ **Psychodynamic therapy:** Focuses on the client expressing feelings derived from early experiences, as these feelings arise during the ongoing relationship between client and therapist.

- ✔ **Systemic therapy:** Commonly used with families and couples, this emphasises the idea that emotional problems are the product of a dysfunctional system, for example a family or relationship.

- ✔ **Interpersonal therapy (IPT):** Focuses on changes in life roles, grief, and disputes with significant others. IPT is another proven treatment for depression and some eating disorders.

Meeting the experts

Lots of mental health professionals are able to provide general counselling and support. If you specifically want CBT, don't hesitate to say so. Many psychiatrists, psychologists, and nurses have had some training in CBT, but you'd be wise to find out the extent of her training and experience. Ideally, choose someone who's had specialist training in CBT. *Specialist training* means that the therapist has obtained a degree, diploma, or Master's qualification in CBT from a university or recognised training institute.

Ask your therapist if she is accredited with either the UKCP (United Kingdom Council for Psychotherapy) or BABCP (British Association for Behavioural and Cognitive Psychotherapies), if you live in the UK (contact details for these organisations are listed in Appendix A). You can also ask your therapist to tell you where and when she studied, and if you're sceptical, you can check this information out with the educational bodies they list. Some therapists have their certificates, which outline their qualifications, on display. If you are referred to a therapist by a psychiatrist, the psychiatrist may be able to give you more details about your therapist's credentials, or to verify the information that a therapist gives you.

In the UK, anyone can call themselves a counsellor or psychotherapist, regardless of whether they have any professional training. A therapist with a recognised professional qualification will not be offended if you ask about their relevant training. You have every right to satisfy your desire to know about your therapist's background and training, because this is *your* treatment. If you know that you want CBT as part of your treatment, you must ask about the CBT specifics of your therapist's training and experience.

In case you're a bit flummoxed by the range of different professionals offering help, here's a little breakdown of them:

- ✔ *Psychiatrists* are medical doctors who specialise in psychological problems. They can prescribe medication and typically are more knowledgeable than family doctors about the drugs used to treat psychiatric illness. Not all psychiatrists are trained in CBT, although many can refer you to a CBT therapist who they're familiar with.

- ✔ *Clinical psychologists* have usually studied a broad range of therapies and have basic training in how to apply therapeutic principles to specific problems. Many can offer CBT but may not have specialist training.

- ✔ *Counselling psychologists* have been trained in basic counselling and different types of psychotherapy. Like clinical psychologists, most counselling psychologists have no specialist training in CBT, but they may offer it as part of the techniques they use.

- ✔ *Nurse therapists* are originally trained in psychiatric nursing. They have a more in-depth understanding of psychological processes and disorders than general nurses. Psychiatric nurses in the UK may have undergone further training to specialise in CBT.

✔ *Counsellors* are usually trained in listening and helping skills. They may hold a certificate in basic counselling, or be more specialised in certain problem areas, such as addiction. They do not always have a psychology degree, or in-depth knowledge of psychological problems. Often, counsellors will not be specialised in a specific psychotherapeutic orientation like CBT.

✔ *Psychotherapists* have normally specialised in a specific school of therapy, for example CBT or person-centred therapy. The level of training and experience, however, can vary widely.

You have the right to ask your therapist or other mental health professional (such as community based nurses, social workers, and occupational therapists), how much experience they have of using CBT and to what level they have trained. You can also ask them how much experience they have of dealing with your specific problems, such as depression, panic disorder, or obsessive-compulsive disorder (OCD). If you're not satisfied with the answers you receive, take the matter further. In most cases you can request a referral to another therapist either through your GP or psychiatrist.

Tracking Down the Right CBT Therapist for You

After you've decided to search specifically for a therapist with CBT training, you may have a bewildering number of questions to ask both yourself and potential therapists. This section poses, and helps you begin to answer, these questions.

Asking yourself the right questions

Sifting through directories of CBT therapists can be quite a daunting prospect. You may feel like there's a lot you want to find out about but aren't sure exactly how to ask for the information.

To help locate and select the best CBT therapist for you, consider the following questions:

✔ **Where can I find a CBT-trained therapist?** Begin by asking for recommendations from your doctor, psychiatrist, or friends. Many practitioners are listed in the telephone directory, although you may need to call them to find out more about their backgrounds. Additionally, you can look on Web sites (see Appendix A) for accredited CBT therapists. *Accredited therapists* have usually reached a recognised level of training and experience. In the United Kingdom, therapists are accredited by the BABCP or the UKCP (or both). In the United States, therapists are licensed by the State in which they practise.

✔ **How much can I afford to pay?** In the UK, CBT is sometimes available on the NHS, but you may probably be placed on a waiting list first. Your GP is your best first port of call. Unfortunately, relatively few GP surgeries offer CBT treatment on site. You do have a right to appropriate treatment through the NHS. If your doctor recommends you for CBT, then technically the NHS needs to provide it for you. If you have done some background research on your specific problems and have articles outlining CBT as the recommended treatment, you can show these to your doctor and request a referral.

Fees for private CBT vary from practitioner to practitioner, depending on location, training, and experience. In general, the more experienced and highly trained the therapist, the higher the fees. But, shopping around can save you money. Some practitioners have a limited number of lower-fee sessions for people on low incomes. Sometimes, trainee CBT therapists may not charge, or they may offer a reduced rate. Many trainees are very competent and provide good-quality service. However, before beginning therapy with a trainee, find out who she reports to, her arrangements for consulting, and who monitors her professional supervision. Then, you know who to talk to if you have any concerns or complaints about the treatment your trainee therapist provides.

✔ **Would I prefer a male or female practitioner?** When you're selecting a therapist, try to be open-minded about their sex. However, some people, perhaps because they have issues with sexual abuse or relationships, may prefer either a male or a female therapist. If you feel the sex of your therapist impairs your ability to discuss your problems openly, raise your concerns with them or your doctor, who should then refer you to another therapist.

You may also wish to have therapy with someone who is from the same cultural background as you are. Ask your doctor if they can recommend a local service that may be able to get you some culturally specific counselling.

✔ **Does the therapist have the appropriate experience or training?** If you have a specific problem, such as panic attacks, addiction, or OCD, you're best looking for a therapist with experience in treating your specific disorder. If you find a practitioner who you like but who doesn't have experience in your disorder, ask whether they're prepared to find out more about your problem. If not, find another therapist.

✔ **How many sessions do I need?** Estimating the number of therapy sessions you may need is difficult. In general, CBT is briefer than psychoanalysis or psychodynamic therapy, which typically involves regular sessions for a year or a number of years. In general, unless your problem is very specific, such as snake phobia, we suggest initially trying six sessions and then reviewing the treatment progress with your therapist.

A common estimate for CBT is between 8 and 20 sessions. You will normally start off with weekly sessions and build in bigger gaps as you progress. However, for complex and longstanding problems, CBT can last two years or more, with multiple sessions per week. Ask your therapist to give you a rough idea of how many sessions she believes you need after her initial assessment of your problems.

Your therapist can also regularly review your treatment with you, which may help give you a clearer sense of how many more sessions you need.

Ultimately, you – not your therapist – must determine how long you choose to stick with CBT treatment.

✔ **Can I take along my copy of *CBT For Dummies* or another self-help book?** As we mention earlier, CBT therapists often suggest self-help material and can usually help you work through a self-help book. If you've been using a book that you find useful, take it along to your first sessions. Your therapist may already be familiar with the resource; if not, she may be prepared to read through it.

Speaking to the specialists

Make the most out of your initial phone contact with possible therapists by asking about whatever questions are on your mind. Once you make an assessment appointment with a therapist, you may want to list a few things that you want to discuss during your first meeting. Here are some ideas of what questions to ask your therapist:

Although CBT therapists vary as to how much they're prepared to discuss over the phone before your first meeting, the following questions are reasonable after you identify a potential therapist:

✔ How much do you charge [if the therapist is a private practitioner]?

✔ How long are your sessions?

✔ Do you charge a cancellation fee?

✔ Do you have any experience of treating my particular kinds of problems?

✔ Are sessions booked in a fixed time slot each week, or can they vary?

✔ Where do you practise? Do you have a waiting room?

✔ Can I tape-record our sessions?

Fighting your fears about seeking specialist help

We often comment to each other about how strange our jobs are. We like what we do very much, but the reality is that for most people therapy is an unfamiliar experience. Most people don't sit in front of a stranger and tell him about personal problems. Being apprehensive about starting therapy is entirely natural, and you may have some common worries about seeking help, such as the following:

- **What if working with a professional doesn't help me?** Treatment may not have an immediate effect. However, if you're committed to getting better, the treatment will probably have at least some benefit. Proceeding down the professional path may seem like a big risk, but you're very likely to be glad you took it.

- **What if talking about my problems makes them worse?** Good therapy, and/or the right medication, very rarely worsens problems. Sometimes, you may feel a temporary increase in discomfort while on the road to long-term recovery. We discuss this more in Chapters 7 and 9.

- **What if I'm too embarrassed to tell my therapist what's really bothering me?** Tell your therapist if you're feeling embarrassed or ashamed. She may well be able to put your mind at rest by explaining that many of your feelings are normal. You don't have to divulge all to your therapist straightaway (although doing so may be the most efficient route), and you can take some time to build trust between the two of you.

- **What if my therapist thinks I'm mad and wants to keep me in hospital?** Your therapist or psychiatrist is not going to think that you're mad, or judge you negatively for being disturbed. She will frequently see patients with your types of problems. People are assessed to stay in hospital against their will only in extreme circumstances... If you're a danger to yourself or to others, if you're actively suicidal, or are neglecting yourself badly, you may be detained in hospital – but this would be to keep you safe, not to punish you. Most areas in the UK now have home treatment teams so that regular visiting is available to support people in their own homes, so they don't need to go to hospital.

- **What if my therapist passes on my private information to social services or my employer?** The information that you share with any mental health professional is confidential and will not be given to family members, or employers without your explicit (usually written) consent. An exception to this is when very clear risks to yourself, or others – including children – are identified.

Only in very extreme and relatively rare circumstances do therapists ask social services to assess the impact of a mental health problem on a patient's family or children. In all but the most extreme circumstances, your therapist can tell you of his intention to involve any outside agencies.

If you have any of the above worries, voice them with your doctor or therapist. Worrying is normal, and any mental health professional with even the smallest amount of therapy experience can be sensitive to your concerns and discomfort. If they're not sensitive to your needs, consider seeking help from somebody else.

If you're comfortable with the answers you receive from phoning your therapist, seek out answers to the following more detailed questions during your first meeting:

✔ Can you explain your theory about what's maintaining my problems?

✔ What sort of things do you think I need to do to overcome my problems?

✔ How many sessions do you estimate that I need?

✔ What do you expect of me in therapy – and what I can expect from you?

✔ Can you recommend any reading or self-help materials to me?

Making the Most of CBT

So what can you expect from your CBT therapist? As a general rule, a lot! Most likely, you'll end up feeling that you're working hard both during and between sessions.

Discussing issues during sessions

When you meet with your CBT therapist, expect extensive two-way discussion, as well as some challenging questions from your therapist. Topics for collaboration may include the following:

✔ **Treatment goals:** CBT is goal-focused. Your therapist is likely to ask you about your therapeutic goals early in treatment. If your goals are not realistic, your therapist will discuss this with you.

✔ **Specific problems, causes, and solutions:** A skilled CBT therapist can share her ideas about what's perpetuating your problems, and invite you to work with her on what can help you in the long run. You can also expect your therapist to agree *with you* to a treatment strategy, which is likely to include homework assignments.

Although you may, on occasion, feel awkward with your therapist, she's speaking from a place of sound, clinical experience, and knows that some behavioural exercises, although they can be uncomfortable for you in the short term, can get you better in the long term.

Expect your sessions to be focused. Your therapist may interrupt and refocus you if you stray off the point, and do not address the actual issues that brought you to treatment. Additionally, a good CBT therapist may pull you up if you avoid working on your problem areas.

Hallmarks of a good CBT therapist

CBT practitioners exhibit some fairly predictable behaviours in session. You can use the following list of attitudes, actions, and interactions to help you determine whether you're actually receiving CBT treatment, and to assess the standard of your therapy. In general, good CBT therapists:

- Help you define problems and ask about your goals and expectations for therapy.

- Explain a bit about CBT at your first meeting and invite you to ask questions.

- Use scales and measures, such as a *depression inventory* (refer to Chapter 10), to help monitor your progress.

- Evaluate your problems based on the CBT model and explain this process to you so you can do it yourself in the future.

- Ask questions to elicit your thoughts and help you evaluate them.

- Are active in sessions, educating you about CBT and its perspective on your problems, asking questions, writing things down, and making suggestions of ways to try to improve your problems.

- Develop therapy homework exercises with you, to be carried out between sessions.

- Review your homework. If you haven't done it, a thorough therapist can discuss the obstacles that stopped you doing so.

- Regularly review your progress and reassess your goals with you.

- Invite feedback about therapy generally, and openly listen to any constructive criticism you give.

- Invite you to voice any doubts, reservations, and fears you have about aspects of your CBT.

- Challenge your unhelpful beliefs and behaviours and help you to do the same on your own.

- Encourage you to be independent and to take personal responsibility for your mental health.

- Answer most of your questions, and tell you why if they don't or can't answer others.

- Refer you to another professional if you require additional or alternative help.

- Receive regular clinical supervision (in which they have their work listened to or have discussion with other therapists) to improve their practise. Don't be afraid to ask about this: It's important!

Okay, so this list is rather long, but we recommend consulting it if you have any doubts about your CBT therapist. Don't hesitate to take this list to your therapist and ask her to clarify her position on any or all of these points. Even though you may be seeing an experienced or qualified CBT practitioner, attitudes and styles of therapeutic delivery can vary dramatically. Like many therapists, we're always pleased when clients suggest ways in which we can make sessions more helpful.

Overall, your CBT therapist is likely to be pretty human. Your CBT therapist shouldn't give the impression that she considers herself above you, or fundamentally different from you, simply because you're the patient and she's the professional. Most skilled CBT therapists acknowledge that they're the experts on CBT, and possibly on particular psychological problems, but that *you* know *yourself* best. Therefore, they may ask you a lot of questions about your experiences, thoughts, and feelings, rather than telling you what you experience, think, and feel.

Just as you can expect your CBT therapist to be open and honest during sessions, you can get even more from your sessions by being open about your own doubts and reservations. Although doubt is wholly natural, be prepared to reconsider your reluctant feelings about change.

Even if you know intellectually that a new way of thinking or acting is better, you may still have a gut reservation. For example, we often see clients who realise that their perfectionism is highly toxic but still fear that they may perform badly if they give it up. In these cases, we often have to help people see that being more flexible doesn't mean dropping their ideal standards. You can strive for excellence without demanding perfection.

Being active between sessions

CBT is in part educational, so your therapist may use a whiteboard, pen and paper, and various printed forms in your treatment. At some stage, your therapist may give you an ABC form or a thought record sheet (which we explain in Chapter 3).

Some of your homework will be written and some will be behavioural – whatever form it takes, however, you can expect your therapist to give you a solid rationale for any intervention they use, or homework they suggest. Your therapist is also likely to give you handouts and reading matter.

Being ready to engage actively in therapy is a major key to your success, so if you are asked to do an exposure assignment or behavioural experiment that you don't feel ready to take on , say so, and suggest an alternative. You may want to address any ambivalence about therapy using a cost–benefit analysis: Weigh up the costs and benefits of carrying on as you are, versus trying out new ways of thinking and behaving.

In order to make your CBT experience successful, do your homework! We find that whether a client completes therapy assignments or not is the single best predictor of success. CBT involves retraining your attention, changing your behavioural patterns, and adopting new ways of thinking. It takes practice and repetition to break old patterns and to replace them with new ones.

Consider therapy as a temporary experiment. Give your therapist's advice a shot and see what happens. You can always return to your old ways or try out a new strategy if you think therapy isn't working well.

Part V

The Part of Tens

The 5th Wave

By Rich Tennant

In this part . . .

This Part of Tens is a source of vital CBT information. You'll find ten fundamental pointers toward living in an upbeat and enjoyable way, ten books to benefit your library, and ten self-esteem boosters that don't work and alternatives that do.

Chapter 20

Ten Healthy Attitudes for Living

In This Chapter

▶ Philosophising rationally

▶ Taking responsibility for your feelings

▶ Enhancing your psychological health

▶ Staying interested

As we discuss many times in this book, the attitudes you hold about yourself, other people, and the world greatly affect your ability to respond successfully to negative life events. Even in the absence of unusual or difficult circumstances, your core philosophies influence your overall experience of life. People who hold rational philosophies are generally less prone to emotional disturbances, such as anxiety and depression, and are more readily able to solve problems.

This chapter offers ten rational philosophical standpoints that are good for your psychological health. Read them, re-read them, think them through, and test out acting upon them to see for yourself.

Assuming Emotional Responsibility: You Feel the Way You Think

Bad or unfortunate things, such as splitting up from a partner, being made redundant, or having a car accident, can happen to anyone. You may reasonably have negative feelings in response to such events. Experiencing extreme sadness or annoyance in the face of misfortune is wholly understandable.

In some instances, bad things occur through no fault of your own. In other cases, you may have some personal responsibility. We don't suggest that you blame yourself for every bad thing that comes your way. However, try to assess a given situation and determine whether you have any *legitimate responsibility* for its development and look for a resolution.

Even if you're not personally responsible for a negative event, you can still take responsibility for your emotional and behavioural *responses* to the event. People who deny their part in creating their own emotional problems in the face of negative events don't recognise how their thoughts and actions can make a bad situation worse. They hand over their personal power to make things better by waiting passively for someone or something to step into the breach.

When you hold an attitude of personal responsibility for your feelings and actions, you're more able to find creative solutions, and your belief in your ability to cope with adversity is heightened. You empower yourself by focusing on your ability to influence the way you feel even if you can't control events.

On a cheerier note, when good things happen, you can also assess the extent to which they're a result of your own efforts – and then give yourself credit where due. You can appreciate good fortune without sabotaging your positive feelings with worries that your luck may run out.

Thinking Flexibly

Making demands and commands – thinking in terms of 'must', 'should', and 'have to' – about yourself, the world around you, and other people has a fundamental problem: Such thinking limits your flexibility to adapt to reality. The human capacity to adapt creatively to what's going on is one of the hallmarks of the species' success. However, humans are fallible, and the world continues to be an imperfect place. Insisting 'It shouldn't be this way!' can leave you irate, depressed, or anxious and much less able to focus on how to cope with and adapt to reality.

Although circumstances may well be *desirable*, *preferable*, and even *better* if the situation were different, they don't *have* to be a particular way. Accepting reality and striving to improve it where wise and achievable can help you save your energy for creative thought and action. Refer to Chapter 2 for more on demands, and Chapter 12 for more on developing realistic attitudes towards yourself.

Valuing Your Individuality

You can express your individuality in many ways, such as in your dress sense, musical tastes, political opinions, or choice of career. Yet perhaps you're hesitant to express your individuality openly because you fear the reaction of others. People who develop the ability to value their idiosyncrasies and to express them *respectfully* tend to be well-adjusted and content. Accepting that you're an individual and have the right to live your life, just as other people have the right to live theirs, is a pretty good recipe for happiness.

As social animals, humans like to feel part of a group or social structure, and tend to be happier when interacting meaningfully with other humans. However, the ability to go against group mentality when it's at odds with your own personal views or values is a tremendous skill. You can be both socially integrated and true to your values by accepting yourself as an individual and by being a selective non-conformist. Check out Chapter 12 for more on accepting yourself.

Accepting That Life Can Be Unfair

Sometimes, life's just plain unfair. Sometimes, people treat you unjustly and nothing gets done to put the balance right. Bad things happen to the nicest of people, and people who don't seem to have done a deserving thing in their lives get a winning ticket. On top of being unfair, life's unpredictable and uncertain a great deal of the time. And really, that's just the way life is.

What can you do? You can whine and moan and make yourself thoroughly miserable about the lamentable state of the world. Or you can accept things and get on with the business of living. No matter how much you insist that the world should be fair and you should be given certainty about how things are going to pan out, you ain't going to get it.

Life's unfair to pretty much *everyone* from time to time – in which case, perhaps things aren't as desperately unfair as you thought. If you can accept the cold hard reality of injustice and uncertainty, you're far more likely to be able to bounce back when life slaps you in the face with a wet fish. You're also likely to be less anxious about making decisions and taking risks. You can still strive to play fair yourself, but if you accept that unfairness exists you may be less outraged and less horrified if and when justice simply doesn't prevail.

Understanding That Approval from Others Isn't Necessary

Receiving approval from someone important to you is nice. Getting a bit of praise from a boss or a friend can feel good. But if you believe that you *need* the approval of significant others or, indeed, everyone you meet, then you probably spend a lot of time feeling unhappy and unsure of yourself. Many people get depressed because they believe they're only as good as the opinions others hold of them. These people can't feel good about themselves unless they get positive feedback or reassurance from others.

Accept yourself, independent of overt approval from other people in your life. Having a *preference* for being liked, appreciated, and approved of by others – but not believing that you *need* approval – means that your self-opinion can be stable and you can weather disapproval. You may still behave in ways that are more likely to generate approval than disapproval, but you can also assert yourself without fear. You can consider praise and compliments a bonus rather than something you must cling to and work over-hard to maintain.

If you hold the belief that you *need* rather than *desire* approval, you may pay emotionally for it somewhere along the line. You're likely to feel anxious about whether approval's forthcoming – and when you get approval you may worry about losing it. If you fail to get obvious approval or – horror of all horrors – someone criticises you, you're likely to put yourself down and make yourself depressed. Refer to Chapter 9 for more on combating anxiety, and Chapter 10 for tackling depression.

You cannot please all the people all the time – and if that's what you try to do, you're almost certainly going to be overly passive. If you can take the view that disapproval isn't the end of the world, not intolerable, and not an indication that you're less than worthy, you can enjoy approval when you get it and still accept yourself when you don't.

Realising Love's Desirable, Not Essential

Some people would rather be in any relationship – even an unsatisfying or abusive one – than in no relationship at all. This need may stem from a belief that they can't cope with feelings of loneliness or get through life in general if they're alone. Other people consider themselves worthy or lovable only when they're reassured by being in a relationship.

Romantic relationships *can* enhance your enjoyment of life, but they're not essential for you to enjoy life. Holding this attitude can help you to feel good about yourself when you're not part of a couple and may lead you to make more discerning partner choices in future since you will choose, rather than be compelled. Believing that your basic lovability is relatively constant, regardless of whether a significant other actively loves you, can help you to feel secure within a relationship.

People who strongly *prefer* having a partner and yet believe that they can survive a break up tend to experience little romantic jealousy. Jealousy can be a big obstacle to relationship satisfaction – jealous people tend to believe that they *must* keep their partner and end up focusing on signs of infidelity or waning interest rather than on the pleasure of the relationship. Jealousy's turned many a relationship sour. A jealous partner can end up alienating the other person through constant reassurance-seeking or monitoring, leaving both members of the couple feeling that mutual trust doesn't exist between them.

Preferring instead of *demanding* to have a relationship helps you to retain your independence and individuality. Then when you *are* in a relationship, you're less likely to fall into the trap of trying to be the perfect partner – which means you can continue to attend to your own interests while being able to negotiate compromises when appropriate.

Tolerating Short-Term Discomfort

Healthy, robust, and successful people are often able to tolerate temporary discomfort in the pursuit of longer-term goals. They practise self-denial and delay gratification when doing so is in their long-term interests. These people are the ones who are able to eat healthily, exercise regularly, save money, study effectively, and so on.

You *can* experience intense pleasure in the present and the future, but often some degree of pain and effort *today* are necessary to win you greater pleasure *tomorrow*. This will be true for many of the achievements you've already made in life. Putting up with temporary discomfort is also going to be crucial in *reducing* painful feelings of anxiety and depression. Refer to Chapters 9, 10, and 11 for more on overcoming these problems.

Enacting Enlightened Self-Interest

Enlightened self-interest is about putting yourself first most of the time and one, two, or a small handful of selected others a very close second. Enlightened self-interest is about looking after your own needs and interests while also being mindful of the needs of your loved ones and other people living on the planet.

So why put yourself first? When you reach a certain age, you need to look after yourself because nobody else is going to do so for you. If you can keep yourself healthy and content, you are better able to turn your attention to caring for the people in your life that you love.

Many people make the mistake of always suppressing their own needs and end up tired, unhappy, or ill. People may think they're doing the right thing by putting others first all the time, but in fact they're left with very little to give.

Of course you *will* experience times when putting someone else's needs before your own and making personal sacrifices is a good choice. For example, parents frequently put the welfare of their children before their own. But you must still make space for your own pursuits too.

If you're starting to get concerned that 'self-interest' translates to 'selfish beast', stop! To clarify: Self-interest involves taking responsibility for looking after yourself because you understand that you're worth taking care of. Self-interest means being able to care for others very deeply. When you're self-interested, you're able to meet your own needs and take a keen interest in the welfare of other people in the world around you. You can also determine when you're going to put yourself *second* for a period of time because someone else's need is greater than your own – which is where the 'enlightened' part comes into play.

Selfishness is not – we stress, *not!* – the same animal as self-interest. Ultimately, selfish people put their own wants and needs first, *to the exclusion and detriment of other people*. Selfishness is much less about taking responsibility for looking after yourself and much more about demanding that you get what you want, when you want, and to hell with everybody else. The two concepts are very different – so don't be scared. Head to Chapter 16 for more on building a lifestyle that promotes taking care of yourself.

Pursuing Interests and Acting Consistently with Your Values

Loads of evidence indicates that people are happier and healthier if they pursue interests and hobbies. Have you let your life become dominated by work or chores at home, and do you spend your evenings sitting in front of the television as a means of recharging? If your answer to this question is 'Yes!', then you're in extremely good, but not optimally healthy, company.

One of the arts of maximising your happiness is to pursue personally meaningful goals, such as furthering your education, participating in sports and exercise, developing skills, improving relationships, or acting in ways that contribute to the sort of world you'd like to live in, for example by doing some voluntary work. Try to structure your life to ensure that you have some time for personally meaningful pursuits. Check that the things you do in life reflect what you believe is important.

As far as we can tell, life isn't a dress rehearsal. Will you really look back and regret missing a bit of TV because you dragged yourself out to spend time on a hobby, to exercise, to enjoy a night out with your friends, or to participate in some charity work?

Tolerating Uncertainty

Healthy and productive people tend to be prepared to tolerate a degree of risk and uncertainty. Demanding certainty and guarantees in an uncertain world is a sure-fire recipe for worry and inactivity. Safety comes at a cost – fewer rewards, less excitement, fewer new experiences.

The fact that you don't know what the future holds is grounds for *calculated risks* and *experiments*, not avoidance, reassurance-seeking, or safety precautions. You can make educated decisions and take calculated risks, but if you accept that 100 per cent certainty is exceptionally rare, you can reduce undue anxiety and worry.

Chapter 21

Ten Self-Esteem Boosters That Don't Work

In this Chapter

▶ Identifying techniques that are counterproductive to your self-esteem
▶ Substituting healthier self-esteem strategies

*Y*ou may be trying to manage your low self-esteem in ways that are counterproductive, particularly in the long term. This chapter highlights ten techniques that don't boost your self-esteem effectively.

'Why focus on where I'm going wrong?' you may ask. Well, using the strategies we describe in this chapter to boost your self-esteem is like trying to dig your way out of hole. Your first step is to realise you're only digging yourself deeper – so put down that shovel! Only when you stop digging, can you begin to look for other ways to get out of the hole. Fortunately, we include several self-esteem ladders within this book to help you find your way out.

The following ten points describe counterproductive strategies for boosting your self-esteem. We explain why they don't work and suggest more constructive ways of increasing your sense of self-worth.

Putting Others Down

If you measure your self-esteem by comparing yourself with other people and tend to regard yourself as inferior, you may try to boost your worth by putting down other people, whether in your mind, by moaning about them to others, or by criticising them directly.

By increasing your sense of other people's inferiority, you may manage to persuade yourself temporarily that you're less inferior. But, you won't change the underlying problem – your attitude towards yourself. Putting down others is tiring not only for you but also for other people – and doing so does not elicit warm responses from others.

Instead, try respecting your own uniqueness – and that of others. The human race is a species, not a competition. Focus on following your own values and pursuing your own goals. Pay more attention to your own strengths rather than others' weaknesses.

If you feel inferior, re-evaluating your attitude towards yourself is more effective than trying to pull down someone else's self-esteem.

Thinking You're Special

Trying to replace a sense of worthlessness with a feeling of 'specialness' is another common self-defeating technique you can adopt for beating low self-esteem. Look out for times when you tell yourself 'If I'm not different, I'm nothing', or 'Being average or normal is like not existing'.

The problem here is that, as far as the universe is concerned, you're not special. No one is. You may be unique, but so is everyone else. In fact, you may well try so hard to avoid the 'horror' of mediocrity that you end up living an unhappy and unfulfilled life. This tendency largely stems from an extreme form of *all or nothing thinking* (which we explain in Chapter 2) and the mistaken idea that you need to reduce low self-esteem by wildly overcompensating.

Rather than trying to assert that you're special, focus your attention in a more constructive direction. Challenge the idea that you need to be 'special' in order to feel okay about yourself. Accept yourself as a normal, ordinary, worthwhile individual, just like everyone else.

Trying to Get Everyone to Like You

Substituting your dislike of yourself by trying to win the approval of other people is a recipe for anxiety. You can end up feeling anxious about not achieving your goal of being liked by someone or a group. If you do achieve your goal and win approval, you're likely to become anxious about losing your prize.

The real pity is that your imagined 'need' for approval may not help you give off the attractive, self-assured air you would so dearly like. Believing that you need to be liked in order to like yourself can leave you in a desperate position. Allowing people to walk all over you in an attempt to win their approval has a pretty negative impact on your self-esteem, for fairly obvious reasons.

Rather than attempting to win approval, strive for respect. If you respect yourself, you give off an air of being comfortable in your own skin. People with true self-respect are those often most respected by others. You don't have to be a slave to this principle, but seeking respect can help you assert yourself more readily.

Placing Yourself above Criticism

Placing yourself above criticism is a classic tactic if you believe that being criticised reveals you to be inadequate, useless, or a failure. Perfectionism, covering up your weaknesses, and defensiveness are the inevitable result. You try to be flawless so that other people can't criticise you. However, you end up being unduly harsh with yourself for your shortcomings and errors. You may even believe that you can knock yourself into shape by criticising yourself, unwittingly lowering your self-image further.

Instead, try to accept your human fallibility without condemning yourself. Mistakes and flaws are an unavoidable aspect of being human, no matter how hard you try to change things. Don't be ashamed of your shortcomings – everyone else has flaws too. Do you think people really lose respect for you if they find out you're only human? They probably don't. Chances are, they'll be relieved and feel more able to relax in your company. Their respect for you may even grow, because they can accept you, warts and all.

Reveal an imperfection and check out the response you get. Try accepting yourself non-defensively in the face of criticism. If someone criticises you, try asking them for more information. Most people find owning up to their human fallibility a far more productive strategy than striving to be perfect.

Choosing perfection as your goal is setting yourself up to fail because *no one* is capable of being perfect. The more you fail to reach your unrealistic goal, the more you put yourself down. Don't be tempted to try harder to be perfect. Instead, try harder to accept your imperfection.

Avoiding Failure, Disapproval, Rejection, and Other Animals

You may find that you avoid situations, places, or people that trigger your tendency to put yourself down. This approach is very much a way of papering over the cracks. Your underlying attitude towards yourself remains the problem. By avoiding potential failure, you don't change your attitude: You simply postpone setting off your insecurity for a while.

A long-lasting, elegant solution to overcoming poor self-esteem is for you to uncover, examine, and change any unhelpful attitudes you may have developed towards yourself. Then, you can deliberately seek out the things you've been avoiding, while practicing your new self-accepting attitude (head to Chapter 12 for more).

Avoiding Your Emotions

You may try to block out certain emotions because you regard them as a sign of weakness. Although you may try to persuade yourself that you're strong because you can control your emotions, your relationships and psychological health are likely to suffer.

Having a wide range of emotions is part of what makes you human. Try as you might, avoiding these emotions is difficult – and unhealthy. You may end up feeling isolated, cold, and aloof in your relationships, which can rob you of much richer and more satisfying experiences. Begin to accept your feelings and recognise that this acceptance shows courage, not weakness.

Sometimes, experiencing strong negative emotions is a natural response to adversity, a part of the healing process, and a sign of strength in facing up to difficulties.

Attempting to Feel More Significant by Controlling Others

If you try to control others, the underlying assumption is that you need to *prove* your significance by having an affect on other people. The problem is that without this *proof*, you are (in your eyes) insignificant.

Perhaps you immediately offer unsolicited advice or try to convert others to a favourite cause to prove that you are a person of influence? Unfortunately, your lack of respect for others' thoughts, feelings, and behaviours may actually be a turn-off to those other people.

Compulsively trying to influence or affect people actually shows you have a lack of control. You also reinforce a negative self-image by acting as if you have to prove something to be worthwhile or significant.

Imagine how you'd interact with people if you didn't have the need to prove your power or influence. You can use this imagining exercise as a guide to new healthier behaviour.

Over-Defending Your Self-Worth

We don't advocate you being a doormat, but the healthy alternative to being passive is to stay calm in the face of minor slights. Constantly defending your self-worth can lead to verbal or physical aggression. Besides, if you're confident in your self-worth, do you really need to guard it so carefully? Insisting that others must show you respect at all times leads to unhealthy anger. Your compulsive outrage at being disrespected can simply drive you to take people to task for minor assaults on your fragile self-esteem.

Respect yourself regardless of whether other people treat you respectfully. Self-respect affords you the ability to assert yourself appropriately when it's *worth* doing so.

Feeling Superior

You may have superior, equal, and inferior traits compared with other people, but the idea that you are either an inferior or superior *person* is an overgeneralisation. No one is superior *or* inferior to everyone else in every way. We all have different strengths and weaknesses.

Some people can only feel good about themselves when they convince themselves that they are 'the best'. Many people with this tendency try to demonstrate their superiority by showing off their physical or psychological strength. For example, you may feel driven to impress people with your wit, intellect, or other talent. Unfortunately, these solutions are only temporary ones to your underlying feelings of inferiority, which can be your real target for change. At worst, your attempts at superiority serve only to alienate other people and mask your true strengths.

Although the notion of the 'real you' is a bit simplistic, try dropping the superiority. Be as authentic as you can and see how people respond to you.

Blaming Nature or Nuture for Your Problems

Blaming your problems on your past, genetics, hormones, brain chemistry, or other people, does have the distinct advantage of temporarily alleviating any sense that you're stupid, pathetic, or less worthwhile. This blame system stems from the mistaken idea that if you take an appropriate degree of responsibility for your emotional problems, then it means that you're to blame for those problems. Protecting your self-esteem by blaming something or someone else can typically backfire, which makes real change more difficult because you attribute your problems to factors outside of your control.

Half of the people in the Western world experience some kind of significant emotional problem during the course of their lives. So, having an emotional problem simply means you're human.

Use your understanding of your past and your 'make-up' to develop a compassionate, sympathetic perspective towards your current difficulties. Take some personal responsibility for keeping your problems going. Recognising how you may be making your problems worse gives you the power to make changes for the better.

Unhelpful ideas about how to feel good about yourself can stem from childhood messages. Teachers or parents may have told you to 'Be the best', 'Never admit that you're wrong', 'Our family is better than other families', 'Failure is not an option', or 'Big boys don't cry'. Such messages may have been offered to you as words of wisdom, but as an adult you can re-evaluate their truth and helpfulness. You can decide to dump them in favour of updated, self-acceptance and other acceptance beliefs.

Chapter 22

Ten Ways to Lighten Up

In This Chapter

▶ Discovering the benefits of not taking things too seriously

▶ Finding yourself funny

▶ Getting more enjoyment out of life

▶ Throwing caution to the wind

Sometimes you can make life more difficult than necessary by holding an overly serious view of yourself. This chapter lists ten ways to lighten up a little and experience more enjoyment. Go through the list and pick out the headings that apply most to you.

Accept That You Can – and Will – Make Mistakes

> *I'm only human*
>
> *Of flesh and blood I'm made*
>
> *I'm only human*
>
> *Born to make mistakes*
>
> – The Human League

If you take yourself overly seriously, you're more likely to consider your mistakes unacceptable. You may also believe that other people may reject you on the basis of your blunders. Moreover, you probably judge yourself harshly when you make a social faux pas or a poor decision.

Everyone gets things wrong and mucks up from time to time. If you try to hide or ignore your mistakes, you can deny yourself the opportunity to develop from them. By acknowledging mistakes, and accepting yourself for making them, you have the chance to do things differently next time. You'll also become more comfortable with making errors in the first place and are likely to spend less time worrying about whether you get things 'right'. Most people respect someone who can own up to and take responsibility for his clangers.

Try Something New

Perhaps you're reluctant to play a different sport, change your usual holiday destination, or acquire a new language or skill. Maybe you're even reluctant to try a fresh route to work in case you get lost and look foolish. The fear of looking silly can stop many people dead in their tracks. If you can cope with looking a trifle daft now and again, you'll find it a lot easier to discover novel things and to acquire new skills. Even doing small things like eating different cuisines or going on a one-day mediation course (or a course on anything that interests you!) can broaden your horizons.

Doing something foolish doesn't mean you're a fool. It's pretty much impossible for you to learn a new language or how to play the piano, without making lots of grammatical gaffes or hitting the wrong notes. By giving yourself the opportunity to try new things, you may have a lot of fun in the process, even if you don't become a polyglot or a pianist in the Royal Philharmonic.

Stamp on Shame

Taking yourself too seriously can lead you to experience unnecessary emotional upset. For example, if you need to look as though you are in complete control and composed all the time, you're a prime candidate for experiencing frequent bouts of shame.

Feelings of shame and humiliation are often linked to perceiving that your weaknesses, errors, or faults have been exposed. For example, if you fall over while boarding a train, you may experience intense, unpleasant emotions rather than getting appropriately embarrassed. Your feelings of shame about somebody seeing you trip up are likely to last longer than simple embarrassment, and may likely cause you far more distress than any physical injuries you have sustained.

As one of your goals, you can have a go at overcoming your propensity to feel ashamed. Try deliberately exposing yourself to scrutiny using the following four-step technique:

1. **Make yourself conspicuous.** Wear a ridiculous outfit, make animal noises, sing to yourself, wear your underwear on the outside of your normal clothing, ask a really stupid question, or do anything else silly you can think of. Whatever you choose, do it *on purpose* and *in a very public place*. An excellent place to carry out shame-attacking exercises is when you're on public transport.

2. **Stay in the situation long enough for your feelings of shame and general discomfort to subside on their own.** Don't hide yourself away in the corner, run away from the public place, or remove your clown hat, for example. Stay in the situation until you notice that your uncomfortable feelings are beginning to subside (sometimes this may take ten minutes and other times it may take an hour). The important point is to stick with the exercise for whatever length of time it takes for you to feel *less* embarrassed, ashamed, or anxious.

   Don't expect to feel totally calm and happy when you're deliberately doing something ridiculous in public. The idea is for you to see that nothing terrible happens to you when other people look at you like you're weird.

3. **Hold an attitude of self-acceptance throughout the experience.** This means that you act as if you truly believe that being judged as odd or weird is not the end of the world. (This just isn't the case, or the world would have ended long ago.) Tell yourself that you can tolerate uncomfortable feelings, which you associate with possible negative evaluation from others. (You can: Feelings of shame and embarrassment don't kill people.)

4. **Repeat variations of the exercise often and without long gaps in between.** Doing the exercise once is not enough. Repetition is the key to getting yourself desensitised to scrutiny so that you don't feel shame as a result. You can do an exercise like the one above daily for a week, which is a great way to feel less distressed.

Laugh at Yourself

Many people claim that laughter's the best medicine. This adage may well carry a sizeable grain of truth. Finding the funny angle in an otherwise awkward situation can help remove the sting. Sometimes, you can take the horror out of your mistakes and shortcomings by finding them amusing.

If you're able to value yourself as a worthy person *and* recognise your human imperfection, you won't fall into the trap of taking yourself so seriously that you're unable to laugh. Think of people you know who can't take a joke: They're very likely people who take themselves and everything they do far too seriously. Being overly earnest is a bit tragic: Anything that happens to you or anything you do that is, in your mind, less than acceptable has a profound impact on your global opinion of yourself. You can glean much more enjoyment out of life and your personal relationships if you can have a giggle at your own expense.

Don't Take Offence So Easily

If you believe that everyone must respect you and that you're only as good as what others think of you, then you're going to get offended if someone fails to appreciate you. You're pretty much destined to take offence much of the time unless you live in an air-conditioned bubble all on your own. In the real world, sometimes people are rude to each other and fail to behave in a thoughtful, respectful manner.

We're not suggesting that you take the stance of a passive victim when others treat you unacceptably. You can respect yourself and have clear boundaries about the type of people you choose to associate with and the type of behaviour you're prepared to tolerate.

However, you don't need to be impervious to bad behaviour from other people but you don't need to take undue offence to it. You can make your life easier by distinguishing between when, and when not, to bother asserting yourself. For example, if a friend jibes about a recent blunder you made, is it really that dire? Or if someone bumps into you on the street without apologising, don't consider it an assault on your personal worth and respectability – you may find it rude and annoying, but do you really need to take strong offence.

Feeling offended is akin to feeling angry. Anger is tiring and unpleasant. Chances are that if you hold too serious a view of yourself, you're experiencing anger more often than you actually need to (refer to Chapter 13).

Make Good Use of Criticism

Constructive criticism is a vital element of learning. Of course, not all the criticism you receive may be delivered in a skilled or constructive way. Nevertheless, if you can step back from negative feedback long enough to access its validity, you can use it to your advantage. Often, other people can see more clearly than you where you're going 'wrong' – others can have the benefit of an objective viewpoint.

If you believe that you *must* get *everything* right or perfect, and that any indication that you're failing at a task is evidence that you're inadequate, then you can get very disturbed by criticism. Rather than using feedback to evaluate your approach to a specific task, you're likely to use it as a battering tool on your sense of worth. You may become defensive at the first sniff of less-than-positive comments on your performance.

Rather than reacting to critical comments oversensitively, you can develop more tolerance to such comments so that you find them useful. Try the following techniques:

- ✔ Get rid of your defensive stance. Listen openly to what people are saying about you (head to Chapter 16).

- ✔ Understand that you don't *need* to be right every time. You have the option to behave less than perfectly now and again. Accepting that you can be wrong sometimes means that you can find criticism easier to take.

- ✔ Take time to weigh up the validity of the comments made and then to use any legitimate information offered to aid your development.

Settle into Social Situations

When you have an overly serious attitude towards yourself, you're prone to feeling uncomfortable in social settings. The fear that you may say the wrong thing, offend someone, or expose yourself as stupid or boring can lead you to clam up and say little. You may find that you censor much of what you say or rehearse it in your head before you speak. Alternatively, you may try too hard to be witty and entertaining. Either way, you're not relaxing into the occasion and enjoying the interaction. You're probably much more focused on the impression you're making than on what the other people present are actually talking about.

If you fall into this camp, social situations for you are more likely to be something to get through rather than enjoy. You're probably taking more than your fair share of responsibility for the interaction going smoothly. Remember: You're only ever *part* of a social group, even when there are only two of you – the other person or people present also have a part to play in the smooth running of conversation.

To help yourself relax and be 'more yourself' in social settings, try these tips:

- ✔ **Focus your attention away from yourself and on to the other people present.** Really listen to the conversation and observe others.

- ✔ **Say things spontaneously.** Resist the urge to rehearse witty responses in your head before you speak. Take the risk of dropping in comments during the conversation.

- ✔ **Drop your safety behaviours** (refer to Chapter 7 for more on safety behaviours). Avoid sitting on the outside of a group or fiddling with your drink, handbag, or phone when conversation lulls. These types of behaviours may distract you from your feelings of social awkwardness but they also stop you from getting used to natural social interaction.

- ✔ **Express yourself until you feel heard.** If you start to say something and are interrupted, try again in a few moments, maybe a little louder.

- ✔ **Reign yourself in.** If you tend to overcompensate for your social discomfort by talking a lot or putting on a bit of a show, give others the chance to fill in the gaps and silences.

- ✔ **Enjoy yourself.** Above all, remind yourself that social gatherings are meant to be fun. Make enjoying the company and conversation of other people your main reason for socialising.

Encourage Your Creativity to Flow

To act creatively, whether at work or in your personal life, you have to accept the possibility that some of your ideas won't be considered that great. If you've got a suggestion for an advertising campaign at work or a novel way to spice up your sex life, you'll be less inclined to put forward your ideas if you worry too much about them being rejected or going down like a lead balloon.

Creativity is self-generative: If you try out your ideas, they tend to give rise to more ideas. If you constantly suppress your ideas, you may find that the stream of ideas diminishes over time.

Act Adventurously

Breaking your routine can help you to lighten up. Changing a regular pattern can relieve boredom and improve your mood generally. Even the smallest things, such as choosing a different recipe in a cookbook or walking to a place to that which you normally drive, can make a significant difference to your mood.

Following a routine in order to avoid unpredictable outcomes is all too easy. Unfortunately, getting stuck in a rut may mean that you miss out on new, exciting experiences. Urging yourself to do things differently or to risk a foray into unknown territory, can challenge the demands you hold about having control at all times. Most people like to have some degree of control in their lives and to feel that they have some degree of certainty about what they can expect from life. However, in reality, life is unpredictable and our sense of certainty is largely an illusion.

Accepting your limitations to control events and to be certain about the outcome of events, can help you to act more adventurously and live life more fully. Increasing your tolerance for uncertainty and limited control is also likely to help you become more adaptive for when life throws unexpected problems your way. (Head to Chapter 9 for more on coping with anxiety.)

Enjoy Yourself: It's Later than You Think

Enjoy yourself, it's later than you think,

Enjoy yourself while you're still in the pink,

The years go by as quickly as you wink,

Enjoy yourself, enjoy yourself, it's later than you think

– The Specials

There's no time like the present for chilling out and lightening up. If you never get round to making time for pleasurable or novel activities, you may find that you don't ever do them. People who hold a responsible yet light-hearted attitude about themselves, and life in general, are usually far more pleasant to hang around with. These people give off an air of 'seizing the moment'. Making the most of the present moment can keep you young at heart, even as the years go by.

Chapter 23

Ten Books to Add to Your Library

In This Chapter

▶ Self-help books and therapist manuals

▶ Books for learning more about CBT

▶ Book recommendations for tackling specific kinds of problems using CBT

*N*umerous self-help and professional manuals on CBT are available. We've tried to choose books that reflect the diversity of CBT as an approach, and that can add to your armoury of knowledge and skills in tackling disturbing emotions or behaviours.

Cognitive Therapy – Basics and Beyond

This an excellent step by step guide to the basics of CBT. Written by Judith S. Beck (Guilford Press, 1995), *Cognitive Therapy – Basics and Beyond* provides a sound overview of the theory and application of CBT. The book is useful to the CBT practitioner and other mental health professionals interested in using CBT. It also contains enough good, hands-on advice to be useful as a self-help book or to be used in conjunction with a therapist.

Cognitive Therapy and the Emotional Disorders

Cognitive Therapy and the Emotional Disorders by Aaron T. Beck (Penguin Psychology) is the founder of cognitive therapy's original text on his research-based approach to emotional problems. Beck's contribution to the field of CBT has been phenomenal, not least because of the emphasis placed on scientifically evaluating CBT treatments. This is an historic book, and a good introduction to the fundamentals of CT.

Full Catastrophe Living

Full Catastrophe Living: Using the Wisdom of Your Body and Mind to Face Stress, Pain and Illness, by Jon Kabat-Zinn (Delta) is a guide to stress reduction based on the principles of mindfulness meditation. This is part of a new wave in CBT that focuses more on what we *do* with our mind rather than the *content* of the thoughts that go through it. This book helps readers identify different kinds of stress in our daily lives and outlines a programme of mental and physical exercises to help combat stress.

Overcoming . . .

The *Overcoming . . .* books (published by Robinson Press) are an excellent series that attend to specific kinds of problems. These books are usually written by experts in their field and are frequently recommended by professional therapists. The series includes: *Overcoming Childhood Trauma* by Helen Kennerly; *Overcoming Depression* by Paul Gilbert; *Overcoming Obsessive Compulsive Disorder* by David Veale and Rob Willson; *Overcoming Social Anxiety and Shyness* by Gillian Buttler; *Overcoming Traumatic Stress* by Claudia Herbert and Ann Wetmore; and *Overcoming Mood Swings* (bipolar affective disorder) by Jan Scott.

Overcoming Anger

Windy Dryden, author of *Overcoming Anger* (Sheldon Press) has written or edited more than 150 books in the areas of counselling and psychotherapy. In a clear and forceful style, Windy shows how we create our anger with our attitudes and beliefs. He goes on to show how thinking rationally helps overcome unhealthy anger and communication with others.

Oxford Guide to Behavioural Experiments in Cognitive Therapy

The *Oxford Guide to Behavioural Experiments in Cognitive Therapy*, edited by James Bennett-Levy, Gillian Butler, Melanie Fennell, Ann Hackman, Martina Mueller, and David Westbrook (Oxford University Press) is like a distilled essence of CBT. Many cognitive behavioural therapists wish that the book had been written years earlier! Focusing on the 'lets find out' element of CBT, the book covers a huge range of psychological problems, and how to test out the negative thoughts related to them.

Reason and Emotion in Psychotherapy

Dr Albert Ellis, the author of *Reason and Emotion in Psychotherapy: A Comprehensive Method for Treating Human Disturbances, Revised and Updated* (Birch Lane Press), is the true founding father of cognitive behavioural therapy. The rational emotive behaviour therapy approach described in this extensive volume, was the first fully developed cognitive behavioural theory and treatment, dating back to the mid-1950s. This version of Ellis' seminal text gives an insight into the philosophy underpinning the approach and Ellis's phenomenal mind. Anyone interested in how reason and philosophy can be applied to reduce human suffering would do well to read this book.

Reinventing Your Life

Reinventing Your Life: How to Break Free from Negative Life Patterns by Jeffrey E. Young, and Janet S. Klosko (Penguin Putnam Inc, USA) gives an introduction to a variant of CBT called 'schema focused therapy'. This therapy focuses on the 'maps' we develop of the world, ourselves, and others from early in our lives. The book aims to help readers identify their unhelpful long-standing thinking patterns and suggests ways of tackling them.

Status Anxiety

Status Anxiety by Alain De Botton (Hamish Hamilton Penguin Books) explores what De Botton describes as 'the universal anxiety about what others think of us'. The book looks at where our status worries come from historically, showing how society encourages us to link self-worth to achievement.

A Woman in Your Own Right

A Woman in Your Own Right by Anne Dickson (Quartet Books) is a classic self-help book on becoming more assertive. It gives clear and practical guidance on overcoming the need for approval, effective communication, and dealing constructively with criticism. And yes, men can benefit from it too!

Appendix A

Resources

● ●

*T*his appendix lists organisations in the United Kingdom and the United States that you may want to contact for further help, support, and information.

Organisations in the United Kingdom

Action on Smoking and Health (ASH), 109 Gloucester Place, London, W1H 4EJ. Tel: 0171 935 3519

Alcoholics Anonymous, PO Box 1, Stonebow House, Stonebow, York, YO1 2NJ. Tel: 01904 644026 / 7 / 8 / 9

Association of Post-Natal Depression, 25 Jerdan Place, Fulham, London, SW6. Tel: 020 7836 0868

British Association for Behavioural and Cognitive Psychotherapies (BABCP), BABCP General Office, The Globe Centre, PO Box 9, Accrington, BB5 0XB. Tel: 01254 875 277. Fax: 01254 239 114. E-mail: babcp@babcp.com. Web site: www.babcp.org.uk/

Council for Acupuncture, 179 Gloucester Place, London, NW1 6DX. Tel: 0171 724 5756

Depression Alliance, PO Box 1022, London, SE1 7GR. Tel: 020 7721 7672 (recorded information)

First Steps to Freedom, 1 Taylor Close, Kenilworth, CV8 2LW. Tel: 0845 120 2916 (Freephone helpline 10 a.m. – 10 p.m.). E-mail: info@first-steps.org. Web site: www.first-steps.org/

Manic Depression Fellowship, 8–10 High Street, Kingston-Upon-Thames, London, KT1 1EY. Tel: 020 8974 6550 and 020 8546 0323

MIND, The National Association for Mental Health, Granta House, 15–19 Broadway, Stratford, London, E15 4BQ. Tel: 020 8519 2122

National Phobics Society, Zion Community Resource Centre, 339 Stretford Road, Hulme, Manchester, M15 4ZY. Tel: 0870 7700 456. Fax: 0161 227 9862. E-mail: `nationalphobic@btinternet.com`. Web site: `http://www.phobics-society.org.uk/contact.php`

No Panic, 93 Brands Farm Way, Telford, TF3 2JQ. Tel: 01952 590005. Freephone helpline: 0808 808 0545 (10 a.m. – 10 p.m.). E-mail: `ceo@nopanic.org.uk`. Web site: `www.nopanic.org.uk/`

OCD Action, Aberdeen Centre, 22–24 Highbury Grove, London, N5 2EA. Tel: 0207 226 4000. Fax: 0207 288 0828. E-mail: `info@ocdaction.org.uk`. Web site: `www.ocdaction.org.uk/`

Phobia Action, Hornbeam House, Claybury Grounds, Manor Road, Woodford Green, Essex, IG8 8PR. Tel: 0181 559 2551

Seasonal Affective Disorder (SAD) Association, PO Box 989, London, SW7 2PZ

Triumph over Phobia UK, PO Box 3760, Bath, BA2 3WY. Tel: 0845 600 9601. E-mail: `info@triumphoverphobia.org.uk`. Web site: www.triumphover phobia.com

Organisations in the United States

Albert Ellis Institute, 45 East 65th Street, New York, NY 10021-6593. Tel: 212 535-0822. Fax: 212 249-3582. Web site: `www.rebt.org`

American Foundation for Suicide Prevention, 120 Wall Street, 22nd Floor, New York, NY 1005. Tel: 212 363 3500. Web site: `http://www.afsp.org`

American Mental Health Foundation, 2 East 86th Street, New York, NY 1008

Anorexia Nervosa and Related Eating Disorders, Inc, PO Box 5102, Eugene, OR 97405. Tel: 541 344 1144. Web site: `www.anred.com`

Anxiety Disorders Association of America, 8730 Georgia Avenue, Suite 600, Silver Spring, MD 20910. Tel: 240 485-1001. Fax: 240 485-1035. Web site: `www.adaa.org`

Association for the Advancement of Behavior Therapy, 305 Seventh Ave, New York, NY 10001-6008, USA. Tel: 212 647 1890. Web site: `http://server.psyc.vt.edu/aabt/`

Children and Adults with Attention Deficit Disorders, 499 Northwest 70th Avenue, Suite 308, Plantation, FL 33317. Tel: 305 587 3700. Web site: `www.chadd.org`

Kidscope, Obsessive-Compulsive Foundation (children's newsletters), PO Box 70, Milford, CT 06460-0070

National Alliance for the Mentally Ill, 200 N. Glebe Rd., Suite 1015, Arlington, VA 22203-3754. Tel: 800 950 NAMI (800 950 6264)

National Anxiety Foundation, 3135 Custer Drive, Lexington, KY 40517-4001. Tel: 606 272 7166. Web site: `http://lexington-on-line.com/naf.ocd.2.html`

National Association of Anorexia Nervosa and Associated Disorders, Box 7, Highland Park, IL 60035. Tel: 847 831 3438. Web site: `www.healthtouch.com`

National Attention Deficit Disorder Association, PO Box 972, Mentor, OH 44061. Tel: 800 487 2282 or 216 350 9595. Web site: `www.add.org`

National Depressive and Manic-Depressive Association, 730 North Franklin, #501, Chicago, IL 60610. Tel: 800 82N DMDA

National Foundation for Depressive Illness, PO Box 2257, New York, NY 10116. Tel: 800 248 4344

National Institute of Mental Health, 9000 Rockville Pike, Building 10, Room 30–41, Bethesda, MD 20892. Tel: 301 496 3421. Information services: Panic and other anxiety disorders: 800 647 2642. Depression: 800 421 4211

National Mental Health Association, 1201 Prince St, Alexandria, VA 22314-2971. Tel: 703 684 7722

National Mental Health Consumers Self-Help Clearinghouse, 1211 Chestnut St, Philadelphia, PA 19107. Tel: 800 553 4539

Obsessive Compulsive Anonymous, Inc. (OCA), PO Box 215, New Hyde Park, New York 11040. Tel: 516 741 4909. Web site: `http://members.aol.com/west24th/index.html`

Obsessive Compulsive Foundation, 676 State Street, New Haven, CT 06511. Tel: 203 401 2070. Fax: 203 401 2076. E-mail: info@ocfoundation.org. Web site: www.ocfounadtion.org/

Trichotillomania Learning Center, 303 Potrero, Suite 51, Santa Cruz, CA 95060. Tel: 831 457 1004. Web site: www.trich.org/

Other Organisations

The Mood Gym: Developing CBT for treatment of depression. www.moodgym.anu.edu.au

The Organisation for Bi-polar Affective Disorders: www.obad.ca

Appendix B

Forms

●●

*I*n this Appendix you can photocopy these blank forms and fill them in, using the instructions provided here and within specific chapters. You can also print out the forms from www.wiley.com/go/cbt.

The 'Old Meaning–New Meaning' Sheet

The sheet has the three headings. Fill them in as follows:

1. **In the first column, 'Event', record what actually happened.**

2. **Under 'Old Meaning' in the second column, record what you believe the event means about you.**

   This is your unhealthy core belief.

3. **In the 'New Meaning' third column, record a healthier and more accurate meaning for the event.**

   This is the new belief that you can work on strengthening.

Head to Chapter 14 for a worked example of the sheet, and for more about reviewing past events.

Event	Old Meaning	New Meaning

The Cost–Benefit Analysis Form

Carry out a *cost–benefit analysis* (CBA) to examine the pros and cons of some-thing can help galvanise your commitment to change. You can use a CBA to examine the advantages and disadvantages of a number of things, such as:

- ✔ **Behaviours:** How helpful is this action to you? Does it bring short-term or long-term benefits?

- ✔ **Emotions:** How helpful is this feeling? For example, does feeling guilty or angry really help you?

- ✔ **Thoughts, attitudes, or beliefs:** Where does thinking this way get you? How does this belief help you?

- ✔ **Options for solving a practical problem:** How can this solution work out? Is this really the best possible answer to the problem?

Evaluate the pros and cons:

- ✔ In the short-term

- ✔ In the long-term

- ✔ For yourself

- ✔ For other people

Try to write CBA statements in pairs, particularly when you're considering changing the way you feel, act, or think. What are the *advantages* of feeling anxiety? And the *disadvantages*? Write down pairs of statements for what you feel, do, or think *currently,* and for other, healthier alternatives. Head to Chapter 8 for worked examples of the form.

Costs and benefits of:	
Costs (Disadvantages)	*Benefits (Advantages)*

The 'Tic-Toc' Sheet

TICs are *task interfering cognitions*, the thoughts, attitudes, and beliefs that get in the way of your progress. You need to respond with *TOCs – task orienting cognitions*, which are constructive alternatives to TICs. The list of unhelpful attitudes (sand traps) in the nearby sidebar is helpful for getting some ideas about task interfering cognitions.

Fill out the Tic-Toc sheet by following these steps:

1. **Identify the goal or task you want to focus on.**

2. **In the left column (TICs), list your thoughts, attitudes, and beliefs that get in the way of you achieving your aim.**

3. **In the right column (TOCs) put responses to each of your TICs that will help you achieve your goal or task.**

Head to Chapter 17 for more on the Tic-Toc sheet.

Goal or task:	
Task Interfering Cognitions (TICs)	*Task Orienting Cognitions (TOCs)*

The Zigzag Form

1. **Write down in the top left-hand box of the zigzag form a belief that you want to strengthen.**

2. **In the next box down, write your doubts, reservations, or challenges about the healthy belief.**

3. **In the next box, dispute your attack and redefend the healthy belief.**

4. **Repeat Steps 2 and 3 until you exhaust all your attacks on the healthy belief.**

5. **Re-rate, from 0 to 100 per cent, how strongly you endorse the healthy belief after going through all your doubts.**

Refer to Chapter 15 for more information about the zigzag form.

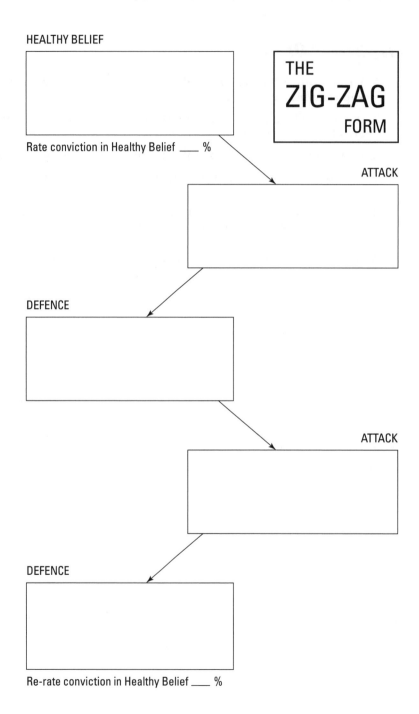

HEALTHY BELIEF

THE
ZIG-ZAG
FORM

Rate conviction in Healthy Belief ___ %

ATTACK

DEFENCE

ATTACK

DEFENCE

Re-rate conviction in Healthy Belief ___ %

The Vicious Flower

1. **In the Trigger box, write down the trigger that makes you feel anxious or upset.**

2. **In the central circle, write down the key thoughts and meanings you attach to the trigger.**

3. **In the flower petals, write down the emotions, behaviours, and sensations you experience when your uncomfortable feeling is triggered. In the top petal, write down what you tend to focus on.**

Chapter 7 has loads more about the vicious flower exercise, and a filled-in example.

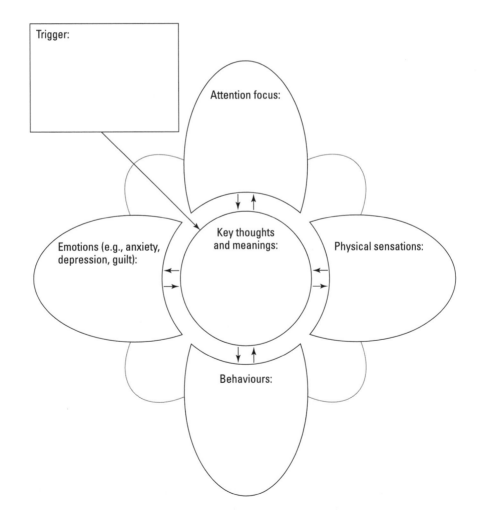

The Task Concentration Sheet

Situation	Attention	Excercise	Feeling	Results
Who were you with? Where were you? What were you doing?	Record your focus of attention. Note what you focused on most. 1. Self % 2. Task % 3. Environment and other people % (Total = 100%)	Use task concentration to direct your attention outward. Remember to focus on your task or environment. Note what you did.	Record how you felt.	Record anything you learned from the excercise. Note how the situation turned out, changes in your anxiety level, and your ability to complete the task.

Head to Chapter 5 for more about the task-concentration exercise, and a filled-in example.

The ABC Form 1

1. **In the 'Consequences' box, point 1, write down the emotion you're feeling.**

2. **In the 'Consequences' box, point 2, write down how you acted.**

3. **In the 'Activating Event' box, write down what triggered your feelings.**

4. **In the 'Beliefs' box, write down your thoughts, attitudes, and beliefs.**

5. **In the 'Thinking Error' box, consider what your thinking errors may be.**

Refer to Chapter 3 for more detailed instructions on filling out the first ABC form.

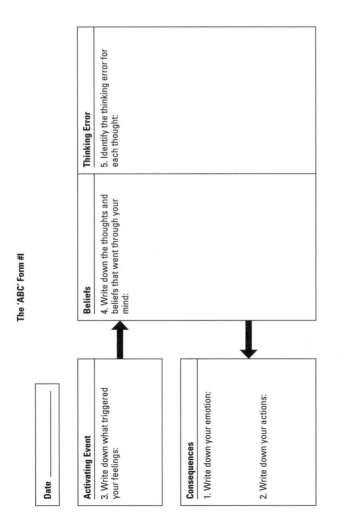

The ABC Form 11

Follow the guidance at the bottom of the form and head to Chapter 3 for more detailed instructions on filling in the second ABC form.

Date _____

The 'ABC' Form #11

Activating Event (Trigger).	Beliefs, thoughts, and attitudes about A.	Consequences of A+B on your emotions and behaviours.	Dispute (question and examine) B and generate alternatives. The questions at the bottom of the form will help you with this.	Effect of alternative thoughts and beliefs (D).
2. Briefly write down what triggered your emotions. (e.g. event, situation, sensation, memory, image)	3. Write down what went through your mind, or what A *meant* to you. B's can be about you, others, the world, the past, or the future.	1. Write down what emotion you felt and how you acted when you felt this emotion. **Emotions** e.g: Depression, guilt, hurt, anger, shame, jealousy, envy, anxiety. Rate intensity 0–100. **Behaviour** e.g. Avoidance, withdrawing, escape, using alcohol or drugs, seeking reassurance, procrastination	4. Write an alternative for each B, using supporting arguments and evidence.	5. Write down how you feel and wish to act as consequence of your alternatives at D. **Emotions** Re-rate 0–100. List any healthy alternative emotion e.g. Sadness, regret, concern. **Alternative Behaviour or Experiment** e.g. Facing situation, increased activity, assertion

Disputing (Questioning and Examining) and Generating Alternative Thoughts, Attitudes, and Beliefs: 1. Identify your 'thinking errors' at **B** (e.g. Mind Reading, Catastrophising, Labelling, Demands etc.). Write them next to the appropriate 'B'. 2. Examine whether the evidence at hand supports that your thought at **B** is 100% true. Consider whether someone whose opinions you respect would totally agree with your conclusions. 3. Evaluate the helpfulness of each **B**. Write down what you think might be a more helpful, balanced and flexible way of looking at **A**. Consider what you would advise a friend to think, what a role model of yours might think, or how you might look at **A** if you were feeling OK. 4. Add evidence and arguments that support your alternative thoughts, attitudes and beliefs. Write as if you were trying to persuade someone you cared about.

Index

• A •

abandonment
  goal setting techniques, 115
  past life experiences, 192
ABC (Activating event, Beliefs, and
    Consequences) form
  Activating Event box, 41–42
  Beliefs box, 42
  Consequences box, 40–41
  constructive alternative approach,
    45–48
  Dispute box, 45–46
  Effect box, 46
  filled-in form example, 47
  how to use, 306–308
  overview, 14–17
  progression techniques, 48
  Thinking Error box, 42–43
abuse
  abusive language, low self-esteem, 171
  past life experiences, 192
accepting compliments, 34
accidental thinking mistakes
  all-or-nothing thinking, 21–23
  black-or-white thinking, 21–23
  catastrophising, 20–21
  disqualifying the positive, 33–34
  emotional reasoning, 26
  fortune telling, 23–24
  inflexibility of demands, 30–31
  labelling, 28–30
  low frustration tolerance, 34–35
  mental filtering, 31–32
  mind-reading tendencies, 24–26
  overgeneralising, 27–28
  overview, 19
  personalising, 35–36
accidents, past life experiences, 192
accurate thoughts and meanings, feeling
    the way you think, 13
acrophobia, 128
acting as if technique, reinforcing beliefs,
    211
acting out, feeling the way you think, 13
Action on Smoking and Health (ASH), 293
action tendencies
  defined, 86
  guilty emotions, 85, 88
  remorse, 86
Activating event, Beliefs, and
    Consequences (ABC). *See* ABC form
active behaviours, feeling the way you
    think, 12
activities, happy lifestyle development,
    224–225
adaptive behaviours, self-acceptance, 165
aggressiveness, obsessional
    problems, 145
agoraphobia
  counterproductive safety
    behaviours, 101
  defined, 128
  overcoming anxiety, 127
aichmophobia, 128
Albert Ellis Institute organisation, 294
alcohol consumption
  low self-esteem, 169
  as problem causing solution, 96
  self-destructive behaviours, 13
Alcoholics Anonymous organisation, 293

all-or-nothing thinking
  discussed, 21
  examples of, 22
  low self-esteem, 276
  recognising, 23
  strategies for, 22
alternative assumption
  behavioural experiments, 53
  reinforcing beliefs, 210
American Foundation for Suicide
    Prevention organisation, 294
American Mental Health Foundation
    organisation, 294
anger
  accepting others, tolerance, 179–180
  annoyance, 175
  assertion skills, 184–185
  behavioural characteristics, 178
  cost-benefit analysis, 183
  criticism, coping with, 185–186
  difficulties in overcoming, 187–188
  disarming technique, 186–187
  FHBs (fallible human beings)
      acceptance, 181
  flexible preferences, 180–181
  frustration tolerance development,
      182–183
  hate, 176
  healthy versus unhealthy, 175–179
  irritability, 175
  low self-esteem, 169
  overgeneralising thinking mistakes, 28
  passive-aggressiveness, 176
  physical sensations of, 90, 177
  rage, 176
  raised heart rates, 177
  revenge, 177
  ridicule, 176
  rigid demands, 176
  self-acceptance, 181–182
  self-righteous, 188

strong preferences, 177
sulking, 177
synonyms for, 74
annoyance
  anger, 175
  healthy and unhealthy emotion
      comparisons, 79–80
antidepressant medication, 129–130
anxiety
  ABC technique, 15
  agoraphobia, 101, 127
  bad events, thinking realistically about,
      119–120
  catastrophic images as, 42
  common anxieties, 125–127
  counterproductive safety
      behaviours, 101
  desensitisation, 122
  dizziness caused by, 51
  extreme thinking, avoiding, 120
  FEAR (Face Everything And Recover)
      technique, 122
  fears, repeatedly confronting, 123
  feeling the way you think, 13
  graded hierarchy of, 124
  health, 54, 146–147
  healthy and unhealthy emotion
      comparisons, 78
  heights, fear of, 102, 127–128
  intrusive thoughts and, 46
  job interviews, 15
  low frustration tolerance, thinking
      mistakes, 35
  panic attacks, 54, 126
  phobias, 128
  physical sensations, 90, 121
  record sheets, 125
  safety-seeking behaviours, 100–101
  social, 126
  synonyms for, 75
  task concentration and, 65–66

thoughts, letting pass by, 69
winning by not fighting technique, 122
worry problems, 126
Anxiety Disorders Association of
    America, 294
appetite variation, depression, 130
approval from others preferences, health
    attitudes, 270
arachibutyrophobia, 128
arachnophobia, 128
art appreciation, happy lifestyle
    development, 224
ASH (Action on Smoking and Health), 293
assertion skills, anger, 184–185
Association of the Advancement of
    Behavior Therapy, 295
attention to detail, task concentration,
    64–65
automatic beliefs, core beliefs, 193
automatonophobia, 128
avoidance behaviours
    body dysmorphic disorder, 148
    discussed, 13
    emotions, 278
    failures, 278
    obsession, 144
    problem causing solutions, 96
awareness
    mindfulness meditation, 68–70
    need for change, 244–246
    task concentration, 62–66

• *B* •

BABCP (British Association for
    Behavioural and Cognitive
    Psychotherapies), 256, 293
background and training specifics,
    professional assistance, 258
bad events, thinking realistically about,
    119–120

barophobia, 128
BDD (body dysmorphic disorder)
    avoidance behaviors, 148
    compulsions associated with, 148
    eating disorders versus, 147
    intrusive thoughts and, 46
Beck, Aaron
    *Cognitive Therapy and the Emotional
        Disorders*, 289
    cognitive therapy founder, 49, 95
Beck, Judith S. *(Cognitive Therapy –
    Basics and Beyond)*, 289
bedroom setup, good sleeping
    habits, 140
behavioural experiments
    alternative theory, 53
    competing theories, 53–54
    experiment execution, 52
    jealousy problems, 54
    no-lose perspectives, 60
    observations, 57
    panic attacks, 54
    predictions, testing out, 50–53
    problem descriptions, 51–52
    reasons for, 50
    record sheets, 58–59
    results, examining, 52–53
    safety signals, 51
    successful experiment considerations,
        57–58
    surveys, conducting, 55–57
    talking treatment, 49
    unambiguous disconfirmation, 50–51
behaviours
    ABC technique, 17
    action, feeling the way you think, 12
    avoidance, 13, 144, 148, 278
    compassion, 172, 220–221, 250
    isolating and mood-depressing, 13
    repeated checking of, 99

behaviours *(continued)*
  self-destructive, 13
  sulking, 12, 177
beliefs, reinforcing
  ABC approach, 15
  acting as if technique, 211
  alternative assumption, 210
  balanced beliefs, 214
  cognitive dissonance, 209–210
  compassion behaviours, 220–221
  doubts and reservations, 215–216
  extreme beliefs, 213
  feeling the way you think, 15
  flexible preference, 210, 214
  global beliefs, 210
  head-to-heart problem, 210
  illogical beliefs, 213
  internalising, 210
  logical beliefs, 214
  positive data logs, 220–221
  rigid beliefs, 213
  self-acceptance, 219
  SOC (strength of conviction), 210
  true beliefs, 214
  unhelpful beliefs, 213
  untrue beliefs, 212
  written exercises, 218–220
  zigzag technique, 216–218, 303–304
Beliefs box, ABC form, 42
bibliophobia, 128
bipolar disorder, 93, 131
black-or-white thinking
  discussed, 21
  examples of, 22
  recognising, 23
  strategies for, 22
blame system, 280
blennophobia, 128
body dysmorphic disorder. *See* BDD

British Association for Behavioural and
    Cognitive Psychotherapies (BABCP),
    256, 293
Buttler, Gillian *(Overcoming Social
    Anxiety and Shyness),* 290

• C •

caffeine and stimulant intake, sleeping
    habits, 139
calming down, positive changes, 250
candles, good sleeping habits, 140
catastrophic images
  anxiety as, 42
  examples of, 20
  safety-seeking behaviours, 101
  strategies for, 21
CBA (cost-benefit analysis)
  goal setting techniques, 111–113
  how to use, 299–300
CBT therapist (Greenberger), 95
certainty, need for, 98–100
certifications, professional
    assistance, 256
challenging situations, task
    concentration, 62
change needs
  awareness, 244–246
  inspiration for, 110–111
  low self-esteem, 168–170
  progression techniques, 240
Children and Adults with Attention
    Deficit Disorders organisation, 295
clarification needs, behavioural
    experiment, 50
claustrophobia, 128
cleaning or washing, obsessional
    problems, 145
clinical psychologists. *See* professional
    assistance

cognitive dissonance, reinforcing beliefs, 210

Cognitive Therapy and the Emotional Disorders (Beck), 289

Cognitive Therapy – Basics and Beyond (Beck), 289

cognitive therapy founder (Beck), 49, 95

communication techniques, happy lifestyle development, 230

compassion behaviours
  beliefs, reinforcing, 220–221
  as positive change, 250
  self-acceptance, 172

competing theories, behavioural experiments, 53–54

compliments, acceptance, 34

compulsions, obsession, 144–147

concentration. *See* task concentration

concern, healthy and unhealthy emotion comparisons, 78, 82–83

confidence, obsessional problems, 150

consequences
  ABC approach, 15
  of emotions, mindfulness meditation, 69
  feeling the way you think, 15

Consequences box, ABC form, 40–41

consistency, acting as if technique, 211

contamination, OCD, 145

contradictions, core beliefs, 199

control
  controlling others, 278–279
  loosening grip on, 97–98

cooking, happy lifestyle development, 224

core beliefs, past life experiences
  automatic beliefs, 193
  abandonment, 192
  about others, 194
  about world events, 194
  about yourself, 194

contradictions, 199

core belief flashcard technique, 203–204

critical parenting, 192

death of loved one, 192

difficult experiences, 192

divorce, 192

downward arrow method, 195–196

dream scenarios, 196–197

filling in the blank method, 197–198

history, revisiting, 205–207

identifying, 192–193

impacts of, 198–200

infidelity, 192

life-threatening illnesses, 192

NATs (negative automatic thoughts), 195–196

neglect, 192

past experience examples, 191–192

physical abuse, 192

prejudice model, 199–200

record sheets, 200–203

starting over, 207–208

themes, tracking, 197

unbiased interpretation, 203

violence, 192

written down statement technique, 203–204

corrective behaviours, self-acceptance, 165

cost-benefit analysis (CBA)
  goal setting techniques, 111–113
  how to use, 299–300

costs, professional assistance, 258

Council for Acupuncture organisation, 293

counseling. *See* professional assistance

counterproductive strategies, problem causing solutions, 95–96

counting, obsessional problems, 145

critical parenting, past life experiences, 192
criticism
  coping with, 185–186
  making good use of, 284–285
  placing yourself above, 277

• *D* •

De Botton, Alain *(Status Anxiety)*, 291
death of loved ones, past life experiences, 192
demand-based thinking
  guilty emotions, 85
  preference-based thinking versus, 86–88
demands, inflexibility of, 30–31
depression
  ABC technique, 15–16
  action provoking thoughts, 131–132
  antidepressant medication, 129–130
  feeling the way you think, 13
  guilty emotions and, 91
  healthy and unhealthy emotion comparisons, 78
  hypomania, 131
  inactivity, 135–136
  positive change needs, 245
  problem solving solutions, 97, 136–138
  rumination, 132–135
  self-neglect, 130, 138
  sleeping habits, 138–140
  suicidal thoughts, 141–142
  symptoms, 130–131
Depression Alliance organisation, 293
desensitisation, anxiety, 122
determination, progression techniques, 237
Dickson, Anne *(A Woman in Your Own Right)*, 291
diligence, progression techniques, 237

disappointment
  emotions, synonyms for, 75
  healthy and unhealthy emotion comparisons, 81
disarming technique, anger, 186–187
disorders
  Anxiety Disorders Association of America, 294
  BDD (body dysmorphic disorder), 46, 147–148
  bipolar, 93, 131
  eating, 147, 226
  feeling the way you think, 10
  OCD (obsessive-compulsive disorder), 46, 97, 145–146
  panic disorder, 97
  PTSD (post-traumatic stress disorder), 97, 101
  SAD (Seasonal Affective Disorder) Association, 294
Dispute box, ABC form, 45–46
disqualifying the positive, thinking mistakes, 33–34
divorce, past life experiences, 192
dizziness, anxiety related, 51
documentation
  anxiety problems, 125
  behavioural experiments, 58–59
  core beliefs, 200–203
  goal setting techniques, 113–114
  task concentration, 66–67, 306
doubt and uncertainty
  beliefs, reinforcing, 215–216
  self-acceptance, 172–173
  tolerance, 150, 273
downward arrow method, core beliefs, 195–196
dream scenarios, core beliefs, 196–197
drug use
  low self-esteem, 169
  problem causing solutions, 96
  self-destructive behaviours, 13

Dryden, Windy
  Overcoming Anger, 290
  self-help thinking methods, 161
DTRs (dysfunctional thought records), 39

• *E* •

eating disorders
  body dysmorphic disorder versus, 147
  happy lifestyle development, 226
educational activities, happy lifestyle
    development, 227–228
Effect box, ABC form, 46
effort, progression techniques, 237
Ellis, Albert
  Albert Ellis Institute organisation, 294
  rational emotive behaviour therapy,
    30, 161
  *Reason and Emotion in Psychotherapy:
    A Comprehensive Method for Treating
    Human Disturbances, Revised and
    Updated*, 291
embarrassed emotions, synonyms for, 75
emetophobia, 128
emotional problems
  problem-solving techniques, 92–94
  psychotherapy and, 11
  rating, 93–94
emotional reasoning, thinking
    mistakes, 26
emotional responsibility, feeling the way
    you think, 14, 267–268
emotions
  ABC technique, 17
  anatomy of, 76–77
  avoiding, 278
  consequences and, 40–41, 69
  demand-based thinking, 86–88
  emotive terminology, 74–75
  guilt-based action tendencies, 88

healthy and unhealthy comparisons,
    78–83
  meta-emotions, 91
  physical sensations, emotion
    similarities in, 90–91
  preference-based thinking, 86–88
  thinking what you feel, 75–76
empathy, disarming technique, 186
encouragement, progression
    techniques, 237
endorphins, 138
enjoyment, lightening up
  blame system, 282–283
  criticism, making good use of, 284–285
  laughing at yourself, 283–284
  making mistakes, acceptance, 281–282
  new skill sets, 282
  present moment response, 287
  socialising, 285–286
enlightened self-interest, healthy
    attitudes, 272
environment triggers, need for change,
    246–247
envy
  emotions, synonyms for, 75
  healthy and unhealthy emotion
    comparisons, 83
esteem. *See* low-self esteem; self-
    acceptance
events
  ABC technique, 17
  emphasising meanings attached to, 13
excited emotions, physical sensations, 90
exercise
  happy lifestyle development, 226–227
  rumination, 134–135
experiments, behavioural
  alternative theory, 53
  competing theories, 53–54
  experiment execution, 52

experiments, behavioural *(continued)*
  jealousy problems, 54
  no-lose perspectives, 60
  observations, 57
  panic attacks, 54
  prediction formulation, 50–53
  problem descriptions, 51–52
  reasons for, 50
  record sheets, 58–59
  results, examining, 52–53
  safety signals, 51
  successful experiment considerations,
    57–58
  surveys, conducting, 55–57
  talking treatment, 49
  unambiguous disconfirmation, 50–51
exposure and response prevention,
    obsessional problems, 153–154
external and practice criteria,
    obsessional problems, 152
extreme beliefs, 213
extreme reactions, self-acceptance, 167
extreme thinking, avoiding, 120

• F •

Face Everything And Recover
    (FEAR), 122
failure
  avoiding, 278
  fear of, mental filtering thinking
    mistakes, 32
fallible human beings (FHBs), 181
family and friend acceptance, self-
    acceptance, 171–172
FEAR (Face Everything And
    Recover), 122
fears
  avoidance behaviours, 13
  of change, progression techniques, 240
  of failure, 32

of heights, 102, 127–128
  manageable exposure, 123–124
  repeatedly confronting, 123
  traveling, 35
  worst-feared situations, 124
feeling the way you think
  ABC format approach, 14–16
  accurate thoughts and meanings, 13
  acting out, 13
  active behaviours, 12
  beliefs, 15
  consequences, 15
  disorders, 10
  emotional responsibility, 14, 267–268
  focused approach, 12
  healthy versus unhealthy emotions,
    75–76
  personal meanings, 15
  research methods, 9–10
  sulking behaviour, 12
feelings
  defining how you feel, 109
  thought-feeling link, 40
female versus male practitioner
    preference, 258
FHBs (fallible human beings), 181
First Steps to Freedom organisation, 293
flaws, self-acceptance techniques,
    162–163
flexible behaviours
  anger, 180–181
  beliefs, reinforcing, 210, 214
  as healthy attitude, 268
  obsessional problems, 151
  as positive change, 243–244
  self-acceptance, 163–164
focused approach, feeling the way you
    think, 12
fortune telling, thinking mistakes, 23–24
founder of cognitive therapy (Beck), 49

friend and family acceptance, self-acceptance, 171–172
frustration
  HFT (high frustration tolerance), 168
  LFT (low frustration tolerance), 168
  thinking mistakes, 34–35
  tolerance development, anger and, 182–183
Full Catastrophe Living: Using the Wisdom of Your Body and Mind to Face Stress, Pain and Illness (Kabat-Zinn), 290

• *G* •

Gilbert, Paul (*Overcoming Depression*), 290
global beliefs, reinforcing beliefs, 210
goal setting techniques
  abandonment, 115
  CBA (cost-benefit analysis), 111–113
  goal statements, 110
  long-term goals, 111, 168, 238
  motivation techniques, 110–114
  problem statements, 108–109
  procrastination, 115
  progression techniques, 238
  record sheets, 113–114
  short-term goals, 111, 168, 238
  SPORT (Specific, Positive, Observable, Realistic, Time) acronym, 107
graded hierarchy of anxiety, 124
graded practice exercise, task concentration, 64
Greenberger, Dennis (CBT therapist), 95
guilt emotions
  action tendencies, 85, 88
  demand-based thinking, 85
  depression and, 91, 130
  healthy and unhealthy emotion comparisons, 83–84
  personalising, thinking mistakes, 36–37

progression techniques, 234–235
synonyms for, 75

• *H* •

habituation, 122
haemophobia, 128
happy lifestyle development
  activities and hobbies, 224–225
  communication techniques, 230
  eating habits, 226
  educational activities, 227–228
  exercising, 226–227
  intimate relationships, 229–232
  leisure time, 226
  pampering, 225
  personal time, 225
  physical appearance, 227
  recreational pursuits, 225
  relapses, 223–224
  resource management, 226
  sex drive, 230–232
  social contact, 226
  special interest groups, 226
  spiritual satisfaction, 228
  talking the talk, 229
  vitally-absorbing interests, 226
  walking the walk, 227–228
hate, anger, 176
head-to-heart problem, reinforcing beliefs, 210
health anxiety
  compulsions associated with, 146–147
  discussed, 54
healthy attitudes, rational standpoints
  approval from others preferences, 270
  emotional responsibility, feeling the way you think, 267
  enlightened self-interest, 272
  flexible behaviours, 268
  individuality, valuing, 269

healthy attitudes, rational standpoints
(continued)
  interests, pursuing, 273
  life's unfair acceptance, 269
  loving and romantic relationships,
    270–271
  short-term discomfort tolerance, 271
  uncertainty, tolerating, 273
heights, fear of
  counterproductive safety
    behaviours, 102
  overcoming anxiety, 127–128
Herbert, Claudia (Overcoming Traumatic
    Stress), 290
HFT (high frustration tolerance), 168
hoarding, obsessional problems, 145–146
hobbies, happy lifestyle development,
    224–225
hopelessness, feelings of, 130
hurt emotions
  healthy and unhealthy emotion
    comparisons, 81
  synonyms for, 75
hypomanic states, 93, 131
hypothesis, scientific research, 11

• *I* •

icons, need for change, 111
illness, past life experiences, 192
illogical beliefs, 213
inactivity, depression, 135–136
inappropriate emotional response, self-
    acceptance, 167
independent worth, self-acceptance
    techniques, 161–162
individuality, valuing, 269
infidelity, past life experiences, 192
inflexibility of demands, thinking
    mistakes, 30–31
influencing others, need for certainty
    demands, 100
inspirational stories, need for
    change, 110
interests, healthy attitudes, 273
internalising, reinforcing beliefs, 210
interpersonal therapy (IPT), 255
intimate relationships, happy lifestyle
    development, 229–232
intrinsic values, self-acceptance, 160
irritability
  anger, 175
  depression, 130
isolating and mood-depressing
    behaviours, 13

• *J* •

jealousy emotions
  behavioural experiments, 54
  healthy and unhealthy emotion
    comparisons, 82
  intrusive thoughts and, 46
  problem causing solutions, 104
  synonyms for, 75
job interviews, anxiety and, 15
judgmental behaviours, self-
    acceptance, 171

• *K* •

Kabat-Zinn, Jon (Full Catastrophe Living:
    Using the Wisdom of Your Body and
    Mind to Face Stress, Pain and
    Illness), 290
Kennerly, Helen (Overcoming Childhood
    Trauma), 290
Kidscope, Obsessive-Compulsive
    Foundation, 295

Klosko, Janet S. *(Reinventing Your Life: How to Break Free from Negative Life Patterns)*, 291

• *L* •

labelling
  examples of, 29
  letting go of, 162
  low self-esteem, 28, 159–160
  strategies for, 29–30
lack of concentration, depression, 130
laughing at yourself, lightening up, 283–284
leisure time, happy lifestyle development, 226
LFT (low frustration tolerance), 168
libido, loss of, 130
life's unfair acceptance, healthy attitudes, 269
lifestyle changes, seeking happiness
  activities and hobbies, 224–225
  communication techniques, 230
  eating habits, 226
  educational activities, 227–228
  exercising, 226–227
  intimate relationships, 229–232
  leisure time, 226
  pampering, 225
  personal time, 225
  physical appearance, 227
  recreational pursuits, 225
  relapses, 223–224
  resource management, 226
  sex drive, 230–232
  social contact, 226
  special interest groups, 226
  spiritual satisfaction, 228
  talking the talk, 229
  vitally-absorbing interests, 226
  walking the walk, 227–228

life-threatening illness, past life experiences, 192
lightening up, enjoyment
  blame system, 282–283
  criticism, making good use of, 284–285
  laughing at yourself, 283–284
  making mistakes, acceptance, 281–282
  new skill sets, 282
  present moment response, 287
  socialising, 285–286
listening exercise, task concentration, 63
lockiophobia, 128
logical beliefs, 214
long-term goal techniques
  discussed, 111
  progression techniques, 238
  self-acceptance, 168
loving emotions
  healthy attitudes, 270–271
  physical sensations, 90
  synonyms for, 75
low frustration tolerance (LFT), 168
low self-esteem. *See also* self-acceptance
  all-or-nothing thinking, 276
  change needs, 168–170
  labelling, 159–160
  name calling, 171
  putting others down, 275–276
  self-abusive language, 171
  self-downing, 159–160
  self-talk strategies, 170–171
  temporary conditions, 159
lutraphobia, 128
lyssophobia, 128

• *M* •

male versus female practitioner preference, 258
manageable exposure to fears, 123–124
Manic Depression Fellowship organisation, 293

medical assistance, suicidal
    thoughts, 141
medication, antidepressants, 129–130
meditation
    consequences of emotions, 69
    daily strengthening tasks, 70
    observations, 69
    presence in the moment, 68
    thoughts, letting pass by, 68–69
memory problems, depression, 130
mental filtering, thinking mistakes
    examples of, 31–32
    strategies for, 32
mental health, American Mental Health
    Foundation organisation, 294
meta-emotions, 91
metaphors, need for change, 111
MIND organisation, 294
mindfulness mediation
    consequences of emotions, 69
    daily strengthening tasks, 70
    observations, 69
    presence in the moment, 68
    thoughts, letting pass by, 68–69
mind-reading tendencies, thinking
    mistakes, 24–26
mistakes, lightening up, 281–282
The Mood Gym organisation, 296
moral misinterpretation, obsessional
    problems, 151
motivation
    decreased, 130
    goal setting techniques, 110–114
    progression techniques, 241
muscular tension, anger, 177

• *N* •

name calling, low self-esteem, 171
National Alliance for the Mentally Ill
    organisation, 295

National Anxiety Foundation, 295
National Association for Anorexia
    Nervosa and Associated Disorders
    organisation, 295
National Attention Deficit Disorder
    Association, 295
National Depressive and Manic-
    Depressive Association, 295
National Foundation for Depressive
    Illness organisation, 295
National Institute of Mental Health, 295
National Mental Health Association, 295
National Mental Health Consumers
    Self-Help Clearinghouse
    organisation, 295
National Phobics Society organisation, 294
NATs (negative automatic thoughts)
    core beliefs, 195–196
    self assurance, 39–40
natural oils and herbs, good sleeping
    habits, 140
necrophobia, 128
neglect, past life experiences, 192
No Panic organisation, 294
noctiphobia, 128
nurse therapists. *See* professional
    assistance

• *O* •

OBAD (Organisation for Bi-polar
    Affective Disorders), 296
observations
    behavioural experiments, 57
    mindfulness meditation, 69
obsessional problems
    aggressiveness, 145
    avoidance behaviours, 144
    cleaning or washing, 145
    compulsions, 144, 146–147

counting, 145
doubt and uncertainty, tolerance, 150
exposure and response prevention,
    153–154
external and practical criteria
    toward, 152
flexible behaviours, 151
health anxiety, 146–147
hoarding, 145
identifying, 149
moral misinterpretation, 151
physical sensations, normalising, 153
poor memory confidence, 150
preoccupation, 144
probability misinterpretation, 151
professional assistance, 158
religious, 145
repeating actions, 145
responsibility, being realistic about,
    151, 155–157
rituals, 144, 154–155
sexual, 145
subclinical problems, 143
terms associated with, 144
violence, 145
Obsessive Compulsive Foundation, 296
OCA (Obsessive Compulsive
    Anonymous, Inc.), 295
Occam's razor scientific principle, 53
OCD (obsessive-compulsive disorder)
    common obsessions in, 145
    compulsions associated with, 145
    contamination, fear of, 145
    control, loosening grip on, 97
    intrusive thoughts and, 46
    prevalence of, 146
OCD Action organisation, 294
Old Meaning – New Meaning form,
    297–298
ombrophobia, 128

optimism, progression techniques, 238
Organisation for Bi-polar Affective
    Disorders (OBAD), 296
Overcoming Anger (Dryden), 290
Overcoming Childhood Trauma
    (Kennerly), 290
Overcoming Depression (Gilbert), 290
Overcoming Mood Swings (Scott), 290
*Overcoming Obsessive Compulsive
    Disorder* (Veale and Willson), 290
Overcoming Social Anxiety and Shyness
    (Buttler), 290
Overcoming Traumatic Stress (Herbert
    and Wetmore), 290
overgeneralising, thinking mistakes
    discussed, 27
    how to recognise, 28
    strategies for, 28
overreacting, catastrophising, 20–21
*Oxford Guide to Behavioural Experiments
    in Cognitive Therapy* (Oxford
    University Press), 290

• *P* •

painting activities, happy lifestyle
    development, 224
pampering, happy lifestyle
    development, 225
panic attacks
    behavioural experiments, 54
    control, loosening grip on, 97
    counterproductive safety
        behaviours, 101
    overcoming anxiety, 126
parental control, past life
    experiences, 192
passive personalities, progression
    techniques, 240
passive-aggressiveness, anger, 176

past life experiences, core beliefs
  abandonment, 192
  automatic beliefs, 193
  contradictions, 199
  core belief flashcard technique,
    203–204
  critical parenting, 192
  death of loved one, 192
  difficult experiences, 192
  divorce, 192
  downward arrow method, 195–196
  dream scenarios, 196–197
  filling in the blank method, 197–198
  history, revisiting, 205–207
  identifying, 192–193
  impacts of, 198–200
  infidelity, 192
  life-threatening illnesses, 192
  NATs (negative automatic thoughts),
    195–196
  neglect, 192
  about others, 194
  past experience examples, 191–192
  physical abuse, 192
  prejudice model, 199–200
  record sheets, 200–203
  starting over, 207–208
  themes, tracking, 197
  unbiased interpretation, 203
  violence, 192
  about world events, 194
  written down statement technique,
    203–204
  about yourself, 194
perseverance, progression techniques,
  239
personal meanings, feeling the way you
  think, 15
personal time, happy lifestyle
  development, 225

personalising, thinking mistakes, 35–36
person-centered therapy, 255
pets, happy lifestyle development, 224
philosophical studies, 11–12
phobias, 128
physical abuse, past life experiences, 192
physical activity, rumination elimination,
  134–135
physical appearance, happy lifestyle
  development, 227
physical sensations
  anger, 177
  of anxiety, 121
  obsessional problems, 153
  vicious flower exercise, 104–105
positive attitudes
  compliments, acceptance, 34
  disqualifying the positive, thinking
    mistakes, 33–34
positive changes. *See also* progression
    techniques
  awareness, need for change, 244–246
  calming down, 250
  compassion, 250
  depression, 245
  environment triggers, identifying,
    246–247
  flexible thinking behaviours, 243–244
  realistic goals, 250
  recurrent problems, 247–248
positive data logs, reinforcing beliefs,
  220–221
post-traumatic stress disorder (PTSD),
  97, 101
predictions, behavioural experiments,
  50–53
preference-based thinking
  demand-based thinking versus, 86–88
  remorse, 86
prejudice model, core beliefs, 199–200

preoccupation, obsession, 144
presence in the moment, mindfulness meditation, 68
pride-based attributes, progression techniques, 235–236
probability misinterpretation, obsessional problems, 151
problem causing solutions
  alcohol and drug consumption, 96
  avoidance, 96
  certainty, need for, 98–100
  control, loosening grip on, 97–98
  counterproductive strategies, 95–96
  dealing with problems, putting off, 96
  depression, 97, 136–138
  examples of, 96
  excessive safety-seeking, 100–102
  jealousy emotions, 104
  superstitious rituals, 99
  thought suppression, 103–104
  vicious flower exercise, 104–105
  worrying behaviours, 102–103
problem descriptions, behavioural experiments, 51–52
problem statements, goal setting techniques, 108–109
procrastination
  goal setting benefits, 115
  low frustration tolerance, 35
professional assistance
  accredited therapists, 257
  background and training specifics, 258
  certifications, 256
  clinical psychologists, 256
  costs, 258
  counselling psychologists, 256
  fears about, 260
  female versus male preference, 258
  good therapy traits, 262
  IPT (interpersonal therapy), 255
  nurse therapists, 256

obsessional problems, 158
person-centered therapy, 255
progression techniques, 235
psychiatrists, 256
psychodynamic therapy, 255
selection considerations, 257–261
sessions with, 261–264
systemic therapy, 255
transactional analysis, 255
treatment goals, 261
UKCP (United Kingdom Council for Psychotherapy), 256
when to seek, 253–255
progression techniques. *See also* positive changes
ABC forms and, 48
determination, 237
diligence, 237
effort, 237
encouragement, 237
fear or change, 240
goal setting, 238
guilt emotions, 234–235
motivation, 241
optimism, 238
passive personalities, 240
perseverance, 239
pride-based attributes, 235–236
professional assistance, 235
progress paralysis, 235
repetition, 237, 239
shame, 234–235
sidestepping traps, 240
task-interfering thoughts, 239–240
proverbs, need for change, 111
psychiatrists. *See* professional assistance
psychodynamic therapy, 255
psychologists. *See* professional assistance

psychotherapist. *See* professional
assistance
psychotherapy, emotional problems
and, 11
PTSD (post-traumatic stress disorder),
97, 101
public speaking, avoidance
behaviours, 13
publications
Cognitive Therapy – Basics and Beyond
(Beck), 289
*Cognitive Therapy and the Emotional
Disorders* (Beck), 289
*Full Catastrophe Living: Using the
Wisdom of Your Body and Mind to
Face Stress, Pain and Illness* (Kabat-
Zinn), 290
Overcoming Anger (Dryden), 290
Overcoming Childhood Trauma
(Kennerly), 290
Overcoming Depression (Gilbert), 290
Overcoming Mood Swings (Scott), 290
*Overcoming Obsessive Compulsive
Disorder* (Veale and Willson), 290
Overcoming Social Anxiety and Shyness
(Buttler), 290
Overcoming Traumatic Stress (Herbert
and Wetmore), 290
*Oxford Guide to Behavioural
Experiments in Cognitive Therapy*
(Oxford University Press), 290
*Reason and Emotion in Psychotherapy:
A Comprehensive Method for Treating
Human Disturbances, Revised and
Updated* (Ellis), 291
*Reinventing Your Life: How to Break Free
from Negative Life Patterns* (Klosko
and Young), 291
Status Anxiety (De Botton), 291
A Woman in Your Own Right
(Dickson), 291

• Q •

quotes, need for change, 111

• R •

rage, anger, 176
raised heart rates, anger, 177
rape, past life experiences, 192
rational emotive behaviour therapy
(Ellis), 30, 161
rational standpoints, healthy attitudes
approval from others preferences, 270
emotional responsibility, 267–268
enlightened self-interest, 272
flexible behaviours, 268
individuality, valuing, 269
interests, pursuing, 273
life's unfair acceptance, 269
loving and romantic relationships,
270–271
short-term discomfort tolerance, 271
uncertainty, tolerating, 273
reading, happy lifestyle
development, 224
realism
all-or-nothing thinking mistakes, 22
as positive change, 250
*Reason and Emotion in Psychotherapy:
A Comprehensive Method for Treating
Human Disturbances, Revised and
Updated* (Ellis), 291
reasoning skills, all-or-nothing thinking
mistakes, 22
reassurance, requests for, 99
record sheets
anxiety problems, 125
behavioural experiments, 58–59
core beliefs, 200–203
goal setting techniques, 113–114
task concentration, 66–67, 306

recreational pursuits, happy lifestyle development, 225

recurrent problems, positive change needs, 247–248

regret, healthy and unhealthy emotion comparisons, 80–81

reinforcement, beliefs
 ABC approach, 15
 acting as if technique, 211
 alternative assumption, 210
 balanced beliefs, 214
 cognitive dissonance, 209–210
 compassion behaviours, 220–221
 doubts and reservations, 215–216
 extreme beliefs, 213
 feeling the way you think, 15
 flexible preference, 210, 214
 global beliefs, 210
 head-to-heart problem, 210
 illogical beliefs, 213
 internalising, 210
 logical beliefs, 214
 positive data logs, 220–221
 rigid beliefs, 213
 self-acceptance, 219
 SOC (strength of conviction), 210
 true beliefs, 214
 unhelpful beliefs, 213
 untrue beliefs, 212
 written exercises, 218–220
 zigzag technique, 216–218, 303–304

Reinventing Your Life: How to Break Free from Negative Life Patterns (Klosko and Young), 291

relapses, happy lifestyle development, 223–224

relaxation, good sleeping habits, 139

religious obsessions, 145

remorse
 action tendencies, 86
 healthy and unhealthy emotion comparisons, 84
 preference-based thinking, 86

repeated checking of behaviours, 99

repetition
 obsessional problems, 145
 progression techniques, 237, 239

research
 feeling the way you think, 9–10
 philosophical studies, 11–12
 scientific studies, 11

resource management, happy lifestyle development, 226

resources
 United Kingdom organisations, 293–294
 United States organisations, 294–296

responsibility for emotions, feeling the way you think, 267–268

responsibility misinterpretation, obsessional problems, 151, 155–157

results, behavioural experiments, 52–53

revenge, anger, 177

ridicule, anger, 176

rigid beliefs, 213

rigid demands, anger, 176

risk avoidance, need for certainty demands, 100

rituals, obsession
 delaying and modifying, 154–155
 discussed, 144

role models, need for change, 110

rumination
 defined, 132
 effective strategies for, 134–135
 recognising, 132–133

• S •

SAD (Seasonal Affective Disorder) Association, 294

sadness
 emotions, synonyms for, 75
 healthy and unhealthy emotion comparisons, 79

safety-seeking behaviours, problem causing solutions, 51, 100–102
schedules, good sleeping habits, 139
scientific principle, Occam's razor, 53
scientific studies, 11
Scott, Jan (*Overcoming Mood Swings*), 290
Seasonal Affective Disorder (SAD) Association, 294
selective serotonin reuptake inhibitors (SSRIs), 130
self-acceptance. *See also* low self-esteem
  adaptive and corrective behaviours, 165
  anger, 181–182
  assertions, 160–161
  beliefs, reinforcing, 219
  compassion behaviours, 172
  doubt and reservations, 172–173
  extreme reactions, 167
  family and friend acceptance, 171–172
  flaws, defining new roles, 162–163
  flexible attitudes, 163–164
  HFT (high frustration tolerance), 168
  inappropriate emotional response, 167
  independent worth, 161–162
  intrinsic values, 160
  judgmental behaviours, 171
  labelling, letting go of, 162
  LFT (low frustration tolerance), 168
  long-term goals, 168
  self-improvement, 173
  self-uniqueness, 165–166
  short-term goals, 168
  unconditional, 160
self-destructive behaviours, 13
self-downing, low self-esteem, 159–160
self-esteem, low
  all-or-nothing thinking, 276
  change needs, 168–170
  labelling, 159–160

name calling, 171
putting others down, 275–276
self-abusive language, 171
self-downing, 159–160
self-talk strategies, 170–171
temporary conditions, 159
self-help thinking methods (Dryden), 161
self-neglect, depression, 130, 138
self-righteous anger, 188
self-talk strategies, low self-esteem, 170–171
self-worth, over-defending, 279
sessions, professional assistance
  being active between, 263–264
  discussing issues during, 261–263
sex drive
  happy lifestyle development, 230–232
  sexual obsessions, 145
shame
  ashamed emotions, synonyms for, 75
  concealing aspects of, problem causing solutions, 96
  healthy and unhealthy emotion comparisons, 80
  progression techniques, 234–235
short-term discomfort tolerance, healthy attitudes, 271
short-term goal techniques
  discussed, 111
  progression techniques, 238
  self-acceptance, 168
sleeping
  depression, 130, 138–140
  excessive sleeping habits, isolating behaviours, 13
  good sleeping habits, 138–140
SOC (strength of conviction), 210
soceraphobia, 128
social anxiety, 126

social contact, happy lifestyle development, 226
social isolation, depression, 130
social outlining, avoidance behaviours, 13
socialising, lightening up, 285–286
solutions, problem causing
  alcohol and drug consumption, 96
  avoidance, 96
  certainty, need for, 98–100
  control, loosening grip on, 97–98
  counterproductive strategies, 95–96
  dealing with problems, putting off, 96
  depression, 97
  examples of, 96
  excessive safety-seeking, 100–102
  jealousy emotions, 104
  superstitious rituals, 99
  thought suppression, 103–104
  vicious flower exercise, 104–105
  worrying behaviours, 102–103
speaking exercise, task concentration, 64
special interest groups, happy lifestyle development, 226
specialists. *See* professional assistance
spiritual satisfaction, happy lifestyle development, 228
SPORT (Specific, Positive, Observable, Realistic, Time), goal setting techniques, 107–108
sporting activities, happy lifestyle development, 224
SSRIs (selective serotonin reuptake inhibitors), 130
Status Anxiety (De Botton), 291
stimulant intake, good sleeping habits, 139
strength of conviction (SOC), 210
strong preferences, anger, 177
subclinical obsession problems, 143

suicidal thoughts
  discussed, 130
  managing, 141–142
  medical assistance, 141
sulking behaviour
  anger, 177
  feeling the way you think, 12
superstitious rituals, need for certainty demands, 99
surveys, behavioural experiments, 55–57
symptoms, depression, 130–131
systemic therapy, 255

• *T* •

talking the talk, happy lifestyle development, 229
talking treatment
  behavioural experiments, 49
  low self-esteem, 170–171
task concentration
  anxiety and, 65–66
  attention to detail, 64–65
  challenging situations, 62
  graded practice exercise, 64
  listening exercises, 63
  non-threatening situations, 62
  record sheets, 66–67, 306
  for rumination, 134
  speaking exercise, 64
task interfering cognitions (TICs), 301
task orienting cognitions (TOCs), 301
task-interfering thoughts, progression techniques, 239–240
temporary conditions, low self-esteem, 159
theories, behavioural experiments, 53–55
therapists. *See* professional assistance
therapy. *See* professional assistance
Thinking Error box, ABC form, 42–43

thinking mistakes
  all-or-nothing thinking, 21–23
  black-or-white thinking, 21–23
  catastrophising, 20–21
  disqualifying the positive, 33–34
  emotional reasoning, 26
  fortune telling, 23–24
  inflexibility of demands, 30–31
  labelling, 28–30
  low frustration tolerance, 34–35
  mental filtering, 31–32
  mind-reading tendencies, 24–26
  overgeneralising, 27–28
  overview, 19
  personalising, 35–36
thoughts
  catastrophising strategies, 21
  documenting, 40
  extreme thinking, avoiding, 120
  letting pass by, mindfulness mediation,
    68–69
  NATs (negative automatic thoughts),
    39–40
  suppressing, problem causing
    solutions, 103–104
  thought-feeling link, 40
  validating, behavioural experiment
    reasons, 50
thoughts, feeling the way you think
  ABC format approach, 14–16
  accurate thoughts and meanings, 13
  acting out, 13
  active behaviours, 12
  beliefs, 15
  consequences, 15
  disorders, 10
  emotional responsibility, 14, 267–268
  focused approach, 12
  healthy versus unhealthy emotions,
    75–76
  personal meanings, 15

research methods, 9–10
sulking behaviour, 12
TICs (task interfering cognitions), 301
TOCs (task orienting cognitions), 301
tolerance
  accepting others, 179–180
  doubt and uncertainty, 273
  frustration, 182–183
  HFT (high frustration tolerance), 168
  LFT (low frustration tolerance), 168
transactional analysis, 255
trauma, past life experiences, 192
traveling fears, 35
treatment goals, professional
    assistance, 261
Trichotillomania Learning Center, 296
triggers, activating events, 14–15
trypanophobia, 128

• *U* •

UKCP (United Kingdom Council for
    Psychotherapy), 256
unambiguous disconfirmation,
    behavioural experiments, 50–51
unbiased interpretation, past life
    experiences, 203
uncertainty and doubt
  beliefs, reinforcing, 215–216
  self-acceptance, 172–173
  tolerance, 150, 273
unconditional self-acceptance, 160
uniqueness, self-acceptance, 165–166
United Kingdom Council for
    Psychotherapy (UKCP), 256
United Kingdom organisations,
    resources, 293–294
United States organisations, resources,
    294–296
untrue beliefs, 212

• V •

validating thoughts, behavioural experiment reasons, 50
Veale, David *(Overcoming Obsessive Compulsive Disorder),* 290
verbal abuse, low-self esteem, 171
vicious flower exercise, 104–105, 305
violence, obsessional problems, 145
violent attacks, past life experiences, 192
vitally-absorbing interests, happy lifestyle development, 226

• W •

walking the walk, happy lifestyle development, 227–228
Wetmore, Ann *(Overcoming Traumatic Stress),* 290
WHO (World Health Organization), 143
Willson, Rob *(Overcoming Obsessive Compulsive Disorder),* 290

winning by not fighting technique, anxiety, 122
A Woman in Your Own Right (Dickson), 291
worry problems
  intrusive thoughts and, 46
  overcoming anxiety, 126
  problem causing solutions, 102–103
written down statement technique, core beliefs, 203–204

• Y •

Young, Jeffrey E. *(Reinventing Your Life: How to Break Free from Negative Life Patterns),* 291

• Z •

zigzag technique, reinforcing beliefs, 216–218, 303–304

FOR DUMMIES®

Do Anything. Just Add Dummies

UK editions

Buying and Selling a Home
0-7645-7027-7

Renting Out Your Property
0-7645-7016-1

DIY & Home Maintenance ALL-IN-ONE
0-7645-7054-4

PERSONAL FINANCE

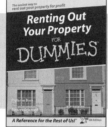

Investing
0-7645-7023-4

Paying Less Tax 2005/2006
0-7645-7053-6

Sorting Out Your Finances
0-7645-7039-0

BUSINESS

Starting a Business
0-7645-7018-8

Understanding Business Accounting
0-7645-7025-0

Business Plans
0-7645-7026-9

Other UK editions now available:

British History
For Dummies
(0-7645-7021-8)

Building Confidence
For Dummies
(0-4700-1669-8)

Buying a Home On A
Budget For Dummies
(0-7645-7035-8)

Cleaning and Stain
Removal For Dummies
(0-7645-7029-3)

CVs For Dummies
(0-7645-7017-X)

Diabetes For Dummies
(0-7645-7019-6)

Divorce For Dummies
(0-7645-7030-7)

eBay.co.uk For Dummies
(0-7645-7059-5)

European History
For Dummies
(0-7645-7060-9)

Formula One Racing
For Dummies
(0-7645-7015-3)

Gardening For Dummies
(0-470-01843-7)

Genealogy Online
For Dummies
(0-7645-7061-7)

Golf For Dummies
(0-470-01811-9)

Irish History
For Dummies
(0-7645-7040-4)

Marketing For Dummies
(0-7645-7056-0)

Neuro-Linguistic
Programming
For Dummies
(0-7645-7028-5)

Nutrition For Dummies
(0-7645-7058-7)

Pregnancy For Dummies
(0-7645-7042-0)

Rugby Union
For Dummies
(0-7645-7020-X)

Small Business
Employment Law
For Dummies
(0-7645-7052-8)

Su Doku For Dummies
(0-4700-189-25)

Sudoku 2 For Dummies
(0-4700-2651-0)

Sudoku 3 For Dummies
(0-4700-2667-7)

Wills, Probate and
Inheritance Tax
For Dummies
(0-7645-7055-2)

FOR DUMMIES®

A world of resources to help you grow

HOBBIES

0-7645-5232-5

0-7645-5137-X

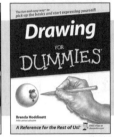

0-7645-5476-X

Also available:

Art For Dummies
(0-7645-5104-3)

Aromatherapy For Dummies
(0-7645-5171-X)

Bridge For Dummies
(0-7645-5015-2)

Card Games For Dummies
(0-7645-9910-0)

Chess For Dummies
(0-7645-5003-9)

Crocheting For Dummies
(0-7645-4151-X)

Improving Your Memory
For Dummies
(0-7645-5435-2)

Massage For Dummies
(0-7645-5172-8)

Meditation For Dummies
(0-7645-5116-7)

Photography For Dummies
(0-7645-4116-1)

Quilting For Dummies
(0-7645-5118-3)

Woodworking For Dummies
(0-7645-3977-9)

EDUCATION

0-7645-7206-7

0-7645-5581-2

0-7645-5422-0

Also available:

Algebra For Dummies
(0-7645-5325-9)

Astronomy For Dummies
(0-7645-8465-0)

Buddhism For Dummies
(0-7645-5359-3)

Calculus For Dummies
(0-7645-2498-4)

Christianity For Dummies
(0-7645-4482-9)

Forensics For Dummies
(0-7645-5580-4)

Islam For Dummies
(0-7645-5503-0)

Philosophy For Dummies
(0-7645-5153-1)

Religion For Dummies
(0-7645-5264-3)

Trigonometry For Dummies
(0-7645-6903-1)

PETS

0-7645-5255-4

0-7645-8418-9

0-7645-5275-9

Also available:

Labrador Retrievers
For Dummies
(0-7645-5281-3)

Aquariums For Dummies
(0-7645-5156-6)

Birds For Dummies
(0-7645-5139-6)

Dogs For Dummies
(0-7645-5274-0)

Ferrets For Dummies
(0-7645-5259-7)

German Shepherds
For Dummies
(0-7645-5280-5)

Golden Retrievers
For Dummies
(0-7645-5267-8)

Horses For Dummies
(0-7645-5138-8)

Jack Russell Terriers
For Dummies
(0-7645-5268-6)

Puppies Raising & Training
Diary For Dummies
(0-7645-0876-8)

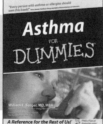

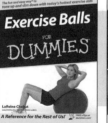

FOR DUMMIES®

The easy way to get more done and have more fun

LANGUAGES

Spanish 0-7645-5194-9

French 0-7645-5193-0

Italian 0-7645-5196-5

Also available:

Chinese For Dummies
(0-4717-8897-X)

Chinese Phrases
For Dummies
(0-7645-8477-4)

French Phrases For Dummies
(0-7645-7202-4)

German For Dummies
(0-7645-5195-7)

Italian Phrases For Dummies
(0-7645-7203-2)

Japanese For Dummies
(0-7645-5429-8)

Latin For Dummies
(0-7645-5431-X)

Spanish Phrases For
Dummies
(0-7645-7204-0)

Hebrew For Dummies
(0-7645-5489-1)

MUSIC AND FILM

Guitar 0-7645-9904-6

Filmmaking 0-7645-2476-3

Piano 0-7645-5105-1

Also available:

Bass Guitar For Dummies
(0-7645-2487-9)

Blues For Dummies
(0-7645-5080-2)

Classical Music For Dummies
(0-7645-5009-8)

Drums For Dummies
(0-7645-5357-7)

Jazz For Dummies
(0-7645-5081-0)

Opera For Dummies
(0-7645-5010-1)

Rock Guitar For Dummies
(0-7645-5356-9)

Screenwriting For Dummies
(0-7645-5486-7)

Songwriting For Dummies
(0-7645-5404-2)

Singing For Dummies
(0-7645-2475-5)

HEALTH, SPORTS & FITNESS

Fitness 0-7645-7851-0

Exercise Balls 0-7645-7851-0

Asthma 0-7645-4233-8

Also available:

Controlling Cholesterol For
Dummies
(0-7645-5440-9)

Dieting For Dummies
(0-7645-5126-4)

High Blood Pressure For
Dummies
(0-7645-5424-7)

Martial Arts For Dummies
(0-7645-5358-5)

Menopause For Dummies
(0-7645-5458-1)

Power Yoga For Dummies
(0-7645-5342-9)

Thyroid For Dummies
(0-7645-5385-2)

Weight Training For Dummies
(0-7645-5168-X)

Yoga For Dummies
(0-7645-5117-5)

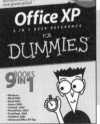